Sacred Writings

THEMES IN RELIGIOUS STUDIES SERIES

Series Editors: Jean Holm, with John Bowker

Other titles

Worship
Making Moral Decisions
Attitudes to Nature
Myth and History
Human Nature and Destiny
Picturing God
Rites of Passage
Women in Religion
Sacred Place

Sacred Writings

Edited by

Jean Holm

with John Bowker

PINTER
PUBLISHERS
LONDON, NEW YORK

Distributed exclusively in the United States and Canada by St. Martin's Press

Pinter Publishers Ltd.
25 Floral Street, London WC2E 9DS, United Kingdom

First published in 1994

Distributed exclusively in the USA and Canada by St. Martin's Press, Inc., Room 400, 175 Fifth Avenue, New York, NY10010, USA

British Library Cataloguing in Publication Data

A CIP catalogue record for this book is available from the British Library

ISBN 1 85567 106 9 (hb)
ISBN 1 85567 107 7 (pb)

Library of Congress Cataloging in Publication Data

Sacred writings / edited by Jean Holm, with John Bowker.
p. cm. – (Themes in religious studies series)
Includes bibliographical references and index.
ISBN 1-85567-106-9. – ISBN 1-85567-107-7 (pbk.)
1. Sacred books – History and criticism. I. Holm, Jean, 1922– .
II. Bowker, John Westerdale. III. Series.
BL71.S23 1994
291.8'2–dc20 94-15113
CIP

Typeset by Mayhew Typesetting, Rhayader, Powys
Printed and bound in Great Britain by Biddles Ltd., Guildford and King's Lynn

Contents

Series Preface
Jean Holm vi

List of Contributors ix

Introduction: Raising the Issues
Jean Holm 1

1. Buddhism
Ulrich Pagel 10

2. Christianity
Douglas Davies 44

3. Hinduism
Gavin D. Flood 71

4. Islam
Martin Forward 101

5. Judaism
Alan Unterman 125

6. Sikhism
Beryl Dhanjal 151

7. Chinese Religions
Xinzhong Yao 173

8. Japanese Religions
Ian Reader 187

Index 199

Series Preface

The person who knows only one religion does not know any religion. This rather startling claim was made in 1873, by Friedrich Max Müller, in his book, *Introduction to the Science of Religion.* He was applying to religion a saying of the poet Goethe: 'He who knows one language, knows none'.

In many ways this series illustrates Max Müller's claim. The diversity among the religious traditions represented in each of the volumes shows how mistaken are those people who assume that the pattern of belief and practice in their own religion is reflected equally in other religions. It is, of course, possible to do a cross-cultural study of the ways in which religions tackle particular issues, such as those which form the titles of the ten books in this series, but it soon becomes obvious that something which is central in one religion may be much less important in another. To take just three examples: the contrast between Islam's and Sikhism's attitudes to pilgrimage, in *Sacred Place*; the whole spectrum of positions on the authority of scriptures illustrated in *Sacred Writings*; and the problem which the titles, *Picturing God* and *Worship*, created for the contributor on Buddhism.

The series offers an introduction to the ways in which the themes are approached within eight religious traditions. Some of the themes relate particularly to the faith and practice of individuals and religious communities (*Picturing God, Worship, Rites of Passage, Sacred Writings, Myth and History, Sacred Place*); others have much wider implications, for society in general as well as for the religious communities themselves (*Attitudes to Nature, Making Moral Decisions, Human Nature and Destiny, Women in Religion*). This distinction, however, is not clear-cut. For instance, the 'sacred places' of Ayodhya and Jerusalem have figured in situations of national and international conflict, and some countries have passed laws regulating, or even banning, religious worship.

Stereotypes of the beliefs and practices of religions are so widespread that a real effort, of both study and imagination, is needed in order to discover what a religion looks – and feels – like to its adherents. We have to bracket out, temporarily, our own beliefs and presuppositions, and 'listen in' to a religion's account of what *it* regards as significant. This is not a straightforward task, and readers of the books in this series will encounter a number of the issues that characterise the study of religions, and that have to be taken into account in any serious attempt to get behind a factual description of a religion to an understanding of the real meaning of the words and actions for its adherents.

First, the problem of language. Islam's insistence that the Arabic of the Qur'ān cannot be 'translated' reflects the impossibility of finding in another language an exact equivalent of many of the most important terms in a religion. The very word, Islam, means something much more positive to a Muslim than is suggested in English by 'submission'. Similarly, it can be misleading to use 'incarnation' for *avatāra* in Hinduism, or 'suffering' for *dukkha* in Buddhism, or 'law' for Torah in Judaism, or 'gods' for *kami* in Shinto, or 'heaven' for *T'ien* in Taoism, or 'name' for *Nām* in Sikhism.

Next, the problem of defining – drawing a line round – a religion. Religions don't exist in a vacuum; they are influenced by the social and cultural context in which they are set. This can affect what they strenuously reject as well as what they may absorb into their pattern of belief and practice. And such influence is continuous, from a religion's origins (even though we may have no records from that period), through significant historical developments (which sometimes lead to the rise of new movements or sects), to its contemporary situation, especially when a religion is transplanted into a different region. For example, anyone who has studied Hinduism in India will be quite unprepared for the form of Hinduism they will meet in the island of Bali.

Even speaking of a 'religion' may be problematic. The term, 'Hinduism', for example, was invented by western scholars, and would not be recognised or understood by most 'Hindus'. A different example is provided by the religious situation in Japan, and the consequent debate among scholars as to whether they should speak of Japanese 'religion' or Japanese 'religions'.

Finally, it can be misleading to encounter only one aspect of a religion's teaching. The themes in this series are part of a whole interrelated network of beliefs and practices within each religious tradition, and need to be seen in this wider context. The reading lists at the end of each chapter point readers to general studies of the religions as well as to books which are helpful for further reading on the themes themselves.

Jean Holm
November 1993

List of Contributors

Jean Holm (EDITOR) was formerly Principal Lecturer in Religious Studies at Homerton College, Cambridge, teaching mainly Judaism and Hinduism. Her interests include relationships between religions; the relationship of culture to religion; and the way in which children are nurtured within a different cultural context. Her publications include *Teaching Religion in School* (Oxford University Press, 1975), *The Study of Religions* (Sheldon, 1977), *Growing up in Judaism* (Longman, 1990), *Growing up in Christianity*, with Romie Ridley (Longman, 1990) and *A Keyguide to Sources of Information on World Religions* (Mansell, 1991). She has edited three previous series: *Issues in Religious Studies*, with Peter Baelz (Sheldon), *Anselm Books*, with Peter Baelz (Lutterworth) and *Growing up in a Religion* (Longman).

John Bowker (EDITOR) was Professor of Religious Studies in Lancaster University, before returning to Cambridge to become Dean and Fellow of Trinity College. He is at present Professor of Divinity at Gresham College in London, and Adjunct Professor at the University of Pennsylvania and at the State University of North Carolina. He is particularly interested in anthropological and sociological approaches to the study of religions. He has done a number of programmes for the BBC, including the *Worlds of Faith* series, and a series on Islam and Hinduism for the World Service. He is the author of many books in the field of Religious Studies, including *The Meanings of Death* (Cambridge University Press, 1991), which was awarded the biennial Harper Collins religious book prize in 1993, in the academic section.

Ulrich Pagel is Curator of the Tibetan Collections in the British

Library. Dr Pagel's research interests include the *bodhisattva*-ideal, (early) Mahāyāna *sūtras*, *Kanjur* research, Buddhist bibliography and history, and Buddhism in Central Asia. In addition to several articles in journals and edited collections, he is author of *The Bodhisattvapiṭaka: Its Doctrines, Practices and their Position in Mahāyāna Literature* (Tring, 1994). He is also co-editor of *The Buddhist Forum*, Lecturer in Tibetan at the School of Oriental and African Studies (SOAS), and contributes to the *Bod rGya Tshig mDzod Chen Mo* Dictionary Project.

Douglas Davies is Professor of Religious Studies in the Department of Theology at the University of Nottingham, where he specialises in teaching the social anthropology of religion. He trained both in theology and social anthropology and his research continues to relate to both disciplines. His interest in theoretical and historical aspects of religious studies is represented in a major study of the sociology of knowledge and religion, published as *Meaning and Salvation in Religious Studies* (Brill, 1984), and in a historical volume, *Frank Byron Jevons 1858–1936, An Evolutionary Realist* (Edwin Mellen Press, 1991). Professor Davies is also very much concerned with practical aspects of religious behaviour and is a leading British scholar of Mormonism and, in addition to various articles, is author of *Mormon Spirituality* (Nottingham and Utah University Press, 1987). He was joint Director of the Rural Church Project, involving one of the largest sociological studies of religion in Britain, published as *Church and Religion in Rural Britain* (with C. Watkins and M. Winter, T. & T. Clark, 1991). As Director of the Cremation Research Project he is conducting basic work on Cremation in Britain and Europe and has already produced some results in *Cremation Today and Tomorrow* (Grove Books, 1990).

Gavin D. Flood is Lecturer in Religious Studies at the University of Wales, Lampeter, where he teaches on courses on Indian Religions and New Religious Movements. His research interests include Śaivism and Hindu Tantra, ritual, and the understandings of the self in Indian religions. He has published articles on Kashmir Śaivism and is author of *Body and Cosmology in Kashmir Śaivism* (Mellen Research University Press, 1993).

Martin Forward is Secretary of the Methodist Church's Committee for Relations with People of Other Faiths, and a Consultant to the Council of Churches for Britain and Ireland's Commission for Inter-Faith relations. He used to work in the Henry Martyn Institute for Islamic Studies, Hyderabad, India. Martin Forward has taught an introductory course on Islam at Leicester University, and now teaches courses on Islam at Bristol University.

Alan Unterman is Minister of the Yeshurun Synagogue, Gatley, Cheshire, and part-time Lecturer in Comparative Religion (Judaism and Hinduism) at the University of Manchester. He studied at the Universities of Birmingham, Oxford and Delhi and at *yeshivot* in London and Jerusalem. He has worked and taught in Israel and Australia. Among his publications are *The Wisdom of the Jewish Mystics*; *Jews: Their Religious Beliefs and Practices*; *Judaism and Art*; 'A Jewish Perspective on the Rushdie Affair' in *The Salman Rushdie Controversy in Interreligious Perspective*; and *A Dictionary of Jewish Lore and Legend.*

Beryl Dhanjal is a Lecturer at Ealing Tertiary College. She works on the programme for teaching ESOL (English to Speakers of Other Languages) and has special responsibility for developing community links, working mainly with people from the new commonwealth and with refugees. She studied Panjabi at the School of African and Oriental Studies, University of London. She has lectured at St Mary's College, Strawberry Hill, and the West London Institute of Higher Education, and has worked in adult education. She has written and translated many books, and particularly enjoys writing books for children and young people – she has written bi-lingual English/Panjabi books for children.

Xinzhong Yao is Lecturer in the Chinese religion and ethics at the University of Wales, Lampeter. His research interests include philosophy, ethics and religion; he is currently focusing on comparative philosophy and comparative religion. Dr Yao is author of *On Moral Activity* (People's University Press, Beijing, 1990), *Ethics and Social Problems* (City Economic Press, Beijing, 1989), co-author of *Comparative Studies on Human Nature* (Tienjin People's Press, Tienjin, 1988) and co-editor of *Applying Ethics* (Jilin People's Press, Changchun, 1994), and main translator of Charles L. Stevenson's *Ethics and Language* (Social Sciences of China Press, Beijing, 1991).

He is a member of the Chinese National Association of Ethics and Deputy Director of the Institute of Ethics, the People's University of China, Beijing.

Ian Reader is Senior Lecturer in Japanese Studies at the University of Stirling in Scotland. He has spent several years in Japan travelling, teaching at Japanese universities and researching into contemporary Japanese religion. His major research interest is in the study of pilgrimage, and he is currently working on a volume on pilgrimage in Japan. Dr Reader is author of *Religion in Contemporary Japan* (Macmillans 1991), and editor (with Tony Walter) of *Pilgrimage in Popular Culture* (Macmillans 1992). He has also published numerous articles in journals and collected editions on Buddhism, Japanese religion, pilgrimage and Japanese popular culture, and is a member of the Editorial Advisory Board of the *Japanese Journal of Religious Studies*.

Introduction: Raising the Issues

Jean Holm

How does one define sacred writings? All religions have sacred literature, or, in the case of non-literate religions, sacred traditions which are handed on orally from generation to generation, but, as the following chapters show, there are vast differences among religions, not only in the nature and authority of their sacred writings, but even more in the amount of the literature and in the ways in which the boundaries of that literature are set.

The concept of 'scripture' is a familiar one in the West. It is used to refer to a canonical body of writings, whose boundaries were fixed long ago, and whose authority within the religion is unquestioned. Christianity is arguably alone among the religions in having its scriptures – the Bible – as its only sacred writing, though, as Beryl Dhanjal illustrates, Sikhism has a clearly defined scripture, the Gurū Granth Sāhib, but recognises a number of other writings which are accepted for reading in the gurdwara.

Some religions have two categories of sacred writings. This can be seen most clearly in Islam: the Qur'ān is uniquely 'scripture' for all Muslims, but it is supplemented by the *Ḥadīth* – the *sunnah*, or accounts of the sayings and actions of the Prophet Muhammad; a firm line is drawn around Qur'ān and *Ḥadīth*, separating them from all other writings. For Judaism, the fundamental sources for the study of the religion are the Bible and the Talmud, the latter being a vast collection of *halakhah* (literally 'walking', legal guidance for living) and *aggadah* (narrative material dealing with ethics and belief); neither Bible nor Talmud stands by itself. However, Alan Unterman, in describing Judaism's two categories as 'written teaching' and 'oral teaching', says, 'The Oral Teaching consists, in its widest sense, of the whole interpretative tradition which bases itself on scripture'.

Moving further along the spectrum, we find the division in Confucianism between *ching* (scripture, or classics) and *shu* (sacred books), though, as Xinzhong Yao points out, since the twelfth century CE the 'Four Books' have acquired a status equal to that of the 'Five Classics'. Hinduism also has two categories of sacred writings: *śruti* ('heard') and *smṛti* ('remembered'), but, as Gavin Flood explains, the boundaries between them are fluid, and there is certainly no recognisable line around the *smṛti* literature. At the other end of the spectrum from Christianity, Buddhism has thousands of sacred writings, but within the total body of literature different regions and different traditions have developed their own canons.

To describe a writing as canonical is to acknowledge its authority, but its authority, of course, only for the adherents of that particular religion, or tradition within a religion. Members of one religion may read and admire the sacred writings of another religion, and even feel that they have gained valuable insights from them, but it is only those who belong to that community of faith who regard the writings as a whole as having authority for the way they live or the beliefs they hold.

'A canon within the canon' is an expression used to refer not to the acceptance as authoritative of a whole body of literature, but to the widespread tendency of individuals or groups to select from a sacred writing those passages which they feel offer support to their particular beliefs or practices. This often leads to people with opposing views appealing to the same 'scriptures', but quoting different passages. The Bible, for example, has been used by Christians in this way in such controversial issues as infant baptism, the role of women in the Church, and whether salvation is possible only through Jesus Christ. The apparent contradictions result from several factors. Hindu, Buddhist, Taoist, Jewish and Christian sacred writings came into being over long periods of time, and therefore many of the writers – or speakers – functioned in different social, political or religious contexts, which influenced the approach they took, and meant that they were often addressing different situations. In some religions there is a recognition of development of beliefs (sometimes called 'progressive revelation' or 'progressive understanding'), so that later teachings may not always accord with earlier ones. This raises an interesting question for such religions: does greater authority lie with later, more developed, writings or with those nearer to the origin of a religion, and, in particular, nearer to the founder?

Revelation is a significant factor in the ascription of authority to sacred writings. Indeed, the broader term 'sacred writings' is not needed for revealed writings. Judaism's Bible, Christianity's Old and New Testaments, Islam's Qur'ān, Sikhism's *Ādi Granth* are simply 'scripture'. So, too, is Hinduism's Veda, though with the major difference that there was no 'revealer': *śruti* means 'heard', but the Veda was 'heard' by the *ṛṣi*s, the early sages, 'in the heart'.

How do sacred writings actually acquire their authority? This is usually a slow process. There is a Buddhist tradition that a council was convened immediately after the Buddha's death to determine the authenticity of the discourses claiming to be his teachings; however, Ulrich Pagel lists the objections to this claim, and concludes that the traditional account of the council 'lacks historical foundation'. Of the major religions, Islam can probably lay claim to having its scripture complied in the shortest time: Muhammad's followers are said to have written down at his dictation the revelations he had received, and after his death in 632 CE, they were gathered together. It was during the time of the third *khalīfah*, 'Uthman (644–656 CE), that the Qur'ān was put into the form with which we are familiar, though, as Martin Forward explains, the debate about some of the details of the text took longer to resolve.

Sometimes it is a powerful individual who draws the boundaries of a religion's sacred writings. Sikhism's tenth Gurū, Govind Singh, added some writings to those which had been collected by the fifth Gurū, and proclaimed that after his death the resulting work would be the Sikh's continuing teacher, or gurū, which is why the *Ādi Granth* is called the Gurū Granth Sāhib. In many of the new religious movements of the nineteenth and twentieth centuries – for example, the Church of the Latter Day Saints (Mormons), Christian Science, the International Society for Krishna Consciousness, the new religions of Japan – it has been the founder who has decided which writings were to be sacred for his or her followers, and these may be completely new works or, more often, particular interpretations of sacred writings of an established religion.

In *Is 'Holy Scripture' Christian?*, Christopher Evans wrote,

'Christianity is unique among the great religions in being born with a Bible in its cradle' (SCM Press, 1971, p. 2). The whole of the Jewish scriptures form the largest part of the Christian scriptures, and only gradually did the Church come to regard the writings of Christians as 'scripture'. The third-century theologian, Origen, in suggesting a definitive list of such writings, took into account those which had gained the greatest acceptance in the various churches. His list varied only slightly from the twenty-seven 'books' which Athanasius included in his pastoral letter of 367 CE, and which became known as the New Testament.

The Christian Church's main criterion for the inclusion of a writing in the New Testament was its apostolic nature, i.e., it was written either by an apostle or by someone associated with the apostles. This emphasis on the importance of nearness to the origin of a religion, particularly to its founder figure, is characteristic of many religions. In Judaism, the Torah, accepted by Orthodox Jews as having been written by Moses, has a higher status than the later *Nevi'im* (Prophets) or *Ketuvim* (Writings). The Mahāyāna was a later development within Buddhism, but it claimed that its teachings were not innovative; rather, they were 'hidden' teachings which were given by the Buddha himself, but not made public because they would not have been understood by people at that time.

Religions have faced the problems of transmission of their texts in various ways. The control of sacred writings has usually been in the hands of leaders of a religion. In early Buddhism, for example, groups of monks (called *bhanaka*s, 'reciters') were responsible for memorising, between them, all the scriptures. However, when writing became widespread the *bhanaka*s lost their tight control over the texts. Islam, as we have seen, fixed the form of the Qur'ān early in its history, but there were greater problems with its second category of sacred writings, the traditions about the Prophet Muhammad. It therefore developed the science of *ḥadīth*, in which scholars recognised as authentic only those *ḥadīth* for which they could trace the handing on of accounts of the actions and sayings of Muhammad in an unbroken chain stretching back to the Prophet's companions.

The copying of texts has always proved a difficult area. Ulrich Pagel explains that Indian copies of Buddhist manuscripts have more errors in them than Chinese copies because scribes in India had a fairly low status and would therefore not have had the professional skills of scribes in China, who were highly regarded. Christian scholars have grouped New Testament manuscripts into 'families', according to the variations which they acquired, usually by being copied in different regions. Judaism keeps strict control of the text of the Torah: the creation of a scroll for use in the synagogue is entrusted only to those who are profoundly religious as well as skilled in writing Hebrew, and such extreme care has to be taken that, for a scroll to be acceptable, it must have no mistakes at all.

Religious leaders, as we saw, give their official approval to their religion's sacred texts, but sometimes non-canonical writings gain great popularity and become sacred writings for many devotees. In Buddhism, for example, ordinary people have taken to their hearts the *Dharmapada* (Pāli, *Dhammapada*), a collection of sayings not specifically Buddhist, and not originally included in the canon. Similarly, the Epics and the *Purāṇa*s are the most popular sacred writings for millions of Hindus who may know nothing of the *śruti* texts.

One reason for this is that sacred writings are often the preserve of specialists – scholars or priests. Many are used in the performance of religious ritual, especially, for example, in the Japanese religions and brahmanical Hinduism. Another reason can be the language that is used. The sacred writings of many religions are not easily accessible to ordinary devotees. Beryl Dhanjal explains that although *Gurmukhī*, the language of the Gurū Granth Sāhib, is written in Panjābi script, it is actually a medieval language from North India. The language of Hinduism's Veda, as Gavin Flood points out, is 'vedic Sanskrit, the sacred language of the gods'. Ian Reader says that Shinto uses an archaic form of the Japanese language, and that Japan's Buddhist writings are mainly in 'Buddhist Chinese'. The language of the Qur'ān is not a problem for those who know Arabic, but Muslims in non-Arabic-speaking countries often have to struggle in order to 'read' the Qur'ān, and do not necessarily gain a thorough understanding of the text.

Translations play an important part in the wider use of the sacred writings of many religions. Buddhism spread east from India to China in the first century CE and to Tibet in the seventh century, and much of the earlier Buddhist literature now exists only in Chinese and Tibetan translations. In the last two centuries Christianity has put a great deal of effort into translating the Bible into most of the world's languages, as part of its missionary activity. However, Islam, the other main missionary religion, has resolutely refused to translate the Qur'ān, on the grounds that the word of God would inevitably be altered in the process of trying to find words in any other language for key Muslim terms and concepts. As Martin Forward points out, Muslims use expressions such as 'meaning' or 'interpretation' rather than 'translation' when the Qur'ān is rendered into another language. However, it is not only Muslims who are aware of this problem. For example, translators of the Christian Bible continually confront the difficulty of conveying the meaning of the original words into another language and into a different cultural context.

All sacred writings are interpreted writings. The easiest way to illustrate this is to point to the material which makes up the Jewish Bible and the Christian Old Testament; the content is identical (apart from the order of the books) but each is interpreted within its own community of faith. For example, Jews would certainly not accept the Christian interpretation of the Suffering Servant in the Book of Isaiah. Even in religions, or in traditions within a religion, where emphasis is placed on the literal meaning of the text, there is a felt need for aids to understanding and for adjudication where possible problems arise. Commentaries on sacred writings are widespread; indeed, Tibetan Buddhist monks often study commentaries rather than the actual texts. Some texts are so important in a religion that they have commentaries written on them by large numbers of scholars. For example, in Hinduism practically all major scholars have written commentaries on the *Brahma-sūtra* and the *Bhagavadgītā*, and Douglas Davies shows how the letter of Paul to the Romans has had commentaries written on it by important Christian scholars from the time of the Reformation.

The use of words such as 'writings' and 'texts' can be misleading. First, because much of what later came to be regarded as sacred writings was originally spoken. Hinduism's Veda was transmitted orally for a thousand years before it was written down, and Buddhist texts for about three hundred years. Similarly, much of the Jewish Bible was handed down orally before taking written form (the teachings of the prophets are actually called 'oracles'), and most of the material about the life and teaching of Jesus was used in the early Church in oral form before being gathered into gospels.

Secondly, it can be misleading because hearing the texts is, in many religions, either more important or more common than reading them. For example, the words of sacred writings are heard in worship. This may take the form of readings. There can be few Christian services without at least one biblical reading, and frequently congregations hear one reading from the Old Testament and one from the New. Readings from the Torah and the Prophets play a most important part in Jewish worship, and it is considered an honour to be 'called up' in the synagogue to the reading of a passage. Sacred writings may also be recited or chanted. Hindu priests chant passages from the Veda as part of all ritual ceremonies, and, as Ian Reader explains, the sacred texts of Shinto are designed mainly for use in ritual. *Ṣalāt*, the prayers Muslims perform five times a day, include reciting passages from the Qur'ān, and Sikh congregational worship involves not only the *granthī* reading from the Gurū Granth Sāhib but the *rāgī*s (musicians) singing its devotional songs.

The use of the Sikh scriptures set to music is a reminder of the importance of the sound of words. In a number of religions the sacred writings are chanted rather than read, especially, for example, in Hinduism and Buddhism. Ian Reader refers to the sacred power of words in both Shinto and Buddhism in Japan, mentioning that the frequently recited *Hannya Shingyo*, the Buddhist *Heart Sūtra*, is regarded as an especially efficacious ritual chant or prayer. Douglas Davies illustrates the role of Christian hymns in making worshippers familiar with biblical themes and imagery, and Xinzhong Yao tells how Confucius set his poems to music. In Judaism, a musical note has been allocated to every syllable of the Torah – a fact which illustrates the demanding nature of the task facing a young boy reading a passage in the synagogue when he becomes Bar-Mitzvah (or, in some Progressive synagogues, when a young girl becomes Bat-Mitzvah).

For ordinary members of a religion, it is the contents of their sacred writings that matter, rather than the history of the canon or the problems of translation or how the authenticity of the text has been guarded. Occasionally one hears it said that all religions are really the same. Other volumes in this series explore both the similarities and the differences in the teachings on particular themes in eight religious traditions; in this volume we are focusing on the actual writings, so we restrict ourselves to noting the nature of their contents, particularly its immense variety.

At one end of the spectrum, Sikhism's Gurū Granth Sāhib consists of devotional poems or songs, prefaced by the *Japjī*, which is used as a morning meditation by devout Sikhs. At the other end of the spectrum, Islam's Qur'ān includes (in addition to a number of poetic *sūrah*s) legislation covering every aspect of life, from personal relationships and religious responsibilities to justice in society and international relations, and this is supplemented in the *Ḥadīth*. The Jewish Bible contains a wide range of types of literature, including legislation, devotional poems or songs, aetiological and other narratives, genealogies, history, court records, prophecy and proverbial sayings, while the Talmud, as we have seen, is a vast collection of rabbinic discussions and commentaries on the Mishnah. Christianity added to the Jewish Bible, which it inherited, gospel narratives about Jesus, letters written by leaders in the early Church, and an apocalyptic work. Key Shinto writings deal with what Ian Reader calls 'mythistory', particularly concerned with the relationship between the *kami* (deities), the Japanese Imperial family and the Japanese people, but the function of many other texts relates to ritual procedures.

As we move on to the other religious traditions represented in this book, any description of the contents of their sacred writings becomes much more problematic, partly because of the quantity and variety of the literature, and partly because of the difficulty in deciding where the boundary of the sacred writings comes. Confucian works include history, poetry, rituals, divination, moral teachings, and guidance for political life, and the enormous corpus of Taoist writings covers every aspect of Taoist belief and practice, with much space devoted to immortality and to expositions of *tao* – the Way. Ulrich Pagel describes the attempts made in the Buddhist tradition to classify its literature, one of the earliest of these being by content, into three 'baskets' (*tipiṭaka*), dealing with doctrine, monastic life, and philosophy. With the development of the Mahāyāna, there was a tremendous expansion of literature, ranging from interpretations of earlier teachings to stories of the life of the Buddha and of his and other *buddha*s' previous lives. Hinduism's Veda focuses on the ritual context, and includes hymns and songs for use in brahmanical rites, while the *Upaniṣad*s are concerned mainly with philosophical speculation. However, once one moves outside the *śruti* texts, the proliferation is enormous, and, as Gavin Flood explains, the literature includes metaphysical systems, interpretations of earlier works, epic poems and an extensive range of mythologies.

The chapters in this volume demonstrate the significant place that sacred writings hold in all religions, but they also reveal the many ways in which such sacred writings differ.

1. Buddhism

Ulrich Pagel

The sacred writings of the Buddhists form a collection of literature of astonishing magnitude. The spiritual fountainhead of all Buddhist scriptures is the Buddha, or to be more precise, the doctrine (*dhamma*) that was taught by him. Most scholars would agree that the teachings of the historical Buddha are recorded in the scriptures of the Theravāda school – the Pāli Canon.

Broadly speaking, the religious texts of Buddhism fall into three categories. First, there is a large body of early canonical writings. Preserved in the Pāli *Tipiṭaka*, their contents are generally accepted to have come from the lips of Śākyamuni Buddha. Secondly, there is a smaller collection of paracanonical works. Chronologically, these texts followed closely on the canonical writings, but failed to find their way into the early canon by the time it became fixed. Thirdly, we have a large number of pseudo-canonical and non-canonical texts. From the historian's point of view, these include the *sūtra*s of the Mahāyāna, the *tantra*s of the Vajrayāna and a large body of commentarial literature that sprang up around the canon. In their own traditions, however, both *sūtra*s and *tantra*s enjoy canonical status as they too are attributed to the Buddha. The commentarial works were mostly composed by prominent Indian scholars and exegetists discussing the contents of canonical writings. Taken together, the three categories of writings build up to a collection of several thousand individual works. The length and scope of all these texts vary greatly, ranging from writings of only a few lines to works comprising many thousands of pages.

Divisions of Buddhist scriptures

Overwhelmed by the magnitude of its literature, Buddhist tradition drew up several modes of scriptural classification. The most common is that into three baskets (*tipiṭaka*), i.e., *Suttapiṭaka*, *Vinayapiṭaka* and *Abhidhammapiṭaka*.[1] Tradition has it that this threefold classification was established at the communal recitation (*saṅgīti*) held soon after the demise of the Buddha. However, since there is only one late reference to someone 'knowing the three *piṭaka*' in the canon itself, this classification was probably introduced *a posteriori* to sanction the lineages of transmission evolving from the *saṅgha*'s division of labour in scripture memorisation.

Most other divisions recorded in Buddhist writings have only theoretical value, since they do not correspond to any true classification. The division that is most frequently cited refers to nine/twelve branches (*aṅga*) of literary genres present in the canon. These are the *sutta* (prose), *geyya* (recitation of prose and verse), *veyyākaraṇa* (prophecies), *gāthā* (verse), *udāna* (solemn utterances), *itivuttaka* (discourses prefixed: 'Thus has been said by the lord'), *jātaka* (birth stories of the Buddha), *abhutadhamma* (descriptions of feats) and *vedalla* (analysis and elaboration). Although books called *Jātaka*, *Udāna* and *Itivuttaka* are included in the Pāli Canon, it is unlikely that their namesakes among the *aṅga* refer to them, but are examples of the types of literature that had gained prominence in Buddhist circles – not specific texts.

The northern Sanskrit tradition of Buddhism augmented the nine branches with three further genres. These are the *nidāna* (short introductions giving the circumstances in which the discourse was delivered), *avadāna* (biographic, faith-inspiring accounts of elders contemporary with the Buddha) and *upadeśa* (explanatory literature on the contents of *sūtra*s). While it is generally correct to associate the twelvefold division with the Mahāyāna, it is important to note that the twelve *aṅga* are also found in Śrāvakayāna Sanskrit works – and vice versa.

Following the fragmentation into schools (third/second century BCE), the division into three baskets was amended to include new sets of writings. The Bahuśrutīya school, for instance, divided its body of scriptures into five categories to comprise, besides the traditional *Sūtra-*, *Vinaya-* and *Abhidharmapiṭaka*, a *Saṃyukta-* and *Bodhisattvapiṭaka*. Mahāsāṃghika followers devised a similar division, only replacing the *Bodhisattvapiṭaka* with a *Dhāraṇīpiṭaka*. The Dharmaguptaka reportedly possessed four baskets of writings, adding a *Bodhisattvapiṭaka* to the established *Tripiṭaka*. Since these collections are not preserved, it is impossible to ascertain the exact contents of the additional baskets.

In translation, the organisation into baskets was only partially implemented. Tibetan translations of the Buddhist canon are divided into two categories, the *bKa'-'gyur* and *bsTan-'gyur*. The *bKa'-'gyur* contains only those texts that are attributed to the Buddha himself. It consists of well over one hundred volumes and is subdivided into five major groupings comprising works of the *Vinaya*, Mahāyāna *sūtra* collections, *dhāraṇī* texts, independent Mahāyāna *sūtra*s (augmented by several pre-Mahāyāna works) and a selection of *tantra*s. In the *bsTan-'gyur*, totalling over two hundred and twenty volumes, the compilers of the Tibetan canon included translations of works belonging to the Indian commentarial Buddhist tradition. Although these writings are non-canonical by Indian standard, they enjoy great authority in Tibet and are regularly studied in conjunction with *bKa'-'gyur* material.

The Chinese Buddhist tradition divided the scriptures from a different viewpoint. First, it included not only works of Indian origin, but also a great number of indigenous Buddhist writings. Secondly, it amended the traditional threefold division by introducing other criteria. Issues such as the author's country of origin, a text's doctrinal orientation (Śrāvakayāna or Mahāyāna), the epoch in which it was translated and the degree of authenticity granted were all considered. What is more, the criteria varied from period to period. Thus, depending on the epoch in which they were drawn up, catalogues show quite different organisations. Today, the Japanese Taisho Shinshu Daizokyo edition of the Chinese canon (subdivided into twenty-four sections and itself based on Korean and Ming readings) is generally used as standard reference work by scholars.

Process of canonisation

Tradition has it that immediately after the demise of the founder steps were taken to safeguard the accurate preservation of the Buddha's teachings. For this purpose, Mahakasyapa, a prominent disciple of the Buddha, reportedly convened a council in Rajagrha, the capital of Magadha. He appointed five-hundred *arahant*s (accomplished monks free of all attachment) to decide on the authenticity of the teachings that were submitted to the council. For the doctrine he called on Ananda, the Buddha's personal attendant known to have heard most sermons, to recite all the discourses (*sutta*) he remembered. For the monastic code, Mahakasyapa summoned Upali, a great expert in the *Vinaya*, and asked him to relate all monastic rules that he heard from the Buddha's lips. Before a discourse or precept was formally authenticated, it was subjected to careful scrutiny and required unanimous approval by all five-hundred *arahants*. Whenever in doubt, the assembly refused admission out of fear that they unwittingly might alter the Buddha's teaching.

Assessment of the scripture's authenticity followed a set of guidelines drawn up by the Buddha himself. Recognising the threat false claims of authenticity could pose to his teaching, he advised his disciples to confirm in every case that a newly introduced text stemmed either directly from his own lips or from that of elders (*sthavira*) of a formally constituted *saṅgha* and that it conformed to the spirit of both the *dhamma* and *Vinaya*. Any text that did not match these four principal 'authorities' was to be rejected as bogus.

Several sources included also the recitation of the *Abhidhamma-piṭaka* in their accounts of this council – some attributing it to Ananda, others to Mahakasyapa himself. The scholastic nature of the *Abhidhammapiṭaka* cast doubt on this claim, although we know that the systematisation of *sutta* material began already very early.

Research by modern scholarship introduced serious reservations about the claims found in the accounts of this council. It is highly questionable whether the monks who were present at the council had access to all the sermons of the Buddha. The texts themselves speak of disciples who refused to endorse the sermons as recalled by Ananda, preferring instead to adhere to the form in which they had memorised them. There must have been many monks in India who, although remembering genuine discourses, either failed to gain admission to the council, or did not reach it in time to have them considered. Furthermore, the earliest version of the account conspicuously lacks a description of the canon whose authenticity it proposes to establish. What is more, the various schools do not agree on the contents of their canon, showing differences in the distribution of the texts and the presence of an *Abhidharmapiṭaka*. Had there been an early codification, it would undoubtedly have been adopted as a common basis by all sects. The claim of codification is further dented by the late composition of some of the *Abhidhamma* works and the enduring controversy surrounding the composition of the *Khuddakanikāya*. In view of these objections, one cannot help but conclude that the traditional account of the Rajagrha council lacks historical foundation. One suspects that while a gathering of scriptures probably took place soon after the demise of the Buddha – for a collection like the Buddhist canon does not come about by chance – the information we are given on this event perhaps reflects how the council was perceived by the order in later times.

The circumstances in which the 'true' gathering of sermons took place are not known. It is widely believed that the collecting of texts was begun already during the lifetime of the Buddha. Progress of the compilation is implicitly documented in the accounts of a second Buddhist council that was held about sixty years after the Buddha's *parinirvāṇa* at Vaisali. At that council, a group of monks was rebuked for practices deviating from the monastic code. Their conduct was condemned on the basis that it contravened what was then regarded as canonical tradition. For this condemnation to be convincing, the majority of the order had to have a very clear idea of what constituted inviolable scripture. Wishing to authenticate their version of the canon and to give the community a body of scriptures that would hold authority in future dissidence, the Rajagrha account might have been inspired by the proceedings at Vaisali.

Contents of the Buddhist canon

Division of the early scriptures into three baskets represents fundamentally an organisation of writings according to contents: the *Suttapiṭaka* contains discourses of the Buddha on the doctrine (*dhamma*), the *Vinayapiṭaka* lists the rules and precepts governing monastic life and the *Abhidhammapiṭaka* consists of scholarly treatises analysing material taken from the *suttas*.

The *Suttapiṭaka* is the main source for the doctrine of the Buddha. Buddhaghosa (fifth century CE), our chief authority on the division of the early Buddhist canon, speaks of the *Suttapiṭaka* as being divided into five groups (*nikāya*) of texts. These are the *Dīghanikāya* (collection of long sayings), *Majjhimanikāya* (collection of middle-length sayings), *Saṃyuttanikāya* (collection of works grouped together according to their contents), *Aṅguttaranikāya* (collection of *sutta*s characterised by numerical groupings of items treated) and *Khuddakanikāya* (collection of minor texts).[2] The discourses of the first four *nikāya* are, for the most part, in prose punctuated with verse. The teaching proper is invariably preceded by a short introduction (*nidāna*) giving the circumstances in which the *sutta* was delivered, starting with a phrase supposedly uttered by Ananda at the first council: 'Thus I have heard, at one time the lord was dwelling at . . .'. The names of the *nikāya* reflect to some extent the length of the *sutta*s they contain, although there is evidence that in some cases the size increased through interpolation. Their present length is thus not necessarily a guide to their original contents. There are several *sutta*s that appear in two or more of the five *nikāya*. This applies especially to the *Khuddakanikāya* (but also to the *Saṃyutta-* and *Aṅguttaranikāya*) which contains much material from the other four *nikāya*. The order of the *nikāya* reflects generally the order of the *sutta*s' age and authenticity, though attempts to disentangle the chronological strands amongst the *sutta*s bore little fruit.

The *Dīghanikāya* contains thirty-four independent *sutta*s which deal with various aspects of the doctrine. In the *Brahmajāla-*, *Sāmmaññaphala-* and *Mahāparinibbānasutta*, it includes several of the most important early Buddhist writings. Apart from containing detailed accounts of the spiritual training of monks, descriptions of ascetic practice and important doctrinal expositions, the *sutta*s of the *Dīghanikāya* are a valuable source for life in ancient India in general. Several of its *sutta*s also provide information on the biography of the Buddha – legendary and historical – that is not found elsewhere in the canon.

In the *Majjhimanikāya*, some one hundred and fifty *sutta*s of medium length are loosely grouped together according to subject matter and title. Like the *Dīghanikāya*, the *Majjhimanikāya* shows little cohesion in content. Its *sutta*s deal with almost all aspects of the Buddhist doctrine, ranging from monastic life, asceticism, morality and meditation to the four noble truths and the eightfold path. Variations in depicting the Buddha suggest substantial differences in the *sutta*s' time of composition. The latest strand is probably found in the *sutta*s of the penultimate group (*vagga*) which foreshadow the trend to systematising typical of the *Aṅguttara-nikāya* and later *Abhidhamma* works.

The *Saṃyuttanikāya* includes almost three thousand mostly

shorter *sutta*s that are arranged according to their contents. It is subdivided into fifty-six collections (*saṃyutta*) arranged into five *vagga*, each of which looks at particular aspects of the doctrine or shares the interlocutor to whom its *sutta*s are addressed. This arrangement rests unmistakably on an editorial intervention stemming from a conscious selection of material. Like those of the preceding *nikāya*, the *sutta*s of the *Saṃyuttanikāya* deal with a broad spectrum of topics. The majority of texts display a slight shift away from the early, 'primitive', method of teaching towards a more scholastic way of exposition. This applies particularly to those *sutta*s that deal with numerical subjects where there is some notable overlapping with the topics treated in the *Aṅguttaranikāya*.

The *Aṅguttaranikāya* consists of over two thousand individual, short *sutta*s. Unlike the *Saṃyuttanikāya*'s subject-oriented approach, the *Aṅguttaranikāya* lists its *sutta*s according to numerical criteria, arranged serially in ascending order. It is subdivided into eleven sections (*nipāta*) organised in about one hundred and sixty *vagga*. Typically, each *nipāta* contains *sutta*s that deal with subjects in a similar fashion and are connected to the number of the section. Most *sutta*s are devoid of narrative elements but employ technical, stereotyped patterns of presentation. Their scholastic propensity ties the *sutta*s of the *Aṅguttaranikāya* to the *Abhidhamma* books of later centuries, and facilitated the interpolation of additional material in the appropriate *nipāta* up to the period of its fixation.

The material that is included in the *Khuddakanikāya* is not recognised as canonical by all schools. It includes the 'inferior' texts that remained outside the four *nikāya*, because they were perceived to be of doubtful authenticity. It is the longest collection of the *nikāya* and comprises fifteen books of varying subjects, contents and character, most of which are written in verse. The titles of these books are (1) *Khuddhakapāṭha*, (2) *Dhammapada*, (3) *Udāna*, (4) *Itivuttaka*, (5) *Suttanipāta*, (6) *Vimānavatthu*, (7) *Petavatthu*, (8) *Theragāthā*, (9) *Therīgāthā*, (10) *Jātaka*, (11) *Niddesa*, (12) *Paṭisambhidāmagga*, (13) *Apadāna*, (14) *Buddhavaṃsa* and (15) *Cariyāpiṭaka*.

Of all five *nikāya*, the *Khuddakanikāya* was always the most fluctuating collection. Even in the Singhalese tradition, its exact composition was long subject to controversy. Although, in its present form, doubtless the most recent part of the canon, several of its originally independent works are of great antiquity. Some of its texts are used as sources for the first four *nikāya* and most have correspondents in Prākrit or Sanskrit. Conceived as poetic works intended to arouse interest in Buddhism, they are not methodical treatises of scholarly stature, but won acclaim for their inspirational value. As a body of literature they are of considerable interest in themselves and they played an important role in the popularisation of Buddhism.

The second basket of the *Tipiṭaka*, the *Vinayapiṭaka*, contains the rules of conduct that were drawn up by the Buddha in response to misbehaviour by his disciples. As a communal law, the *Vinaya*'s prime objective was to guarantee the smooth running of the Buddhist order. For this purpose, it decrees various sets of sanctions meted out in response to violations of accepted parameters of behaviour, and lays down the guidelines for the functioning of the order. Since each rule was formulated in response to an actual offence, the *Vinaya* shows a high degree of realism. The majority of rules address ethical concerns intended to maintain the community's moral standard. More often than not, these rest on ancient Indian conventions of morality complemented by rules that serve the particular requirements of the Buddhist order.

There is, however, more to the *Vinaya* than the dimension of legality and morality. Its precepts are not meant to be followed uncritically, but intended to create an inner awareness of the nature of one's action. Changes in the rules in adjustment to new surroundings suggest that they were primarily seen as a preventive force designed to control the environment of the monks as well as their actions in relation to it. The sanction that is meted out to the offender varies in line with changes in the circumstances relating to the intent and degree of completion of the wrongdoing.

> If (the monk) thinks it is trading when it is trading there is an offence of expiation involving forfeiture. If he is in doubt as to whether it is trading, there is an offence involving forfeiture. If he thinks it is not trading when it is trading, there is an offence of expiation involving forfeiture. If he thinks it is trading when it is not trading, he is guilty of wrong-doing. If he is in doubt as to whether it is not trading, he is guilty of wrong-doing. If he thinks that it is not trading when it is not trading there is no offence.
>
> (*Vinaya* II, 111–12)

Hence, the precepts become a finely tuned set of indications revealing blemish in the monks' mental state. When fully implemented in intuitive observance, they become the ideal representation of the teaching of the *dhamma*.

The *Vinaya* is furthermore the principal means for the Buddhist *saṅgha* to legitimate its status as successors to the Buddha. It sustains the identity and purity of the order as a whole, and holds in balance the delicate relationship to its lay supporters.

As it is known today, the *Vinaya* is divided into three major categories. First, there is *Suttavibhaṅga*, whose core consists of the 227/311 *Pātimokkha* rules for monks and nuns. It always maintained an elevated position in Buddhism and underwent little change. Conceived as a casuistic law, the *Pātimokkha* does not decree broad principles, but lists individual cases as they were decided by the Buddha. The rules themselves fall into eight classes, enumerating the transgressions in descending order of gravity. Governing social behaviour and cultural conventions as well as spiritual concerns, the *Suttavibhaṅga* gives insight into many aspects of life in ancient India and represents a valuable historical source in its own right.

The second portion of the *Vinaya*, the *Khandhaka*, introduces a new wider circle of *Vinaya* rules that complement the *Pātimokkha* precepts. Most of them concern the collected acts of the order and address discord in the communal life. They govern the procedures for major monastic ceremonies and propose a mechanism to resolve the threat of schism. Although largely cast in the context of Sakyamuni's biography, the *Khandhaka* deviates from the order of events because it classifies the rules by subject matter.

The third section of the *Vinaya*, the *Parivāra*, is a collection of auxiliary works of varying dates that sprang up around the *Vinaya* in the centuries following the Buddha's demise. Singling out material from the bulk of *Vinaya* texts and reducing them to surveyable portions, it is used by novices to facilitate the task of mastering the *Vinaya*. Although of canonical status, the *Parivāra* is little more than an appendix to the *Vinaya*.

The *Abhidhammapiṭaka* is later than the *Sutta-* and *Vinayapiṭaka*. Yet, it figures among the earliest known Indian philosophical treatises which reason by means of sets of established logical techniques to establish their propositions. The themes of analysis are always taken from the discourses of the *Suttapiṭaka*. This work of categorisation started during the life-time of the

Buddha, when it was mostly entrusted to Sariputra. Initially, the systematisation consisted of little more than drafting sets of headings (*mātikā*) to serve as notes on the doctrine. This method was retained and most *Abhidhamma* works propose a *mātikā* at the beginning of the treatise as a table of contents on which they then expand. The *Abhidhamma* of the Theravāda tradition consists of seven separate *Abhidhamma* books. Other schools drew up different sets of *Abhidhamma* treatises. In subject, spirit and methodologic approach, however, they all belong to the same scholastic tradition.

The works included in the three *piṭaka* came into existence early enough to attain canonical status. That is to say, they had gained sufficient influence and standing to be considered by the time the canon was closed. Besides these texts, Buddhism recognises several other early works of paracanonical or early post-canonical status. For the *Vinaya*, these are the *Pātimokkhasutta* and the *Karmavācanā*. For the *Suttapiṭaka*, the best-known of these texts are the *Peṭakopadesa*, *Nettippakaraṇa* and *Milindapañha*. While the first works are essentially exegetical treatises aiding scholarly analysis of *sutta* material, the *Milindapañha* shows many strands of popular Buddhism, and it enjoyed great repute among lay followers for its enlightened dialogues.

> Milinda asked: 'Is it through wise attention that people are freed from further rebirth?' 'Yes, that is due to wise attention and also to wisdom and the other wholesome *dharmas*.' 'But is wise attention not the same as wisdom?' 'No, O king. Attention is one thing and wisdom is another. Sheep and goats, oxen and buffaloes, camels and asses possess attention, but wisdom they lack.' 'Well put, Nagasena!'
>
> Milinda asked: 'Which is the characteristic of attention and which is the characteristic of wisdom?' 'Reflection is the characteristic of attention – cutting off is that of wisdom.' 'Why? Please provide a simile.' 'You supposedly know what barley reapers are?' 'Yes, indeed.' 'In which fashion do they reap barley?' 'With the left hand they take hold of a bushel of barley, in the right hand they hold a sickle and then they cut the barley with the sickle.' 'Likewise, O king, the yogin gathers his thought with attention and cuts off defilements by means of wisdom.'
>
> (*Milindapañha* III, 51–2)

Such was its popularity that the *Milindapañha* gained canonical status in the Burmese tradition and was included alongside the

Peṭakopadesa, *Nettippakaraṇa* and *Suttasaṅgaha* in the Burmese *Khuddakanikāya*.

Round about the beginning of the Christian Era, the *sutta*s of early Buddhism began to be supplemented by new works. For those who subscribed to their doctrines and religious ideas, these new texts superseded the old established writings. Like the early *sutta*s, they too claimed the authority of the Buddha. Miraculously emerging from the underworld where they had been hidden for several centuries, they trace their origin to sermons allegedly preached by Śākyamuni in places that were inaccessible to the *śrāvaka* (disciples of the historical Buddha). Hence, they escaped attention at Rajagrha. Starting out with a few scattered texts, the literary output of this new tradition grew swiftly to immense proportions, turning out scriptures of unseen magnitude and philosophical depth.

Unlike their counterparts of early Buddhism, Mahāyāna scriptures are not organised in a methodical classification, but fall into two broad categories. That is to say, they are either part of one of the scriptural collections of the Mahāyāna or belong to the large body of independent *sūtra*s.

The *sūtra* collections of the Mahāyāna are four, viz., the *Prajñāpāramitā*, *Mahāratnakūṭa*, *Buddhāvataṃsaka* and *Mahāsaṃnipāta*. With the exception of the *Prajñāpāramitā*, little is known about the period in which these collections came into existence or the circumstances that gave them their present form.

The *Prajñāpāramitā* is doubtless the earliest and doctrinally most influential of the Mahāyāna collections. Its founding texts, the *Ratnaguṇasaṃcayagāthā* and the prose version thereof, the *Aṣṭasāhasrikā*, represent the earliest strands of the Mahāyāna. Their philosophical visions served as inspiration for many generations of Buddhist thinkers after them. There is probably not a single text among the hundreds of Mahāyāna *sūtra*s whose religio-philosophical thinking they did not affect.

The period of composition of *Prajñāpāramitā* texts lasted well over one thousand years. It began in the century before the Christian Era and came to a close in the twelfth century CE. During the first period, extending roughly from 100 BCE to 100 CE, the basic texts containing the original impulses were elaborated and systematised. In the second period (100–300 CE), these were then expanded to produce new, infinitely larger versions. In the period from 300 to 500 CE, scholars set out to reformulate the basic doctrines of the founding works in short *sūtra*s and versified summaries. In the *Vajracchedikā* and *Hṛdaya Prajñāpāramitā*, this period produced some of the most outstanding examples of Buddhist philosophical writings.

> 'O Subhūti, is there any doctrine that was taught by the Tathāgata?' 'No, indeed, O lord, there is no doctrine that was taught by the Tathāgata.' 'O Subhūti, when you ponder the number of particles of dust in this world system comprising one thousand worlds, would they be many?' 'Yes, O lord, because that which the Tathāgata taught as dust particles, he declared "non particles". Thus, they are called particles of dust. And this world system the Tathāgata declared a "no system". Thus, it is called world system.' 'O Subhūti, what do you think, can the Tathāgata be perceived through the thirty-two marks of the great being?' 'No, indeed.' 'Why?' 'Because the thirty-two marks of the great being that were taught by the Tathāgata are, in reality, "no marks". Thus, they are called the thirty-two marks of the great being.'
>
> (*Vajracchedikā*, 13b–d)

After 600 CE, the creative phase of *Prajñāpāramitā* literature came gradually to a halt. Its teachings were increasingly influenced by ritualistic manifestations of tantric thought and lost much of their philosophical appeal. *Prajñāpāramitā* doctrines were compressed in brief magical spells whose exact meaning was revealed only to a few chosen ones. At an even later stage, *Prajñāpāramitā* became conceptualised as an independent spiritual force. It was given a place in the pantheon of Buddhist deities and declared worthy of veneration.

The *Mahāsaṃnipāta*, as given in the Chinese canon, consists of seventeen *sūtra*s of little religio-philosophical cohesion. Because they share so little apart from a certain preoccupation with magic, scholarship has thus far failed to ascertain the *rationale* behind their grouping into a single collection. The earliest reference to the *Mahāsaṃnipāta* goes back to the second century CE, but it does not reveal the composition of this early version. Today, as a group of texts, the *Mahāsaṃnipāta* is preserved only in Chinese, although its *sūtra*s do appear individually in the Tibetan canon. Information on an Indian prototype of the *Mahāsaṃnipāta* is very scarce indeed. Judging by this lack of references, its composition might have been a local affair that never attracted much attention – if indeed it originated in India.

The *Mahāratnakūṭa* collection as it stands today was edited at the beginning of the eighth century in China by Bodhiruci, a South Indian *Tripiṭaka* master. Before Bodhiruci, the history of the collection is obscure. Little conclusive can be said about the earliest phases in the formation of the 'original' *Ratnakūṭa* collection. It seems certain that the *Ratnakūṭa* was shaped in Central Asia where it grew out of a small collection of informally assembled *sūtra*s. This group, which may have comprised as many as twenty or more *sūtra*s, was rendered into Chinese in the third century by Dharmaraksa. It is probable that by the time Hsuan-tsang visited India in the seventh century CE, they had assumed the shape of a formal collection entitled *Mahāratnakūṭa*. However, since most Indian exegetists seem ignorant of it, one suspects that in India this collection never gained the prominence it achieved in Central Asia.

The earliest references to a collection of *sūtra*s bearing the name *Mahāratnakūṭa* are found in fifth-century Chinese translations of Indo-Buddhist commentarial literature. There we find several references to a *Mahāratnakūṭa* collection, consisting of at least five works from among those presently included. The translations themselves were executed in Chinese Central Asia, suggesting that there the *Ratnakūṭa* was a well-known body of scriptures, possibly as early as the fourth century CE. Five of its *sūtra*s belong to the earliest Mahāyāna texts ever translated into Chinese, among them the influential *Kāśyapaparivarta*. On the *bodhisattva*, the *Kāśyapaparivarta* says:

> O Kāśyapa, there are four [means] to attain the great treasure of *bodhisattva*s. Which four? He rejoices at the presence of the Buddha; he hears the six perfections (*pāramitā*); he meets *Dharma* teachers without malevolent prepense and delights unremittingly in the practice of seclusion.
>
> O Kāśyapa, there are four things that help the *bodhisattva* to transcend all evil. Which four? He retains the thought of enlightenment; he harbours no ill-feeling towards sentient beings; he discerns mistaken views and he despises no one.
>
> O Kāśyapa, there are four things that enable the *bodhisattva* to accumulate roots of virtue. Which four? He takes genuine delight in seclusion; he holds on to the four means of conversion without expectation for reward; he pursues the Doctrine unfettered by concern for body or life and he accumulates roots of virtue without satiety.
>
> O Kāśyapa, there are four adornments of immeasurable merit. Which

four? He teaches the Doctrine with a pure mind; he shows great compassion for people of low character; he imparts the thought of enlightenment to all beings and he bears with those who are languid.

(Stael-Holstein (ed.) § 17–20, pp. 37–43)

Philosophically, the *Kāśyapaparivarta* attracted much attention for the exemplary transparency with which it expounds the Doctrine of Emptiness.

O Kāśyapa, things are empty not because one thinks of them as empty (*śūnya*) – they are empty in themselves. Things are signless not because one thinks of them as signless – they are signless in themselves. Things are wishless not because one thinks of them as wishless – they are wishless in themselves. Things are unaccumulated, unborn, unarisen and without own-being not because one thinks of them as such – they are so in themselves. Furthermore, O Kāśyapa, emptiness does not rest on the disappearance of the existence of individuality (*pudgala*). Individuality itself is emptiness and this emptiness is emptiness in itself, absolute emptiness. . . . O Kāśyapa, take refuge in emptiness – not in individuality. But those who seek refuge in emptiness through the perception of emptiness using the senses, these I declare hopelessly strayed from my Doctrine. O Kāśyapa, it is better to subscribe to the belief of the substantiality (*ātmadṛṣṭi*) – even if it is as large as Mount Sumeru – than to subscribe arrogantly to the view of emptiness (*śūnyatādṛṣṭi*). Why? Because to those who adhere to the belief of the substantiality, emptiness is liberation – but how is one liberated from the view of emptiness?

(Stael-Holstein (ed.) § 63–4, pp. 94–5)

The forty-nine *sūtra*s presently comprising the *Ratnakūṭa* cover the complete spectrum of (early) Mahāyāna thought. Indeed, the impression gained is that the collection may have been compiled as part of an early conversion activity, with the aim to provide a well-balanced cross-section of Buddhist thought. Such a motive for its compilation would account for the almost complete absence of evidence on the formation and existence of an Indian *Ratnakūṭa* collection. Moreover, it would intrinsically link its formation with those Central Asian areas where the earliest traces of the *Ratnakūṭa* literature have been discovered.

The *Buddhāvataṃsaka* is extant in two Chinese recensions, consisting respectively of thirty-four and thirty-nine chapters. Most of the chapters came into existence as separate *sūtra*s that circulated independently for many centuries. The period in which they were gathered together to form a greater collection is not known. The dating of Chinese translations has shown that two of its texts are very early indeed and might go back to the beginning of the Christian Era. However, the first reference to a collection of texts called *Buddhāvataṃsaka* does not appear before the beginning of the fifth century CE. It was in China that the collection attained most attention, eclipsing even the *Mahāratnakūṭa* and *Mahāsaṃnipāta*. Favoured by a shift towards Yogācāra thinking, of which several of its texts are fervent exponents, the *Buddhāvataṃsaka* gained great popularity during the last quarter of the first millennium CE. The best-known and doctrinally most important works of the *Buddhāvataṃsaka* are the *Gaṇḍavyūha* and *Daśabhūmikasūtra*. Judging by the dating of its earliest translation, the *Daśabhūmika* is likely to have preceded the *Gaṇḍavyūha*. Its exposition of the ten stages grew into a landmark for the *bodhisattva* doctrine that affected all later developments in the organisation of the *bodhisattva* path. In contrast, the contribution of the *Gaṇḍavyūha* rests on its value as literary masterpiece. Conceived as a balanced work of art, it combined convincingly the literary dimension with innovative philosophical thought. Embellished by similes, elaborate descriptions and figurative language, the *Gaṇḍavyūha* guides the reader through a maze of narratives without ever neglecting its vision of universal interpenetration. Although often held to display the idealist view of the early Yogācāra, the *Gaṇḍavyūha* carefully avoids statements that would affirm such a position.

The independent Mahāyāna *sūtra*s share with the texts of the four collections a common interest in the *bodhisattva* and Mahāyāna ontology. Taking this interest as point of departure, they set out in many different ways to elaborate, interpret or expand on these themes.

The *Saddharmapuṇḍarīka* is generally regarded to have arisen alongside the early *Prajñāpāramitā*. Almost certainly a composite work, its doctrines touch on many subjects central to Mahāyāna thinking. Above all, it became famous for its treatment of skilful means (*upāyakauśalya*) as the supreme expedient effectuating liberation for all sentient beings. Enlaced in its picturesque language and mythological setting is a fervent criticism of the *śrāvaka*'s limited aspiration. Owing to the *Saddharmapuṇḍarīka*'s immense popularity and its propagation of the 'cult of the book', the *Saddharmapuṇḍarīka* is extant, besides the customary Tibetan and Chinese translations, in numerous Sanskrit redactions.

Another early Mahāyāna *sūtra* of great influence is the *Vimalakīrtinirdeśa*. Doctrinally, it stems from the same philosophical movement as the earliest known recensions of the *Prajñāpāramitā*, *Mahāratnakūṭa*, *Buddhāvataṃsaka*, and *Mahāsaṃnipāta*. Composed at the beginning of the Christian Era, the *Vimalakīrtinirdeśa* became a major source for the ontological thought of the Madhyamaka school. Its greatest contribution to Buddhist thought was, however, its authoritative discussion of the ideal of the lay *bodhisattva*. By ascribing the role of the main protagonist to a lay *bodhisattva* and crediting him with an erudition second to none, the *Vimalakīrtinirdeśa* firmly established the lay *bodhisattva* in the fold of Buddhist saints.

Fine examples of the many philosophically accomplished works are the *Laṅkāvatāra* and *Saṅdhinirmocana*. Both texts contain highly abstract, ontological thought that played a major role in shaping Mahāyāna philosophy. Unmistakably composite *sūtra*s that grew over many decades, they are first attested in their present form in fifth-century China. It was also in China that the *Laṅkāvatāra* and *Saṅdhinirmocana* reached the pinnacle of their popularity, where they became paramount to the Yogācāra movement of the eighth and ninth centuries.

Thematically positioned at the other end of Mahāyāna creativity are the *Bhadrakalpika* and *Suvarṇaprabhāsottama*. The *Bhadrakalpika* stands out for the wealth of mythological material brought together to embellish its biographical accounts of former *buddha*s. This legendary genre prevails also in several other Mahāyāna works, most notably the *Amitābhavyūha*, *Kāraṇḍavyūha* and *Karuṇāpuṇḍarīka*. Consisting typically of picturesque accounts glorifying the powers, conduct and abodes of mythical *buddha*s and *bodhisattva*s, they are virtually devoid of philosophical thought, and serve to stir up sentiment in the devotee. Such mythological *sūtra*s became especially popular in the Far East where they gave rise to several Buddhist movements that were entirely based on faith and devotion (e.g., Pure Land Buddhism).

The composition of the *Suvarṇaprabhāsottama* (fourth century CE) heralded the end of mainstream Mahāyāna. Although doctrinally still very much within the parameter of Mahāyāna thought, its inclusion of magic spells and ritual precepts clearly stepped beyond accepted convention. Enlaced with legends celebrating feats of *bodhisattva*s and goddesses in magico-ritualistic contexts, the *Suvarṇaprabhāsottama* bears many traits foreshadowing the rise of tantric Buddhism.

The scriptures of the Vajrayāna mark the closing phase in the canonical literature of Buddhism. Its output is extremely prolific and comprises several hundred works. The vast majority of *tantra*s are preserved only in their Tibetan and Chinese translations. The earliest examples of tantric literature are short magic formulae, called *dhāraṇī* or *vidyārājñī*, that sprang up from around the third century CE. For the sake of propagation, they were regularly appended to well-known Mahāyāna *sūtra*s. In some instances, *dhāraṇī* became interpolated in specific *sūtra*s which explained their use and praised their magic powers. The exact number of spells is difficult to assess, but just those that were handed down to us amount to several thousand.

From the fourth century onwards, *dhāraṇī* rapidly gained momentum in Mahāyāna writings and developed into more elaborate treatises. Yet it was probably not before the end of the seventh century that the first comprehensive texts on tantric ritual and doctrine came into being. The most important works of this early period are the *Mahāvairocana* and the *Vajroṣṇīṣasūtra*. Following on these *sūtra*s, there emerged a multitude of shorter works which set the foundation for the surge of interest in Vajrayāna in China, Korea and Japan.

According to Tibetan historians, the whole output of tantric literature falls into four categories, each describing specific aspects of tantric practice. First, there are *tantra*s that lay down procedures at ceremonies and 'outer rituals' held in the worship of tantric deities. These are called *Kriyātantra* and make up the lowest, least esoteric, sets of texts. In the second category, the *Caryātantra* class, are those works that describe and characterise the conduct of more advanced tantric practitioners in 'outer ritual' and 'inner yoga'. The third category contains all those texts that set out to explain the working of esoteric and magical practices that spring from 'inner yoga'. As these are chiefly related to yogic trances and meditation, it is called *Yogatantra* class. The majority of *tantra*s fall into this category. The fourth and highest category of *tantra*s, the *Anuttarayogatantra* class, constitutes the most esoteric group of *tantra*s. Describing sexual symbolism in inner yogic practice, its texts are of the highest mystical order and strictly guarded by the initiated.

In order to attain authority and respectability, *tantra*s were designed to share many formal features with their Mahāyāna predecessors. The main protagonist in most *tantra*s is a *buddha* who is also portrayed as the teaching's fountainhead. Only the sites in which *tantra*s were preached differ from the places that are cited in the *sūtra*s. They are no longer historic places in northern India, but became locations of mythical origin. In the *Anuttarayogatantra*s, the 'preaching site' is often the vagina (*bhaga*) of the Buddha's consort, symbolising wisdom (*prajñā*).

Commentarial literature

The revelation of canonical writings was accompanied by a steady growth of commentarial literature. For the most part, commentaries refer to specific texts whose contents they explain on an individual basis. For the Śrāvakayāna, the only works preserved belong to the Theravāda and Sarvāstivāda. The most prolific commentator among the Theravāda was the fifth-century scholar, Buddhaghosa. Besides writing important commentaries on the *Sutta-*, *Vinaya-* and *Abhidhammapiṭaka*, he composed several independent treatises on the Buddhist path. The most important of these is the *Visuddhimagga*, which gives a systematic account of Buddhist meditation and its doctrinal foundations.

The commentaries of the Sarvāstivāda tradition are extant only in their Chinese translations. Unlike their Theravāda counterparts, they are not dominated by the genius of a single person, but were composed by various persons in the course of several centuries. The most noteworthy books are perhaps the *Mahāvibhāṣā*, attributed to Vasumitra, and the Sarvāstivāda commentaries on *Abhidharma* issues, such as the *Abhidharmakośa* by Vasubandhu.

Of the Mahāyāna *sūtra*s, we possess a large body of commentarial literature that has been preserved in Tibetan and Chinese translations. The works are so numerous that they make up most of the second division of the Tibetan canon, the *bsTan-'gyur*. Sanskrit originals are extant in only a few cases. As with the early scripture, they fall into commentaries on specific *sūtra*s and scholastic works of a more general nature. While the scope of the former is typically restricted to issues raised in the root texts, the latter set out to discuss Buddhist doctrine in a broader fashion.

Generally, one speaks of three major doctrinal currents in the exegetico-commentarial writings of the Mahāyāna. First, there are the treatises that were composed by the adherents of the Madhyamaka school of Buddhism. Its founder, Nagarjuna (second century CE), ranks also among the important writers of this school, and many works of great authority are attributed to him. His most influential work is doubtless the *Madhyamakaśāstra*, in which he postulates all the major tenets of Madhyamaka thinking. Besides this foundation-work, Nagarjuna is credited with a large number of exegetical treatises. For the most part, however, these works are apocryphal. Other important texts belonging to the Madhyamaka school are Candrakirti's commentary on the *Madhyamakaśāstra*, the *Prasannapadā*, and Bhavaviveka's *Prajñādīpamūlamadhyamakavṛtti*, which elaborate and interpret Nagarjuna's original propositions.

Treatises by the Yogācāra school represent the second major current in Mahāyāna commentarial literature. The most prolific writers of the Yogācāra were the brothers Asanga and Vasubandhu. Converted from Sarvāstivāda and Mahīśāsaka thought to the Mahāyāna, they composed many of the most important treatises on Yogācāra philosophy. The school's scriptural backbone is formed by a body of texts known as the *Five Works of Maitreya*. Inspired by Maitreya (a celestial *bodhisattva* awaiting his time to return to earth as the next Buddha), but compiled and written down by Asanga, they comprise the *Mahāyānasūtrālaṃkāra*, *Ratnagotravibhāga*, *Madhyāntavibhāga*, *Abhisamayālaṃkāra* and *Dharmadharmatāvibhāga*. While the treatises of Asanga deal typically with a variety of subjects, the works attributed to his brother are more philosophic in nature. Vasubandhu's most important treatises are the *Trisvabhāvanirdeśa* and the *Triṃśikā*- and *Viṃśatikāvijñaptimātratāsiddhi*, in which he refutes criticism on Yogācāra thought and presents the logic behind its own propositions. Comments on these texts by Dharmapala and several other scholars have been combined in the *Vijñaptimātratāsiddhi*, a work that has traditionally served as the chief source for Yogācāra study in Southeast Asia.

The third current in Mahāyāna exegesis is represented by the writings of Dinnaga, Dharmakirti and Dharmapala. In defence of Yogācāra thinking, Dinnaga set out to systematise the foundation of the *Abhidharma* analysis into a sound logical framework.

Proceeding from earlier *Abhidharma* criticism, he and Dharmapala developed the epistemological ideas of the Yogācāra into a general critique of knowledge. Something of a foundation work to this school is Dinnaga's introductory text on logic, the *Nyāyamukha*. Other well-known treatises include the *Marmapradīpavṛtti* and *Pramāṇasamuccaya*. His work was continued by his disciples and successors, Asvabhava and Dharmakirti, who, always following basic Yogācāra propositions, set out to refine his theory and gradually transformed the Yogācāra into a logical tradition in its own right. These advances in epistemology culminated in the writings of Dharmakirti, especially in his *Nyāyabindu* (summing up Dharmakirti's own views on logic) and *Pramāṇavārttika*. Profoundly influential and respected well beyond the Buddhist tradition, his system of logic won pan-Indian acclaim and was adopted by many epistemological schools.

Popular works

In addition to the spectrum of canonical writings and associated commentarial literature, Buddhist pietism produced a large corpus of 'popular' works. We saw that some of them, although apocryphal in origin but of great antiquity, found their way into canonical writings. Others were denied such status and were collected outside the canon proper.

The best known example of this 'popular' genre is the *Dharmapada*. In the Pāli, the *Dharmapada* forms a collection of 423 stanzas drawn from a common stock of floating verse which prevailed in Northern India since ancient times. Parallels to Jaina and brahmanical works indicate that only a few of these verses are of Buddhist origin, but were probably adopted to broaden its popular base. The number of different versions that are preserved of the *Dharmapada* genre attest the popularity of this type of non-sectarian literature. Expeditions in Central Asia brought to light a (longer) Sanskrit version, entitled *Udānavarga*, and an incomplete edition in Gāndhārī Prākrit. Although of different schools, all three have much in common and shared originally perhaps as many as three hundred and sixty verses. The issues that are addressed in them are not specifically Buddhist, but reflect ancient Indian ideals of sanctity and ethics. Notwithstanding its generic origin and contents, the

Dharmapada soon became one of the most celebrated of all Buddhist scriptures.

> If you aspire to honour, wealth, or after death
> A blissful life amongst the gods,
> Then ensure that you fulfil the maxims
> Of moral life.
>
> A discerning man lives a moral life
> When he realises that it leads to four benefits.
> A sense of virtue gives him peace.
> His body is not overburdened.
>
> At night he sleeps a healthy sleep
> And when he wakes he arises with joy.
> A holy man endowed with insight,
> He thrives and prospers in the world.
>
> A man of wisdom who acts exemplarily,
> A man of morals who gives gifts,
> In this world and in the next too,
> He advances to happiness.
>
> His moral habits planted firm,
> His trance and wisdom excellent.
> Untiring, earnest,
> He gains release from suffering forever.
>
> (*Udānavarga*, vi, 1–3, 5, 8)

Its closest rival in popularity is perhaps the *jātaka* genre. Based on themes of Indian fables, *jātaka* stories purport to narrate the previous lives of Gautama Buddha before he gained enlightenment. Their chief task was to inspire faith and confidence in the Buddha. Embedded in folklore, which was adapted by the Buddhists to draw attention to their cause, the *jātaka* genre attained rapid popularity across India. They are regularly depicted in iconography at ancient Buddhist sites and occur in the scriptures of all schools. Verbatim parallels in Sanskrit literature and excerpts in the four *nikāya* indicate that some *jātaka* are of great antiquity. Beside the 547 stories that are included in the *Jātaka* book of the *Khuddakanikāya*, the Buddhist traditions of Southeast Asia preserve outside the canon a collection of fifty apocryphal *jātaka*. Most of them run parallel to the motifs of the Pāli collection, but several have no Pāli equivalent and correspond to recensions of the northern Sanskrit tradition. Some of the northern *jātaka* were compiled in separate collections, e.g., the *Jātakamālā* of Aryasura. Others found their way as illustrations of the Buddha's accomplishment into the *Vinaya* and Mahāyāna *sūtras*. To whichever literature it was appended, the *jātaka* genre played at all times a prominent role in preparing the reception of Buddhist thought and proved an effectual vehicle to circulate and popularise its ideas.

Legends of elders contemporary to the Buddha (*avadāna*) exerted a similar fascination on the minds of ordinary people. In part, this appeal rested on the glorifying tone in which *avadāna* describe the noble conduct of the elders. They inspire imitation of this conduct by showing that even the most minute wholesome act has the potentiality to prompt great results. In the Pāli Canon the *apadāna* (Pāli form of *avadāna*) texts are gathered in *Khuddakanikāya* as an independent collection of well over five hundred stories. Although in character clearly related to the *jātaka* genre, *avadāna* legends differ since they do not refer to the Buddha and abound with mythological material of late origin.

The Sanskrit tradition broadened the concept of the *avadāna* to include, besides the *Avadāna* book of the *Kṣudrakāgama*, a series of semi-historical works professing to retell the course of past – but factual – events. The earliest specimens of this type of literature, marking the beginning of Sanskrit extracanonical literature (second century CE), are the *Aśokāvadāna* and *Avadānaśataka*. Other *avadāna*, such as the *Bodhisattvāvadānakapalatā* and the *Nandimitrāvadāna*, however, are of much later date. Research has shown that the claim to historicity, especially among the earlier *avadāna*, may not be as preposterous as was previously held. In time and style, these early *avadāna* stand between the original canonical writings and Mahāyāna literature. Citing whole passages from the early *sūtras*, but rejecting stylistic practices imposed by Prākrit prototypes, *avadāna* introduce whole series of new set phrases and formulae that occur otherwise only in the Mahāyāna. The combination of panegyric legends enlaced with canonical material assured the *avadāna* genre a secure place in Buddhist popular literature. Whenever told, it generated awe, admiration, faith and a sense of cultural identity in the audience, and flourished as a major source of Buddhist pietism.

Modes of transmission

The process of transmission of the Buddhist scriptures falls into two major phases. At first, for about three hundred years *Anno Buddhae*, all texts were transmitted orally. During this period, the task of preserving the Buddhist canon was the responsibility of the *saṅgha*. Realising that the number of texts remembered was too vast to be memorised by a single person, the monks followed the example set by the brahmins and divided the canon into more manageable collections (*nikāya*).

Buddhaghosa reports that the grouping of scriptures into *nikāya* was initiated at the council in Rajagrha. Although the naming of individual *nikāya* at Rajagrha is probably an anachronism, it is quite conceivable that the collecting of discourses by length and contents began at that time – if not earlier. Once their contents had been determined, the collections were allotted to groups of monks for transmission to their pupils.

The desire for accurate preservation and the enormous size of the canon necessitated a carefully developed system of oral transmission. Already at an early age, monks in charge of *sutta*-conservation were subjected to a demanding training in memorisation. Entrusted with the *Dhamma*, and well-educated, the reciters (*bhāṇaka*) gained a leading influence on scriptural matters and high standing in the community.

It is not known for how many centuries the *bhāṇaka* system was upheld. Buddhaghosa refers to it as if still practised in his time. Today, the practice of assigning groups of texts for oral preservation to *bhāṇaka* has receded. The reason behind this discontinuation is obvious. The widespread practice of writing and the rising popularity of manuscripts rendered oral transmission through *bhāṇaka* superfluous to the preservation of scripture.

According to Singhalese chronicles, the writing down of the canon started in the middle of the first century BCE. The reasons of war and famine leading up to that important change are plausible and probably genuine. Apparently, in Sri Lanka the number of monks had dropped so low that the *bhāṇaka* system approached collapse. Steps were therefore taken to compile the whole *Tipiṭaka* in writing.

The progressive use of writing increased public access to the scriptures. Although still kept in monasteries, they gradually eluded the control of the *saṅgha* and became available to everyone who showed sufficient perseverance to gain admission to the libraries. Once the exclusive right to maintaining the Buddha's sermons was taken away from the monks, a new phenomenon of immense reverberation emerged in Buddhism.

Thus far, the monastic community was able to control tightly the contents of the canon. Prior to its admittance in the *Tipiṭaka*, every newly proposed text had to be approved by the *bhāṇaka*. A work that failed to meet their criteria, whatever its claim to genuineness, was denied acceptance. This meant that nonconformist texts had little chance of survival, since there was no organisation outside the *saṅgha* that could secure their transmission. The laity, however devoted, could not possibly achieve its preservation as they lacked the training and organisation needed for such a task.

This all changed with the introduction of writing. No longer was the chief requirement for a text's preservation conformity to the views of the establishment. Even the most obscure and neglected manuscript in a monastic library could be picked up and read, even translated, by a curious browser or visiting scholar. This gave a real chance of survival to every new text – irrespective of its doctrinal position – and weakened irrevocably the influence of orthodoxy.

By no coincidence, it is roughly from the first century BCE onwards that Buddhism experienced a large increase in its scriptures. With astonishing speed, numerous new works purporting (like the texts of early Buddhism) to disclose the word of the Buddha appeared. Referring to themselves as discourses of the 'great vehicle' (*mahāyāna*), these new texts were of course the first exponents of Mahāyāna literature. In view of the fervent criticism they directed at the *arahant* and their dubious claim to authenticity, it is questionable whether they would have survived before the advent of writing.

Continuing revelation of scriptures

More than just allowing the rise of the Mahāyāna, the introduction of writing opened up the Buddhist canon to the possibility of 'continuing revelation'. It meant that from then onwards practically every text confident enough to plead *buddhavacana* could legitimately insist on canonicity. We saw that the first recorded assertions to this effect came from the Mahāyāna, beginning with its early *sūtra*s and persisting right through to the *tantra*s. Whether any such claim was ever made before the introduction of writing, we shall never know, as its scriptural basis was destined to be ephemeral. Of the texts which were written down, we know that they traced their origin often – though not invariably – to the historical Buddha, typically having been concealed in mythological realms, *stūpa* or caves. Fear for their transmission at the hands of ill-prepared, philosophically immature Buddhists is the reason that is traditionally cited to explain their concealment. The transitional period between their composition and eventual discovery frequently covered several centuries. The texts' re-emergence was generally 'held back' until people wise enough to understand their teachings correctly would prevail. Once brought to light, the texts were typically given a high profile which – bolstered by the mysterious circumstances of their discovery – helped their rapid dissemination. Judging by the immense literary output of the Mahāyāna, this new mechanism cannot but have gained swift and widespread acceptance across India.

The boldest claim to canonicity, however, came from the Tibetan Buddhist tradition. While generally very conscientious in assessing scriptural authenticity – requesting a Sanskrit original as proof of genuineness – some Tibetans departed from this tested method and claimed canonicity for a series of 'revealed' works (*gter-ma*) for which no Indian original could be produced. Analogous to their Indian predecessors, it was claimed that these texts had been deposited in secret places in former centuries to safeguard their transmission or to prevent untimely circulation. Recent research has shown that some of the earliest *gter-ma* are indeed very ancient. However, their case was somewhat weakened by the great frequency with which *gter-ma* were brought to light well into modern times. Leaving aside the question of their authenticity (an issue which, in substance, does not differ from the claims of the Mahāyāna), Tibetan *gter-ma* are today the only surviving tradition of 'continuing revelation' in Buddhism.

Editions and scribes

The first reference to a written edition of the Buddhist canon goes back to the fourth century CE. It is found in the Singhalese chronicles stating that the Theravāda Pāli canon was recorded in writing during the first century BCE. This early edition is long lost. On the mainland the process of committing Buddhist scriptures to writing began in roughly the same period, although not with the scale and organisation with which it was undertaken in Sri Lanka. Of these early Indian writings too, no specimen is known to have survived in its entirety. The dried palm leaves on which they were written – a resilient fibre which is long-lasting under favourable conditions, but susceptible to humidity, mildew and insects – failed to withstand the test of time and perished probably long ago.

The oldest Indian editions that survived to modern times go back to the sixth/seventh century CE. They belong to the Sanskrit tradition of northern India that flourished under the patronage of the Pāla-dynasty in Bengal. In addition to these early witnesses, a sizable number of Sanskrit manuscripts were preserved in the monastic archives of Nepal. These manuscripts date mostly from the eighteenth and nineteenth centuries. The value of these copies is somewhat marred by the multitude of scribal errors that found their way into the manuscripts in the process of transmission.

Beyond India, expeditions to Central Asia uncovered manuscripts at famous ancient Buddhist sites. Written in Sanskrit or Prākrits, many of them go back to the fifth or sixth century CE. However, since most are extant only in fragments and still have not been deciphered, Central Asian manuscripts are seldom used as main-readings, but are consulted chiefly as collateral material.

In China, manuscript editions are rare since printing was soon adopted for disseminating the Buddhist canon. Starting out with manuscripts on silk or paper, Chinese Buddhists drew early on advances in wood-carving, and commissioned in the tenth century the carving on to wooden blocks of the entire canon. With the availability of printed editions, manuscript copying was no longer required, since copies of the xylographic version could be circulated with ease throughout China. Once the idea of printing had gained acceptance among Chinese Buddhists, great prestige accrued to those who participated in the production. Vying for status and fame, Chinese craftsmen produced no less than fourteen blockprint editions in the course of one millennium.

Tibetan Buddhists followed in the footsteps of their Chinese counterparts. Initially, they too adopted the Indian model of text preservation. However, held back by Tibet's orientation towards

Indian culture, its scribes continued to copy out manuscripts well after the Chinese had introduced printing. Thus the monks of the Narthang monastery worked as late as the thirteenth century with hand-written manuscripts when they established the first Tibetan canon. Tellingly, the first printed edition of the Tibetan canon was not made in Tibet, but was carried out by the craftsmen of the Yuan court in Peking. It consisted only of the *bKa'-'gyur*, but was soon supplemented by the *bsTan-'gyur* in ensuing blockprint editions of Tibetan origin. As with the Chinese canon, once the advantages of printing had become apparent, printed editions became the norm and prevailed to the present day as the standard format of the Tibetan canon.

These cultural differences in scriptural transmission rest, in part, on the professional status awarded to the people who held a key role in the process of preservation – the scribes. In India, scribes occupied a low position. Their involvement in the reproduction of texts was poorly valued and their education did not extend beyond the art of writing. Hence, Indian scribes were in plentiful supply and received little financial reward for their service.

In China, in contrast, writing was a skill reserved to the learned, since it involved, even for the most trivial text, exacting knowledge of complex character formation. In view of these difficulties, copying of important Buddhist manuscripts was entrusted only to the most skilled calligraphers. The high professional standard of the copyist meant, of course, that far fewer scribal errors found their way into Chinese manuscripts. Emphasis on precision became imperative with the introduction of printing methods, since mistakes once carved in the block were difficult to correct. The use of printing from the tenth century onwards helped, therefore, to further contain the number of variant readings. Once the first printed edition was established, a model had been set for all subsequent editions. Such high standards in the field of copying imbue modern xylographs with great textual authority, since their readings are likely to be close to their ancient predecessors which recorded the *ur*-translation two thousand years ago.

The same cannot be said of the scribal tradition in South and Southeast Asia where the prestige remained with hand-written copies, and printing of the canon was never taken up. As a result, manuscripts frequently show inconsistent readings and copying mistakes introduced by poorly trained scribes.

Buddhist languages

The languages in which the editions of the Buddhist canon are preserved fall into two categories. First, there are the languages and dialects in which the texts circulated in India. These include local Prākrits such as Māgadhī, Pāli, and the North-Western Prākrit as well as Sanskrit and its prakritised derivatives. Secondly, we have numerous languages of translation that preserved the canon outside India. The most important of these are Chinese and Tibetan.

The Buddha himself denied preference to any one language and adopted for his preaching the local dialects of the regions through which he travelled. Thus, it is incorrect to speak of an original language of Buddhism and observations about early Buddhist languages cannot but proceed on a text-to-text basis. However, since much of the preaching activity took place in the principality of old Magadha, it is probably true to say that the Buddha's discourses were based on an early variety of Old Māgadhī. Except for a few archaic root forms, no traces of Old Māgadhī have survived. After his demise, the sermons were gradually transposed into other dialects as part of the diffusion process.

A variation of Old Māgadhī is still preserved in the language of the Theravāda canon – Pāli. Originally from the region of Vidisa, it was employed by the missionaries who brought Buddhism to Sri Lanka to memorise the sermons, and it became accepted by the Singhalese tradition as the 'language of the texts' (*pālibhāsā*). Although Pāli underwent morphologic and phonetic change in the course of several revisions, it is perhaps the closest approximation to the 'original' language of Buddhism.

With the beginning of the Christian Era, Prākrits became increasingly rivalled by the use of Sanskrit. Initially, Prākrit texts were interspersed with Sanskrit word-forms rather crudely. Achieving increasing sophistication as the *Dharma* was transmitted, this blend established itself and led to the peculiar hybrid that is found only in Buddhist writings. Modern scholars refer to this cross-breed as Buddhist Hybrid Sanskrit. In essence, Buddhist Hybrid Sanskrit is thus an amalgamation of languages, juxtaposing Sanskrit forms with Prākrit equivalents. Linguistic complexities suggest that its evolution is best credited to authors of considerable linguistic dexterity and not, as it was proposed, to poorly educated authors unable to write correct Sanskrit.

Yielding to the increasing popularisation of Sanskrit, Prākrits and Buddhist Hybrid Sanskrit were gradually replaced by a more correct form of Sanskrit. This process began in the second century CE and made itself felt first in northern India from where it travelled slowly into the south. In time, all the sects of the Indian mainland adopted Sanskrit as the vehicle for their scriptures. Texts that were conceived after this adjustment were of course directly composed in Sanskrit, but many of the earlier works needed to be transposed. Traces of this adaptation are preserved in the many composite works that include linguistic strands of Prākrits and Sanskrit proper.

Of the numerous languages of translation, Tibetan and Chinese are the most important as they constitute the only languages into which the Indian texts were directly transmitted. Most other languages (with the exception of modern scholarly translations from the Sanskrit and Pāli) are secondary in the sense that they are based on either Tibetan or Chinese. This privileged position is reinforced by the towering volume of Tibetan and Chinese Buddhist writings, for no other culture has preserved nearly as many scriptures in its language. Above all, Tibetan translations stand out for their great accuracy and consistency, which were achieved by adapting the Tibetan language in translation specifically to Buddhist terminology. Hence, in Buddhist research Tibetan and Chinese rank on almost equal footing with the Indian languages.

In Buddhism, the concept of a sacred language is of little immediate applicability. Common perception requires for a language to become sacred unanimous acceptance by the adherents of that faith. Moreover, in most cases it will be the tongue in which the divine revealed itself to man. Neither of these conditions is met in Buddhism. We saw that the Buddha himself refused to give preference to any speech. His stance was widely adopted by his followers and there is indeed no single language that is read by all Buddhists. Nevertheless, undercurrents proposing allegiance to one language above others do exist. This is particularly true of Pāli, the language of the Theravāda canon. In the whole of Southeast Asia and Sri Lanka, Pāli is highly esteemed as the original language of Buddhism and given special status in the transmission of the canon. In the process of copying the canon, for instance, Southeast Asian scribes – yielding to the prestige of Pāli – will go to great lengths to preserve the phonology of Pāli in the regional script of their tradition.

In China, Japan and Korea, faith in the efficacy of sound is not shown to Pāli but to Sanskrit. There, in some circles, Buddhists chant routinely short *sūtra*s and magic formulae in the original idiom, convinced that reproduction of sound alone suffices to bring about salvation. Often ill-instructed in the wording of the chant, they trustingly place their fate in the hands of Sanskrit phonetics. If belief in the power of sound is anything to go by, Buddhism clearly has in Pāli and Sanskrit two tongues approaching the concept of a sacred language. However, as neither of them is accepted by all Buddhists they cannot be regarded unreservedly as such.

Utilisation of scriptures

The areas in which sacred writings came to be used varied considerably in Buddhist history. During the first few centuries, the scriptural tradition of Buddhism must have been a very active one. All texts were probably regularly recited and intensely studied, as the mechanisms of oral transmission do not allow for a text to fall into oblivion. Because their preservation was entrusted to the *saṅgha*, it is reasonable to assume that much of these literary pursuits centred on monastic establishments. The growth in *Abhidharma* treatises suggests that the scholarly investigation of texts lasted well into the Christian Era. Lay access to the writings, restricted by the Buddha himself, was granted to only a few selected texts.

With the introduction of writing, these restrictions could no longer be enforced. The speed with which this change began to show is not known. Chronologic discrepancies in the evolutionary process of the nascent Mahāyāna *sūtra*s and their manifestations in lay pietism indicate a delay of several centuries before the new ideas were transmitted to popular culture. We do not know the reason behind this delay. Judging by earlier practices, we may suspect a continuing monastic control on the textual tradition long after the introduction of writing.

The earliest traces of non-scholarly use of Buddhist scriptures go back to the second century BCE. It is found at Bharhut and Sanci in the iconographic depictions of *jātaka* narratives. Engraved in the walls of temples and *stūpa*, these illustrations received probably little scholarly attention but were designed to inspire piety in visitors and to disseminate the stories.

Another use of Buddhist writings is recorded in several early Mahāyāna *sūtra*s which speak of a 'cult of the book'. Expedited by the increasing use of manuscripts and their role in sustaining Mahāyāna thinking, its texts became subject to cultic veneration at *stūpa*, where at first they were typically kept. The beginnings of this cult are only thinly documented. Besides a few references to this practice in the texts themselves, no corroborating evidence of its origins has been uncovered. According to reports by Chinese pilgrims, the concealing of scriptures in *stūpa* had become common practice by the fifth century CE. Recent finds of manuscript fragments underneath collapsed *stūpa* from that period confirm their accounts.

The foundations of scripture-worship go back to early Buddhism. The Buddha himself is reported to have endorsed the occasional use of protective texts (*paritta*) in order to forestall impending calamity. Once Buddhists had subscribed to the idea that a text possesses intrinsic magical powers, the ground was prepared for the cultic devotion of scripture prevalent in the Far East. An example of this cultic practice is found in a passage of Hsuan-tsang's biography, relating how Hsuan-tsang resorted to chanting his favourite text when confronted with danger on his travels. Among many Buddhists of China, Korea and Japan this devotional attitude to scriptures is still widespread. Elaborate invocations in great numbers held in artistically furnished temples, and the recitation and copying of *sūtra*s, assume to the present day an important place in the daily routines of Far Eastern Buddhists. The contents of the texts moved thereby gradually into the background, making way for magical and aesthetic dimensions. In some periods, many a recitation was enjoyed as a purely aesthetic activity, leading to competitions where beauty of melody and voice became the chief focus.

To the present day, for many East Asian Buddhists the most revered text is the *Saddharmapuṇḍarīka*. Numerous tales attest to the efficacy of faith in, reciting and copying of, and generally promulgating its contents – activities which are held to be sufficient for salvation. Turning early away from academic pursuits, its devotees place emphasis on devotional practices springing from the belief in the supreme power of the Buddha and its manifestations in scripture.

In Sri Lanka, belief in the intrinsic power of scripture is less pronounced. From its earliest days in the third century BCE, the Theravāda *saṅgha* set scriptural learning among its main tasks. Moulded by the academic tradition of Indian scholasticism, the monks soon assumed the role of educators for the Sinhala people. Literacy was taught at village temples or monasteries and the materials used in teaching were invariably Buddhist. Responding to social requirements, Singhalese monks became thus from early on scholars and teachers whose primary task consisted of studying the canon and its commentaries. Withdrawal from monastic learning in favour of seclusion or lay preaching was granted only after completion of a comprehensive course in canonical studies. Since it played an important role in general education and monastic training, the canon became quite naturally an object of learning and scholarly investigation.

This is true for all but a small portion of the canon, consisting of protective spells (*paritta*). Valued for their efficacy as charms or exorcisms for one's physical and material well-being, *paritta* grew to be carefully studied by ceremonial specialists who also supervised their recitation at public services. Although *paritta* chanting is not documented before the tenth century, it is undoubtedly a very ancient custom. In order to accommodate the spiritual needs of a laity clamouring for magic and ritual, they came to be vigorously promoted in monastic studies, and today, *paritta* training plays an important part in the education of practically every monk. However, as *paritta* studies are specifically aimed at lay needs, they never superseded monastic learning as the main purpose to which the canon was put.

In Tibetan Buddhism, depending on the sectarian contexts, the use to which sacred writings are put varies in kind and degree. In the dGe-lugs-pa order – the most academic of all schools – the study of Buddhist scriptures is a cornerstone in the monastic education and is regarded as a *sine qua non* for spiritual progress. Although the canonical texts are at all times available in superbly stocked libraries, it is relatively rare that a monk will study them. In practice, much of his reading material will consist of texts from the large corpus of highly esteemed commentarial writings. For the most part, these treatises rework material found in the *bKa'-'gyur*, which they reduce in size and cast into a more digestible format. The degree to which scriptures of any kind are studied depends, of course, also on the aspirations of the individual. Monks who show tenuous inclination to scholarly pursuits will meet with little exposure to sacred writings, while those who aspire to academic distinction are expected to undergo a long and demanding course of study.

Apart from scholarly contexts, virtually all monks encounter sacred scriptures at the numerous religious ceremonies that punctuate monastic life. At such occasions the texts are generally read aloud and relate directly to the purpose of the ceremony. They are invariably recited in Tibetan and their audience is expected to absorb their contents.

Belief in the intrinsic power of sound is less widespread in Tibet and restricted to the ritual context. There, it does play an important role and is regularly found. Typically, it is applied to short spells and formulae designed to secure magically the successful completion of the ritual. Encoded in cryptic language of little independent meaning, the spells are usually recited in their original idiom. Tapping a source of immense power, devotees attach great value to the correct intonation of individual syllables, since mistakes therein are feared to lead to great calamity. Spells of this kind are particularly frequent in tantric ritual where they assume a key role in the empowerment process. The exact purpose to which they are put varies greatly, ranging from the summoning of chief deities to the appeasing of local spiritual forces.

Finally, emulating their Indian predecessors, Tibetans will often deposit sacred scriptures on altars, holy places and, above all, in *stūpa* commemorating events of religious importance. Representing the word of the Buddha, their presence is fundamental to the aura of holiness that surrounds these sites and turns them into places of worship and pilgrimage.

Apart from specifically commissioned *sūtra* recitation, scripture-worship is for the majority of the laity the only contact they will ever have with canonical writings. Constrained by a widespread unavailability of alternative instruction, the laity depend on monks for *sūtra* schooling, which is invariably channelled through monastic institutions. Like their ancient Indian predecessors, Tibetan lay Buddhists are mostly instructed in carefully drafted teaching-texts which touch only on points of immediate relevance to the lay path. Detailed study of canonical material – although theoretically open to all – is in practice left to the religious expert.

NOTES

1. All references to the early Buddhist scriptures relate to the canon of the Theravāda tradition and are therefore given in Pāli.
2. In the Sanskrit tradition, the corresponding categories are called *Dīrghāgama*, *Madhyamāgama*, *Saṃyuktāgama*, *Ekottarāgama* and *Kṣudrakāgama*. These categories of texts represent the canon as it was known to the Sanskrit schools of northern India. Today, little of their canon is preserved in the original idiom. Most of it is found in translation in the Chinese *Tripiṭaka*. While the *āgama* are fundamentally Sanskrit counterparts to the Pāli *nikāya*, they exhibit several differences. First, the number of works included in the *āgama* is greater than that in their Pāli correspondents. Secondly, the arrangement of the *āgama* and their *sūtra*s does not always match that of the *nikāya*. Thirdly, the texts themselves differ in contents and structure, depending on whether they appear in the *āgama* or *nikāya*. In most cases, the differences in contents are limited to the method of expression and arrangements of subjects. The doctrinal base itself is very uniform in both collections. The question whether these variants go back to deviations in the oral tradition or to deliberate modification based on written documents is, as yet, unresolved.

FURTHER READING

Beal, S. (1882) *Buddhist Literature in China*, London, Trübner & Co.
Bechert, H. (ed.) (1980) *Die Sprache der ältesten buddhistischen Überlieferung* (*The Language of the Earliest Buddhist Tradition*), AAWG, Van den Hoeck & Ruprecht, Göttingen.
Bechert, H. (ed.) (1985–87) *Zur Schulzugehörigkeit von Werken der Hīnayāna Literatur*, AAWG, Van den Hoeck & Ruprecht, Göttingen.
Conze, E. (1978) *Prajñāpāramitā Literature*, Tokyo, The Reiyukai Library.
Frauwallner, E. (1956) *The Earliest Vinaya and the Beginnings of Buddhist Literature*, Rome, Serie Orientale Roma, 8.
Law, B.C. (1933) *A History of Pāli Literature* (2 vols), London, Routledge & Kegan Paul.
Norman, K.R. (1983) *Pāli Literature*, Wiesbaden, Otto Harrassowitz.
Ruegg, D.S. (1981) *The Literature of the Madhyamaka School of Philosophy in India*, Wiesbaden, Otto Harrassowitz.
Stael-Holstein, Baron Anton von (ed.) (1926) *The Kāśyapaparivarta: A Mahāyāna Sūtra of the Ratnakūṭa Class*, Shanghai.
Winternitz, M. (1933) *A History of Indian Literature*, vol. 2, Calcutta.

2. Christianity

Douglas Davies

Christianity, along with other great world religions, especially Islam and Sikhism, has a book – in this case the Bible – close to the centre of its life. It even shares a large part of these scriptures with Judaism, for what Christians call the Old Testament the ancient Hebrews and modern Jews have long held as their own scriptures. To share scriptures in this way means, among other things, that there is a focus for both agreement and disagreement between Christians and Jews.

The Bible has been translated from its original texts into many other languages, and this involves trying to grasp what the original authors meant in their own day, and then seeking to communicate those ideas for other societies. This involves the difficult task of 'cultural translation', running alongside the obvious task of interpreting words, of getting the right degree of fit between the original message and the message for today. Through its missionary ventures Christianity has given itself extensively to this task because of its commitment to translate the Bible into the languages of as many people in the world as it possibly can. The belief that ordinary church members as well as church leaders should be able to read the Bible in their own language has motivated both Bible translation and educational programmes teaching people to read in many parts of the world. Christians believed that knowledge of God could be gained from reading the Bible both publicly in church and also in private worship. The Society for Promoting Christian Knowledge (SPCK), for example, was founded in 1698 to build schools for educational purposes in England and Wales and to distribute Bibles throughout the world.

Accurate or intelligible translations?

The issue of interpretation, or hermeneutics, has never been more important than at present, because twentieth-century scholars have become more aware than ever of the social and personal factors influencing authors and readers of texts. Also of great importance is the context in which sacred scriptures serve their purpose, the setting where they come into their own and are perceived as sacred. A Bible on a bookshop shelf may have the title Holy Bible written on it but be viewed as just another book; once it is placed in a church and read, or used as part of an individual's private devotions, it comes to be something far more significant. One decision Christian leaders have to take involves balancing accuracy of translating the Bible from its original languages against making it easily understood in the language of the reader. This is especially important for people who are normally unfamiliar with books or whose level of education in reading and literature is low. Even in Britain, for example, some religious organisations use films, videos, slides, and comic-strip papers, to convey the message and stories of the Bible.

Scriptures in context

Christian worship is so closely linked with sacred scriptures that it is almost impossible to think of any formal Christian service taking place without some use of the Bible. This centrality of the Bible is due to the fact that Christianity stresses its past through the belief that God's self-revelation has occurred within history at particular times and places, through religious leaders such as prophets, but most especially through Jesus of Nazareth. The Bible is the central deposit of witness to this divine revelation.

Because Christianity grew out of the Jewish religion of the time of Jesus, its first sacred writings were those of Judaism. Not only would most of the first Christians, as Jews, have been familiar with having the sacred scriptures of their Jewish tradition regularly read in the synagogue, but they would also have been accustomed to those scriptures being studied and debated, especially by the rabbis. As time went on, Christians drew a distinction between the writings of the Jewish religion prior to the life of Jesus and those writings which

Christian communities produced for their own purpose. The former were not abandoned but came to form what was called the Old Testament, in contrast to the New Testament writings produced by early Christian leaders. So it is that the Bible known to modern Christians is made up of pre-Christian Jewish material seen as a foundation for the new Christian writings. Getting the actual separate books together into an authorised and accepted collection was neither a simple nor a rapid task. The authoritative list, or Canon of Scripture as it is called, of the Jewish scriptures, did not take its final form until about the end of the first century of the Christian Era. It took nearly four hundred years after the birth of Christ before the emerging Christian Church produced its own definite list, including both Old Testament and New Testament sections. This collection came to be called the Bible, from the Greek word *biblia*, meaning books. Subsequent generations of Christians saw the Bible as a special book that was, in some way, inspired by God, and containing truths vital for instruction in living the Christian life, with both Old and New Testaments having their part to play in drawing the picture of divine activity and purpose.

At the heart of Jewish scriptures for Jews lay the idea of the Torah, or divine law, believed to have been given by God through Moses and focused in the Pentateuch, the five books of *Genesis*, *Exodus*, *Leviticus*, *Numbers* and *Deuteronomy*. At the time of Jesus this group of 'Torah' scriptures – The Law – along with those of 'The Prophets', were clearly identified as sacred scripture, while some other 'Writings' were deemed less authoritative; these included all the other books presently in the Old Testament as used by most Christians, plus Ecclesiasticus, Tobit and Maccabees, which were later excluded by Jews.

One of the interesting facts of early Christianity is that it relatively quickly produced written documents of its own. Paul (a convert to Christianity from Judaism), who was a highly educated and literate person, saw himself as having been charged by the risen Christ to take the gospel message to the non-Jewish world. This he did by a series of missionary journeys, by preaching and debating not only with fellow Jews but also with gentiles, the name Jews gave to non-Jews. He later wrote to these new Christian congregations he had helped to create, and in his letters, or Epistles, spelled out his beliefs concerning the significance of Jesus of Nazareth viewed as God's chosen and anointed One or Messiah (or Christ – *christos* in Greek). Christ fulfilled God's promises to the Jews and, through his death and resurrection, also opened up the divine plan of redemption for the gentile world. The message of Christianity focused on a divine plan of salvation motivated by God's love for humankind, executed through the man Jesus, who was believed to be God's Son in some special way, and experienced through the power of the divine Spirit within the company of believers. The very use of the terms Old Testament and New Testament reflects the idea that God has established a relationship of salvation with humankind, since the word 'testament' comes from the Latin word for 'covenant'.

A New Testament sketch

The New Testament is made up of epistles, four gospels, the account of the Acts of the Apostles and, finally, the Apocalypse. Of these twenty-seven New Testament documents some twenty-one are epistles. Their authorship varies and the actual author of some of them is disputed or unknown, even when an epistle stands under the name of a particular apostle. As to their content, it also varies from clear affirmations of faith and expressions of doctrine to pastoral encouragement and moral instruction. The following selections drawn from each basic type of New Testament document illustrate this variety of early Christianity's self-understanding.

Epistles

CHRISTIANS AT CORINTH

The First Epistle to the Corinthians presents a sweep of Christian understanding. Based on the belief that Paul was 'called by the will of God to be an apostle of Christ Jesus' (1:1), whose cross is the power of God for salvation (1:17), it is grounded in the message of 'Jesus Christ and him crucified' (2:2). His hearers are no mere audience but are God's temple where God's Spirit dwells (3:16). But Paul has heard that in this community of the saved there are members living immorally, including an incestuous relationship (5:1). He calls them all to moral living and gives advice about marriage. There is some suggestion in the text that Paul thinks that the period of the Christian Church's existence will be short, given the fact that Christ may return to judge and change the way the world is run; given the shortness of the duration of things, even those who are married might live as if they were unmarried (7:29). Even so he is concerned that they should know that Christians have a great deal of freedom from a multiplicity of religious regulations because of Christ, but they should not use their freedom for selfish ends. So, too, in connection with idols and non-Christian religions, a Christian may eat food that has been offered to idols because it is of no importance to the believer, but if non-believers see some problem in it then the believer should desist from eating because of the other person's conscience (10:28). This kind of ethical approach to life reflects Paul's view of the universe as an ordered scheme of things, from God, through Christ, to men and then to women (11:3–16). The life of the Christian group must also express this sense of order, which is why dissensions and divisions are wrong and why worship should be an orderly affair and not a time of chaos. This is especially true when they meet to break bread together. He emphasises his status as an apostle in touch with Christ when he tells them that what he received from the Lord he gave to them, that 'the Lord Jesus on the night when he was betrayed took bread, and when he had given thanks, he broke it, and said "This is my body which is broken for you. Do this in remembrance of me"' (11:23). This element of tradition is important for Paul because it links the historical life of Jesus with the present-day life of the Christian community: 'You are the body of Christ and individually members of it' (12:27).

Some of the Christians at Corinth possess religious experiences which are publicly significant because they speak in tongues, possess gifts of healing etc. These expressions of spiritual power must, he says, be put to good use and not cause disunity among believers. Indeed, the way to live as a member of this community is by the ethic of love. In the famous chapter thirteen of the epistle, Paul tells of the 'more excellent way' of love.

> . . . if I have all prophetic powers, and understand all mysteries and all knowledge, and if I have all faith, so as to move mountains, but have not love, I am nothing.
>
> (13:2–3)

> So faith, hope, and love abide, these three, and the greatest of these is love.
>
> (13:13)

Love must be used to build up the Christian community of believers, a community which stands entirely on the basis of the death of Jesus for the sins of the world and his resurrection from the dead. If chapter thirteen stands as the prime Christian expression of the ethic of love, then chapter fifteen is the foundation document for the Christian belief in the resurrection of Christ. We have seen how Paul said that he delivered to the Corinthians what he had received as far as the breaking of bread was concerned (11:23); we now find him saying that he also delivered to them 'as of first importance what I also received, that Christ died for our sins in accordance with the scriptures, that he was buried, that he was raised on the third day . . . and that he appeared' (15:3–5). He appeared to Peter, to the Twelve, to five hundred or so others, and finally to Paul himself when he was converted on the road to Damascus, an account of which is given in the Acts of the Apostles (9:3–9). Paul ends his letter with some practical instructions on his hopes for future journeys and visits and shows how mobile and active were his plans as the apostle to the Mediterranean world of the first century.

CHRISTIANS AT ROME

The letter to the Romans focuses on the similarity between the faith of Abraham, expressing the heart of the Old Covenant, and the faith of Christians in the New Covenant. God's deity is known through the created world (1:20) but humankind preferred idolatry to true worship, and idolatry involved immorality. God's wrath is stirred up by this human wickedness, a wickedness which becomes increasingly apparent through the Law of the Old Covenant, which portrays God's righteousness at the same time as it shows humankind's sinfulness. All humans stand sinful before God until they are forgiven through having faith in Jesus. Through him peace comes to exist between believers and God, they are 'justified by faith' (5:1). God's initiative lies at the heart of this process of salvation: 'while we were still weak, at the right time, Christ died for the ungodly'

(5:6). Paul compares Adam, as the first man who sinned, and Jesus, as the second Adam who did not sin. The epistle is full of opposites of this sort, as in arguing that believers were once enemies of God but now are friends, once they lived in sin but now they must live by the Spirit of God. He speaks of the old self which, as it were, has died along with Christ so that the new life of righteousness could begin. Even so, the life of faith possesses a certain tension between the old life in the flesh and the new life in the Spirit: the good I want to do I cannot and the evil I do not want to do is exactly what I do (7:19). But God is on the side of such poor creatures and has 'sent his own Son in the likeness of sinful flesh . . . to condemn sin in the flesh' (8:3). Even the universe itself groans under the power of evil and awaits a new day when God will transform it (8:22). The Spirit of God helps us in our weakness, and by faith believers are convinced that nothing will separate them from God's love (8:39). Paul is sad that the great majority of his fellow Jews do not see that God has acted in Jesus to bring about the New Covenant, but even so he believes God has a plan that is inscrutable for he cannot see that God would ever reject the chosen people of Israel. The thoughts about God's ways bring Paul to poetic worship: 'O the depth of the riches and wisdom and knowledge of God! How unsearchable his judgments and how inscrutable his ways!' (11:33). This sense of God's great goodness draws from the apostle a call to believers to present their own bodies 'as a living sacrifice, holy and acceptable to God' (12:1). They are to be transformed in their thinking rather than conformed to the world, and they must show this in their obedience to human authorities (13:1), just as they do through their humility in welcoming those who are weak in faith (14:1), for 'We who are strong ought to bear with the failings of the weak, and not to please ourselves' (15:1). He ends his letter with various greetings, showing how important human relationships were in the communities of early Christians.

Romans in Christian history

This Epistle to the Romans has been of particular significance in practically every phase of the history of Christianity to date because of the way it influenced the spiritual development of several important church leaders and through them millions of others. Augustine, for example, was finally prompted in his conversion to

Christianity in 386 CE by reading from the end of chapter thirteen, 'let us conduct ourselves becomingly as in the day, not in revelling and drunkenness . . .' (13:13). So too with Martin Luther, whose work was basic to the Reformation. He lectured on Romans between 1515 and 1516, placing great emphasis upon the idea of justification by faith, and on the need for God to act in saving humankind from its wickedness. No amount of human religiosity could yield the kind of faith which leads to a person being justified; God alone can bring this about, as Luther makes clear in saying that:

> A monkey can imitate human actions beautifully but he is not a man because of this. Were he to become a man, this would happen without a doubt not by virtue of the actions by which he emulated man but by virtue of a completely different action, namely, God's. But, being made a man he certainly would perform human actions in the right way.
>
> (Rom. 3:19–20)

In a similar way a person is justified not because the right actions are performed but because of a divine act which allows a person to believe in a way that matches the operation of divine grace. This idea of justification by faith was a freeing belief for Luther, and has continued to be radically important in the life of Protestant Christianity. The best example of its influence came in the conversion of John Wesley on 24 May 1738, when he heard Luther's Preface to The Epistle to the Romans read at a religious meeting in London when, as he put it, his heart was 'strangely warmed'.

In the modern world, it was a commentary on Romans that the Swiss pastor and theologian, Karl Barth (1886–1968), published in 1919 that triggered a new and creative period of theology. Turning his back on the liberal interpretation of Christianity associated with biblical criticism that had become common in the nineteenth century, Barth believed that the transcendent God confronts men and women today through the divine word present in Jesus, present in scripture, and present in the preaching of the Christian message. He went on to write a massive study of Christian doctrine entitled *Church Dogmatics* which owes a great deal to biblical influence but which is a systematic and formal discussion of doctrine. His Romans commentary itself reads more like a sermon than a critical analysis of a text; it comes straight at the reader in the way that Barth believed God does address humankind, as is seen in this brief excerpt from his comments on part of chapter eight, verse ten:

> The body is dead because of sin: but the Spirit is life because of righteousness.
>
> Christ is our freedom, our advance beyond the frontier of human life, the transfiguration of life's meaning, and the appearance of its new and veritable reality. In Christ is uttered the external decision that flesh is flesh, world is world, man is man – because sin is sin; that the existence of the man of this world . . . must become non-existence, must in fact, when it encounters God, die . . . .

Many other theologians have drawn extensively from the Bible, but Romans has continued to stand out as a significant book, while New Testament scholars have themselves seen the writing of a commentary on Romans as an important goal expressing their own maturity as a biblical commentator.

Other biblical commentaries

As with Romans, so with practically every other book in the Bible; they have all attracted the attention of pastors, scholars, and church leaders, who have written commentaries on them. Biblical commentaries are valuable because they help shed light on the meaning of a text, they serve to inspire or encourage the reader in the life of faith, but they also show how scholars, in any generation, approach the Bible. In some Protestant traditions, where the Bible itself is the major focus of religious knowledge, many commentaries have played an important part both as an extension of sermons and also as a means of helping some ministers prepare their own sermons. John Calvin, for example, wrote extensive commentaries as a quite separate exercise from writing his formal theology, while John Wesley, late in his life (1754), wrote a commentary on the whole New Testament, aimed at 'plain, unlettered men, who understand only their mother-tongue, and yet reverence and love the word of God, and have a desire to save their souls'.

Gospels

Despite the fact that many of the epistles were probably written earlier than the gospels, it is still the gospels which are among the best known sacred writings of Christianity. This is probably because they give an account of the life of Jesus in a story form, and because the religious teaching in them is often easy to grasp in the story or parable form in which it is depicted. Stories like that of the Good Samaritan (Luke 10:29–37), who helped someone not of his own natural group who had been attacked and robbed and who had been left unhelped by those of his own background, have put the Christian ideal of service and care in concrete form. Another example is the account of the Prodigal Son (Luke 15:11–32) who claims his inheritance, leaves home, wastes his money, comes to ruin before coming to his senses and returns home to be met by his loving father and selfish brother.

There are four gospels. Three of them – Matthew, Mark and Luke – are called synoptic gospels because they take a similar perspective on the life of Jesus and share such significantly large amounts of similar material that they could be organised in matching columns in a kind of 'synopsis'. John's Gospel, by contrast, takes a different approach, and contains many passages, such as chapter seventeen, which are not in the other gospels and which express very definite and carefully composed theological ideas about the nature of Jesus.

Critical study of the gospels and Bible

The gospels have not been used simply as a means of feeding the public and private worship of Christians; they have also come under the scrutiny of biblical scholars. The striking similarities between Matthew, Mark and Luke attracted detailed study in the nineteenth and early twentieth centuries by scholars who explored the relationships between these gospels to see whether, for example, Mark was the earliest gospel subsequently used by Matthew and Luke, or whether perhaps some material in Matthew and Luke that is not in Mark might have belonged to an independent source, often called 'Q' and no longer known to us as an independent document. Some examples are the accounts of the temptation of Christ (Luke 4:2–13 and Matt. 4:2–11), and some passages referring to John the Baptist

(Luke 7:18–23 and Matt. 11:2–6). All these questions are sometimes placed together and called the 'Synoptic Problem', constituting part of the total field of biblical analysis and critical scholarship. Other kinds of critical study have followed, concerning themselves with possible early traditions of Christianity from which particular arguments have been born, and also with the sociological conditions surrounding early Christianity.

Acts and Apocalypse

Two other and rather different sorts of New Testament material are found in the Acts of the Apostles and the Revelation of St John the Divine. They differ from each other quite considerably in that Acts is very much an account of events occurring in the world of every-day life, while the Apocalypse is set in the realm of heaven and spiritual powers.

THE ACTS OF THE APOSTLES

The Acts of the Apostles is an interesting book because it is widely thought to have been written by Luke. The gospel of Luke ends with the risen Jesus telling his disciples that they must stay at Jerusalem until they are 'clothed with power from on high' (Luke 24:49), to enable them to be witnesses to the resurrection and to announce the message of repentance and forgiveness. Acts begins with a statement about the resurrection of Jesus and then focuses on the dramatic coming of this power from God:

> And suddenly a sound came from heaven like the rush of a mighty wind, and it filled all the house where they were sitting. And there appeared tongues as of fire . . . resting on each one of them. And they were all filled with the Holy Spirit and began to speak in other tongues. . . .
>
> (Acts 2:2–4)

With this dynamic motivation the followers of Jesus begin to preach to Jews and then to non-Jews, and move from Jerusalem out across the ancient world of Mediterranean culture. A firm picture is given of the apostle Peter leading the followers of Jesus, as on the day just mentioned, when 'Peter, standing with the eleven, lifted up his voice and addressed them . . . Repent and be baptized' (Acts 2:14–38). This call to repentance came after he had outlined an Old Testament prophecy that God would one day pour out his Spirit on all people, proclaimed that God had already raised Jesus from the dead and, through him, had now given this powerful Spirit to humankind, who needed to be baptised for the forgiveness of sins.

Acts portrays a community that sensed a deep unity of purpose as they 'devoted themselves to the apostles' teaching and fellowship, to the breaking of bread and the prayers . . . And all who believed were together and had all things in common; and they sold their possessions and goods and distributed to all, as any had need' (Acts 2:42, 44–45). One story tells of a flaw in this community as a man and wife, Ananias and Sapphira, sell some property and pretend they have given all the proceeds to the apostles while they have really kept part of it back for themselves, and both end up dead as a result of their deceit (Acts 5:1–11). The church community grows rapidly and an increase in organisation occurs (Acts 6).

Jewish opposition increases and the first martyr, Stephen, is stoned to death (Acts 7), in an event which introduces the figure of Paul to the story. Paul, or Saul as he still is called in his pre-conversion identity, sets out to persecute the Christians with full authority, but amidst his fervent activity he encounters the risen Christ in a vision while on the road to Damascus (Acts 9:1–31). He is radically converted and becomes a central figure for the rest of the Acts of the Apostles, figuring as a late entry to the inner circle of disciples who had known Jesus when he was still alive, in his earthly ministry.

Paul is the disciple of the resurrected Christ, and is called to preach to the gentile world. The distinction between Jews and gentiles becomes critical at the Council at Jerusalem (Acts 15), where the apostles gather to discuss whether gentiles need to observe the Jewish law or whether faith is a state of life that does not depend upon the former pattern of Jewish life. They come out in favour of faith as freeing people from responsibility to live according to Jewish tradition. Paul goes on to travel far and wide in a series of missionary journeys until he finally arrives in Rome as a prisoner for the gospel's sake. His travels provide the opportunity for the writer of Acts to produce sermons, speeches, and legal defences made by Paul in many different contexts, all of which spell out many aspects of the Christian faith. A central point is the way in which the message concerning God's salvation, brought about through the risen Jesus, opens the love and forgiveness of God to all people, and not only to Jews. This message creates a new people; indeed Acts pinpoints the fact in rather concrete terms: 'It was in Antioch that the disciples were first called Christians' (Acts 11:26). Acts ends with a typical speech in which Paul returns to the theme of the Holy Spirit and to the worldwide mission of the Christian Church: 'Let it be known then that this salvation of God has been sent to the Gentiles: they will listen' (Acts 28:28).

APOCALYPSE

The word 'apocalypse' is the Greek word for revelation, which itself means an unveiling. Apocalyptic literature pulls back the veil to show what will happen in God's plan and in God's own time. Jews were familiar with apocalyptic material from the Book of Daniel, written about a hundred and seventy or so years before the time of Jesus, a time of persecution of the Jews in which they needed encouragement, and the belief that all was ultimately in God's hands no matter how bad things appeared to be on earth.

There are numerous apocalyptic books which were not given the status of scripture by Jews, including the Book of Enoch, the Book of Jubilees, and the Testaments of the Twelve Patriarchs. Against this background it is not surprising to find that one of the books, one that was not finally included in the canon or approved list of New Testament documents until after many of the others, is an Apocalypse.

This revelation claims to be given by Jesus, 'to show to his servants what must soon take place' (Rev. 1:1). It begins in the form of a letter addressed to seven churches, calling them to faithfulness despite the problems they are suffering. Then the author speaks of being caught up into heaven where he sees the throne of God and various supernatural beings about it, including the

> four living creatures, each of them with six wings, and full of eyes all round and within, and day and night they never cease to sing, 'Holy, holy, holy, is the Lord God Almighty, who was and is and is to come'.
>
> (Rev. 4:8)

Basic to these visionary insights is the image of Jesus as the Lamb of God lying at the centre of all God's activities, not least the judgements passed upon evil in the earth and upon Satan (Rev. 12:9). The account of God's wrath being poured out on evil is occasionally interrupted with hymns of praise to God and to the Lamb for all these acts of power:

> Just art thou in these thy judgements, . . . for men have shed the blood of saints and prophets, and thou hast given them blood to drink. It is their due.
>
> (Rev. 16:5–6)

> Hallelujah! For the Lord our God
> the Almighty reigns.
> Let us rejoice and exult and
> give him the glory.
>
> (Rev. 19:6–7)

The Apocalypse ends with the vision of a 'new heaven and a new earth; for the first heaven and the first earth had passed away' (Rev. 21:1). This brings a picture of heaven in which flows the river of the water of life, along with the tree of life whose leaves are for the healing of the nations. The ending is an ending of expectation, as Jesus tells his followers that he will soon come to them: '"Surely I am coming soon". Amen. Come, Lord Jesus!' (Rev. 22:20).

Apocryphal writings

Apocalyptic literature, which reckons to tell of future things, should not be confused with apocryphal literature, which deals with 'hidden' (or apocryphal) things. There are numerous documents not included in the Bible which have the form of gospels or epistles but which were not ultimately included in the Bible as it is known to Christians. Some of these have been discovered only recently, as in the case of the Gospel of Thomas, which was discovered initially as some papyrus fragments in 1897 but which came into its own with major discoveries of more extensive records in 1945–46 in Egypt. It includes some sayings of Jesus not contained in the Bible such as, 'It is not possible for a man to ride two horses, or to draw two bows'.

Authority, interpretation and study of the Bible

The fact that some apocryphal and some apocalyptic literature was not included in the official list of biblical books raises the important question of authority. As the central sacred text of Christianity, the Bible is viewed as authoritative in matters of religion and truth for a variety of reasons which some Christian traditions stress more than others. Protestant traditions emphasise the authority of the Bible because it is believed to have been inspired by God in its production. Those who wrote or composed its constituent parts as a sort of editor are believed to have been guided by God in some way. For these, the Bible is sacred because it is the very word of God. Catholic traditions also value the Bible as the record of God's dealings with humanity, and because the church, in the sense of early Christian generations, accepted these writings as from God.

In the fundamentalist stream of Christian life this leads to a belief that there can be no wrong or contradictory material in the Bible, and that all should accept and believe what it says in a rather direct way. But those of a more liberal tradition see the Bible as a collection of human documents reflecting upon people's experience and insights about God and the way God works. These argue strongly that the context out of which the gospels, epistles and other literature came, influences what is said to a marked extent. What is then important is the question of interpretation, but interpretation, or hermeneutics as it is sometimes called from the Greek word for a translator – itself derived from the idea of Hermes as the messenger of the gods – is far from being a simple task. The fundamentalist prefers the plain meaning of the text while the liberal goes for a much wider meaning, giving full place to metaphor and analogy.

Another important difference surrounding the interpretation of the Bible concerns the Catholic and Protestant attitudes to the Bible. The Bible was a very important element in the Reformation period in the sixteenth century because Martin Luther and others argued that the teaching of the Bible should take precedence over the teaching of the Catholic Church in defining Christian doctrine. This led to a division between those who see the Bible as supreme in matters of faith, and those who see the Church as central. The latter argue that it is Christian teachers, i.e., the Church, who actually interpret the Bible and therefore are ultimately more significant and authoritative. This tradition has grown to the point where the Pope, as the leader of the

Catholic Church and as one who is believed to be St Peter's successor, is infallible when speaking officially and authoritatively on matters of doctrine. Protestants, by contrast, tend to argue that Christians sit beneath the words of scripture and are formed by it, and in this sense it is scripture which is paramount.

The last two hundred years have witnessed an incredible growth in the study of the Bible by linguists, historians and theologians. It is almost certainly the one book that has been studied more than any other in the history of humankind, as is obvious from the thousands of commentaries that have been written on the Bible. Such biblical commentaries are an important source of study for many educated Christian people, especially ministers, priests and other church leaders. Their very existence shows the importance of the biblical texts as foundation documents of all the Christian churches.

Scholarly opinion often offers its own account of how the biblical documents came together and, for some people, this kind of explanation, which focuses on human processes of development, has meant a decline in the intrinsic authority of the Bible. Even so, whatever the view taken of how the Bible came together in the first place, all Christian churches and movements use it in worship. This means that for many people, and in practical terms, the Bible carries great power and is viewed as a sacred text. The proof of the status of the Bible lies in its place in worship and spirituality. This is an important point because it is sometimes easy to think that the proper use of the Bible lies in scholarly and critical study and not in the context of congregational worship and private devotion. But the Bible came into existence to be used for the purposes of faith and not to be the basis for someone's academic career as a biblical or textual scholar. Having said that, however, it must be recognised that the growth of the academic analysis of the Bible since the middle of the nineteenth century has led to an immense body of knowledge which forms a subject all of its own, quite apart from the role the Bible plays in church life and the life of faith. Even so, there is a great overlap between this academic study of the Bible for the sake of knowledge alone, and the application of that knowledge within the religious life of church groups. The sacred scriptures of Christianity exist in this double world of scholarship and piety.

In what is called 'biblical theology', some of this knowledge of the structure and content of the Bible is used to construct a pattern of doctrine which describes what is in the Bible and tries to show how it may be applied within the Christian life. This is the task of theologians within the tradition of active church life. Biblical theology starts with the assumption that the Bible is the vehicle by which God communicates with men and women, and tries to treat it in a way that is appropriate to its nature. Even so, different individuals and groups give different emphases to the text and arrive at varied patterns of belief.

There was a great fear in the nineteenth century that too many scholars wanted to analyse the Bible through the literary and historical factors that had influenced its growth. 'Source Criticism' and 'Form Criticism' were two examples of explanations that focused on the sources from which texts came, and the forms or types of literature into which various passages might be fitted. Originally starting on the Old Testament, this sort of work extended into the New Testament in the early twentieth century. This form of study was elaborate and sophisticated, and was open only to experts. In many ways the ordinary Christian was put at a distance from the Bible. Whereas the Reformation in the sixteenth century had brought the Bible close to ordinary Christians, the nineteenth-century growth of critical scholarship took it away again. But there were several responses to this.

One lay in the new form of orthodoxy associated with the Swiss theologian Karl Barth, whose commentary on Romans we have already discussed as a new emphasis upon the dynamic entry of God into the human life. He called for an attitude towards the Bible in which the Bible brought believers to a kind of crisis, a creative judgement in which they came to see how God confronted them through the words of the sacred scriptures. Three other responses also worth sketching are those of the Fundamentalists, of Liberation Theology originating in Latin America, and of Narrative Theology.

Fundamentalism

Academic interest in critical study of the Bible has not been universally accepted within Christian churches. At the beginning of the twentieth century there was a move on the part of a group of Christians in the United States of America to affirm very strongly their belief that the Bible was the infallible world of God. In a series of tracts, beginning in 1909, some evangelical scholars placed great stress on certain doctrines, including the atonement for sin won by

Jesus as a substitute for sinners, the imminent return of Jesus Christ, and the personal need for salvation and an assurance of salvation. Their belief in the vital importance of the Bible for doctrine and in the inerrancy of the scriptures was the central conviction in what was to be called the Fundamentalist position.

Fundamentalists tend to avoid interpretations of scripture which depend upon ideas of social influence on texts. They speak of the direct and literal meaning of texts. This way of approaching the Bible is useful for individuals without any extensive theological training, since it enables them to see the Bible as the means by which God can communicate with them as individuals in a direct and immediate way in their private study of the Bible. In a similar way, it allows preachers to approach the text with a minimum of scholarly intrusion into biblical passages.

Liberation and Narrative theologies

Some fifty years after the first Fundamentalist tracts and Barth's Romans, in the 1960s and 1970s, another approach to the Bible followed, alongside the growth of Liberation Theology in Latin America. Liberation theologians argued that ordinary people needed to work out their own beliefs as they lived and worked together, along with Christian leaders and thinkers, in the process of gaining justice and political freedom. The Bible was a powerful tool in their hands, as they saw themselves as a part of the long history of God's people being set free in an oppressive world. Gustavo Gutierrez wrote an influential book called *A Theology of Liberation* (1971) in which the Bible plays an important part in providing an understanding of history, justice, faith, and loving God by loving one's neighbour.

Another very similar way of using the Bible, which has extended this view, has been called Narrative Theology. This encourages Christians to use biblical stories about God's dealings with humanity as the framework for their own church groups. In some ways this is a relatively simple task and it may be seen as a way of putting the Bible back into the hands of ordinary Christians so that it can be used for directing the life of faith. Some have seen the late eighteenth and nineteenth centuries as a period when biblical scholarship became increasingly technical and so scholarly that ordinary people could no longer expect to understand what the Bible was about.

Barth's neo-orthodoxy, along with Liberation and Narrative theologies, have all tended to put the Bible back into the heart of ordinary church life.

Bible and worship

The Bible sits at the heart of congregational worship in Christianity in several ways. In the Liturgy of Orthodox, Catholic and Protestant Churches, the Bible is chanted or read as part of the total pattern of the service. In many modern liturgies of major Christian denominations there are likely to be several readings, including one from the Old Testament, one from the gospels, and one from other New Testament sources, especially the epistles.

The emphasis on the importance of the Bible is often made dramatically clear in the reading of the gospel because in churches of a Catholic tradition all the people are likely to stand and face the reader and there may even be a procession of the clergy and others into the centre of the church, carrying the Bible, as the focus of activity; the priest may even kiss the book as a sign of honour. Instead of being read in an ordinary way, the gospel may even be chanted or sung to indicate its special status, one that is greater than the readings from the Old Testament or the epistles, which are likely to be read in a more ordinary style.

In churches of the Protestant tradition the authority of the Bible is portrayed through the sermon and the pulpit. The pulpit, from where the sermon is preached, can be located at a physical height above the people to symbolise that God's word of scripture stands above humans and comes down to us. Much time and care may be taken in the preparation of the sermon, especially if it takes the form of a biblical exegesis, which is an explanation and interpretation of the meaning of the Bible for the congregation. In many Protestant churches the pulpit takes the place that is occupied by the altar in more Catholic churches. This is a dramatic expression of the primacy of the Bible over the Eucharist.

Psalms in hymns

Perhaps the single most influential part of the Bible as far as worship is concerned is the Book of Psalms from the Old Testament. From early days Christians sang the psalms in a continuation of the practice of the Jewish synagogue. As time went on the psalms became especially important in the life of monks and nuns whose day and week composed a special pattern of worship. In the *Rule of St Benedict* all one hundred and fifty psalms were divided throughout these services in such a way that all of them would be covered in the space of a week. In some churches the hundred and fifty psalms are collected into a separate book called a Psalter, and are specially marked, or pointed as it is called, to make it easier for them to be sung. After the Reformation in the sixteenth century, when there was a great decline in the religious life of monastic houses, the psalms became more widespread in their use as laypeople began to take them up. Metrical forms of the psalms were prepared in the sixteenth century to make the psalm into a patterned form that was easier to sing, and so the psalms came to be a kind of hymn.

They were widely used in this form by some of the churches of the Protestant Reformation, especially by John Calvin's church in Geneva from where the influence of metrical psalm-singing spread to reformed churches in England, Holland and Scotland. The increased popularity of psalm-singing that developed in English parish churches in the seventeenth century still has something of a presence at the parish level, but in the twentieth century it is in the cathedrals of the Anglican Church, especially in the Church of England, that psalm-singing has been developed into a distinctive musical form, traditionally following a pattern which sings through all the hundred and fifty psalms at Morning and Evening Prayer services during the course of each month.

Many Christians find the psalms of real benefit in their private prayer and devotion because they represent a wide range of human emotion and religious experience. Christians also tend to interpret them in the light of Jesus and his ministry, which means that some psalms come to have a different significance from that of their Jewish context. The beginning of Psalm 22 offers a good example: 'My God, my God, look upon me; why hast thou forsaken me: and art so far from my health, and from the words of my complaint?'. For a Christian, these words, and much else in the same psalm, are likely to be read as a commentary on the passion and death of Jesus precisely because, in the gospels (Mark 15:34, Matt. 27:46), these words are said to have been used by Jesus as he died on the cross. Later verses (16–18) of the same psalm reinforce this Jesus-focus in its use: 'They pierced my hands and my feet; I may tell all my bones: they stand staring and looking upon me. They part my garments among them: and cast lots upon my vesture'.

Hymns, as general songs for laypeople to sing, probably began in about the thirteenth century but it was from the sixteenth century on, with the birth of the Reformation, that hymn-writing and hymn-singing became a more central part of Christian worship and life. The Methodist Revival in Britain in the eighteenth century marked a vitally important change as hymns, alongside sermons, became a central means of expressing doctrine and faith. Developing from metrical psalm-singing, hymns expressed the doctrines of new religious outlooks in language that could be deeply biblical but could also use non-biblical expressions to great effect. Many hymns took biblical ideas and presented them for use in this new form of popular worship. This was especially true in the nineteenth century which was the century when hymns fully entered the life of the great majority of churches in Britain.

It is possible to find hymns enshrining texts or stories drawn from nearly every part of the Bible, as this brief list of biblical texts and the hymns based on them shows:

Genesis 1:3 God said, Let there be light: and there was light.

Thou whose almighty word,
Chaos and Darkness heard,
And took their flight;
Hear us we humbly pray,
And where the gospel-day
Sheds not its glorious ray
Let there be light.

Exodus 23:19 The first fruits of your land you shall bring into the house of the Lord your God.

Fair waved the golden corn
In Canaan's pleasant land. . .
Like Israel, Lord, we give,
Our earliest fruits to Thee,
And pray that, long as we shall live,
We may thy children be.

I Samuel 3:9 If he calls you you shall say, Speak Lord for your servant hears.

Hushed was the evening hymn,
The temple doors were dark;
The lamp was burning dim,
Before the sacred ark;
When suddenly a voice divine
Rang through the silence of the shrine.

Isaiah 49:15 Can a woman forget her sucking child?

Hark my soul it is the Lord. . .
Can a woman's tender care,
Cease towards the child she bare?
Yes, she may forgetful be,
Yet will I remember thee.

Matthew 3:1 John the Baptist preached.

On Jordan's bank the Baptist's cry,
Announces that the Lord is nigh.

Romans 8:35 Who shall separate us from the love of Christ?

The saviour died, but rose again,
Triumphant from the grave. . .
Nor death nor life, nor earth nor hell,
Nor time's destroying sway,
Can e'er efface us from his heart,
Or make his love decay.

But, although many parts of the Bible have served as a basis for hymns, none can overtake the psalms in popularity or frequency of use. They stand out as the bedrock of Christian hymnody as this short list of hymns indicates:

The Lord's my Shepherd, I'll not want.	(23:1)
Lift up your heads, ye mighty gates.	(24:7)
As pants the hart for cooling streams.	(42:1)
A safe stronghold our God is still.	(46:1)
O God our help in ages past.	(90:1)

O worship the Lord in the beauty of holiness. (96:9)
Unto the hills around do I lift up. (121:1)

Although the Bible has been a major source of inspiration for hymns and for the worship and doctrine of the mainstream Christian churches, and in that sense has helped unite Christians in worship, it has also been the cause of disagreement among Christians on points of doctrine. This is one of the problems of written texts as they come to have a life of their own, often separated from their original context, and certainly made to apply to later and very different situations.

Bible for all

The Reformation brought the Bible out from the control of priests and scholarly church leadership and made it widely available for ordinary men and women to read. As time went on, the consequences of this shift were dramatically significant: not only could ordinary church members study the Bible as part of their own religious devotion, but they could also question its meaning. More than this, the Bible sometimes seemed to impress particular individuals with a religious message that differed from that of the traditionally established churches. Believed to be sacred scripture, the Bible gave to some creative, yet often relatively uneducated, people ideas that were new and exciting. Sometimes these ideas grew and developed and formed the basis for a new religious movement. This was especially the case with parts of the Bible that were not immediately intelligible and which seemed mysterious in some way. The books of Ezekiel, Daniel and Revelation, for example, have all been interpreted in distinctive ways by groups believing the end of the world to be near. Both the eighteenth and nineteenth centuries were periods when many such millennial movements were born. These groups read with interest those passages that spoke of Christ returning to earth and setting up a divine kingdom.

It has often been the case that leaders of new religious movements have interpreted the Bible in ways that diverged quite dramatically from established patterns. Such people often believe that they have been given special gifts from God enabling them to interpret scripture in a true way that is hidden from recognised church leaders. One major example, focusing on the Mormons, will show

how important the Bible has been as a pattern of divine revelation and source of authority.

The case of Mormon Churches offers an important insight into the power of sacred scriptures in moulding religious life. Joseph Smith, who founded the Church of Jesus Christ of Latter Day Saints in 1830, believed God had granted him access to a written history of early American civilisations that had initially originated in the Holy Land. He was given power to translate these, and published them as *The Book of Mormon*. Divided into named books of particular prophets, very much like the Old Testament, and also into chapters and verses just like the Bible, it contains many answers to religious issues current at the time of Joseph Smith. Instead of engaging in debate over points of doctrine and rites such as infant baptism, early Mormons could use *The Book of Mormon* for an authoritative judgement. So it was that Mormons came to view this book as an additional witness to the Bible and to use it as a source of religious teaching and spiritual fulfilment. In all practical terms this is also a sacred text and of great significance in ordinary Mormon life. This shows how the idea of a sacred text can be extended to embrace other scriptures and to impart a sacred character to them.

Another branch of the overall Mormon Restoration movement is called the Reorganized Church of Jesus Christ of Latter Day Saints, which is not based in Utah and is led by a descendant of the prophet, Joseph Smith. It also uses *The Inspired Version* of the Bible, which Joseph Smith is believed to have partly translated from the King James Version of the Bible by special divine power which enabled faults and errors that had crept into earlier translations to be rectified. A further volume of writings used by both the Utah Church and the Reorganized Church is *The Doctrine and Covenants*, containing what are believed to be revelations given to the prophet by God. A distinctive difference between the Utah Church and the Reorganized Mormon Church lies in the fact that while the Utah version contains only early prophecies, the Reorganized Church each year adds to its *Doctrine and Covenants* new revelations that come to their living prophet. Here again is another kind of sacred writing believed to have divine authority.

Many other groups have highly valued key books or, as in the case of the Jehovah's Witnesses, their own version of the Bible. So, for example, Mary Baker Eddy (1821–1910), who founded the Christian Science Church in the 1870s and 1880s in New England, produced *Science and Health with Key to the Scriptures* as an explanation of the Bible as she understood it, in relation to healing through a process of thought which she called mental healing. In this case, as in that of the Mormons and numerous other groups with a strong Protestant cultural background, the idea of an authoritative book is very powerful.

Translations of the Bible

The great majority of the writings now in the Old Testament were originally written in Hebrew, but several centuries BCE these Hebrew scriptures were translated into Greek for the use of Jews in the largely Greek-speaking Mediterranean world. This translation is called the Septuagint (often shortened to LXX) because of a tradition that it was the work of seventy-two translators. It was this version of the ancient Jewish scriptures that the early Christian Church possessed. The LXX had added to it some books not in the Hebrew scriptures; these form the Apocrypha in the Protestant English Bible.

Many, though not all, of those authors whose epistles and gospels would come to form the New Testament, used the LXX when quoting from the 'Old Testament'. Very occasionally this led to slight shifts of meaning, as in Matthew 1:23 which quotes from Isaiah 7:14. Christians are familiar with the words, 'a virgin will conceive and bear a son', a translation that came about because the LXX used the Greek word for virgin to translate a Hebrew word for a young woman of marriageable age. The Hebrew in Isaiah does not intend any idea of a miraculous virgin birth, but early Christians interpreted the birth of Jesus in the light of their knowledge of the Greek Septuagint text which did say 'virgin'. Many of the early Church Fathers used the LXX as their standard Old Testament reference book.

A Latin version of the Bible, commonly called the Vulgate, was produced by Jerome during the late fourth and early fifth century. Jerome came to see the superiority of the Hebrew texts of the 'Old Testament' and increasingly worked from them rather than from the Greek Septuagint. The first printed edition was not published until 1456; it is called the Gutenburg Bible.

These dates of publication of the Septuagint and Vulgate translations of the Bible mark the beginning of European printing in the fifteenth and sixteenth centuries. The discovery of the printing press, coinciding with the emergence of the Reformation, marked a dramatic change in European communication and debate. The Reformers wanted people to possess the Bible in their own language. This led Luther to translate the Bible into German in the early sixteenth century and to set a new trend in a more modern style of German language.

William Tyndale published an English New Testament in Germany in 1526, and a complete English Bible was published by Miles Coverdale in 1585 in England. William Caxton had had a printing press set up at Westminster in London from 1477, but religious and political aspects of the Reformation often led to Protestant material being published on the Continent before appearing in Britain. It was, for example, in a New Testament published in English in Geneva in 1557 that the text was first divided into verses. Perhaps the best known of all English Bible translations is that of the Authorised Version, prepared under the authority of King James I and published in 1611. It became all the better known because this was the version used as the basis for all the readings from the epistles and gospels in the *Book of Common Prayer* of 1662. This is a very good example of Bible translation, in a language understood by the general population, being combined with a book of worship intended for all the people of a nation. Interestingly, the Psalms in that Prayer Book were kept in the Coverdale translation.

With the growth of scholarship and biblical knowledge over the eighteenth century, and especially in the nineteenth century, it was inevitable that new translations should be sought. *The Revised Version* was one important outcome of that desire, and represented the work of some of the greatest of English biblical scholars of the nineteenth century; the New Testament section was published in 1881 and the Old Testament in 1885. Numerous other translations have followed in the twentieth century, including the American *Revised Standard Version*, and the British *New English Bible* (and its 1989 successor, the *Revised English Bible*), which aims at a direct yet more conservative style of language, unlike *Today's English Version*, or the *Good News* version which uses language of an even more vernacular style. All these translations demonstrate Christianity's conviction that the Bible is a vital component in understanding God and that the life of faith is intimately connected with its sacred scriptures.

FURTHER READING

Barr, J. (1973) *The Bible in the Modern World*, London, SCM Press.
—— (1981) *Fundamentalism*, London, SCM Press.
Coggins, R.J. and Houlden, J.L. (eds) (1990) *A Dictionary of Biblical Interpretation*, London, SCM Press.
Goody, J. (1986) *The Logic of Writing and the Organization of Society*, Cambridge, Cambridge University Press.
Grant, R.M. and Tracy, D. (1965) *A Short History of the Interpretation of the Bible*, London, SCM Press.
Muddiman, J. (1983) *The Bible, Fountain and Well of Truth*, London, The Society for Promoting Christian Knowledge (SPCK).
Nineham, D. (ed.) (1963) *The Church's Use of the Bible Past and Present*, London, SPCK.
Rogerson, J.W., Rowland, C. and Lindars, B. (1988) *The Study and Use of the Bible*, Basingstoke, Marshall Pickering.

3. Hinduism

Gavin D. Flood

The sacred writings of Hinduism constitute a vast body of literature, composed mostly in Sanskrit, but also in other Indian languages, particularly Tamil. The earliest layers of the most authoritative of this literature, the Vedas, stretch back over three thousand years, while compositions by modern holy men and women are also regarded as sacred by their devotees. The category of 'sacred writings' therefore tends to have more fluid boundaries within Hinduism than in most other traditions. This does not mean that Hinduism has not developed categories for understanding its own sacred scriptures; it has, but the lines between these categories are sometimes blurred. Nor does this fluidity of boundaries mean that there are no constraints controlling a particular text, rather that 'controls' operating within a text may be harder to specify; but there can be no 'random' texts. This fluidity of boundaries is seen particularly, though not exclusively, with regard to sacred texts of human authorship, as opposed to the eternal, revealed texts.

It has been recently observed that the western understanding of sacred scripture in Hinduism, as indeed in Buddhism and Jainism, has been deeply influenced by the text and function of the Bible within Christianity (Timm 1992: 2). But in contrast to western religious scriptures, one of the most striking features of the Hindu 'revealed' texts is that they were not put into writing for perhaps as long as a thousand years after their origin. Indeed the oldest text, the *Ṛg-veda*, was only printed as a 'book' in the nineteenth century at the instigation of a European scholar, F. Max Müller, an event which Wilfred Cantwell-Smith describes as 'an entrancing instance of nineteenth-century Western cultural imperialism . . . quietly imposing the western sense of scripture' (Cantwell-Smith in Levering, M. (ed.) 1989: 35).

It needs to be borne in mind, therefore, that the category of 'sacred writings' is a western one and that the emphasis in Hinduism has always been not on the canonised, written word, but on the 'heard' word received through the tradition in an unbroken succession from teacher (*guru*) to disciple. Indeed, to write, as Staal and others have observed, was regarded among some Brahmans as a ritually polluting activity. Staal quotes the *Aitareya Āraṇyaka* (5.5.3) which states that a pupil should not recite the Veda 'if he has eaten flesh, or seen blood, or a dead body, or done what is unlawful . . . or had intercourse or written' (Staal 1989: 371; also quoted by Coburn 1989: 104). This quotation reminds us that the recitation of the Veda by the Brahmans must be located in the context of brahmanical ritual and a life lived maintaining, and within the boundaries of, Hindu *dharma*, one's social and moral duty concerned with preserving the boundaries of the cosmic, ethical order (see 'Hinduism' in *Making Moral Decisions* in this series).

That which is heard

Revealed scripture, 'that which is heard', and its use in a ritual context, is at the heart of 'orthoprax' Hinduism. Indeed, acceptance of the body of texts collectively called the Veda ('knowledge') as authoritative revelation could be said to be a characteristic implied by the term 'Hindu'[1] (notwithstanding views which regard the very term 'Hinduism' as a misnomer). Although these texts have had a seminal influence on Indian philosophical and ritual traditions, most Hindus would not have known their 'Hinduism' through these revealed texts, but rather through ritual traditions and the mythologies of the *smṛti* literature. Bharati makes the point (though without giving a source for his figures) that 'less than five percent of all Hindus ever knew these texts even by name, and much less than one percent knew even parts of their content'.

Śruti, the Hindu revelation, is thought to be the eternal word (*śabda*) or sound, which is not composed or uttered by any human, or even, according to some Hindus, divine, being. This 'word' was 'heard' by the ancient sages (*ṛṣis*) and passed down orally through the generations in the form of the Veda, a vast body of texts composed in vedic Sanskrit, the sacred language of the gods. The

Veda comprises four large groups or layers of texts, the *Saṃhitās*, the *Brāhmaṇas*, the *Āraṇyakas* and the *Upaniṣads*. Another way of regarding this scheme is that the term 'Veda' refers only to the collections of the four *Saṃhitās*: the *Ṛg*, *Sāma*, *Yajur* and *Atharva*, each of which has its own *Brāhmaṇas*, *Āraṇyakas* and *Upaniṣads*. These layers represent the rough chronological order of their composition, thus the earliest texts are the hymns of the *Ṛg-veda*, while the latest are the *Upaniṣads*.[2]

Various theological schools are important in the classification of the Veda. Different families of Brahmans, the only class qualified by virtue of their pure social status to learn the Veda, would specialise in learning portions of the text, and the layers of the texts are related to each other through these schools or 'branches' (*śākhā*). A particular Veda will have associated with it a number of branches. For example, the male members of a particular Brahman family might specialise in the *Taittirīya* branch, comprising the *Taittirīya Saṃhitā* of the Black Yajur Veda, the *Taittirīya Brāhmaṇa*, *Taittirīya Āraṇyaka* and *Taittirīya Upaniṣad*. These 'branches' are the diachronic means whereby the texts are transmitted through the generations. This structure can be portrayed diagramatically (only the *Taittirīya* branch is recorded here by way of illustration):

Saṃhitā:	*Ṛg*	*Sāma*	*Yajur*		*Atharva*
			white YV	black YV	
'Branch' (*śākhā*)				*Taittirīya*	
Brāhmaṇa				*Taittirīya B.*	
Āraṇyaka				*Taittirīya A.*	
Upaniṣad				*Taittirīya U.*	

The *Saṃhitā* portion of the Veda comprises the *Ṛg*, *Sāma*, *Yajur* and *Atharva* Vedas. The *Ṛg-veda* is a collection (*saṃhitā*) of ten books (*maṇḍalas*) of 1,028 hymns made up of 'verses' (*ṛcs*) to various deities. Composed over a period of several hundred years, probably from as early as 1200 BCE, by bardic families, these texts are the most important source of our knowledge of vedic religion. Within these hymns we find the cosmos divided into three broad spheres, the sky (*svar*), the atmosphere (*bhūvas*) and the earth (*bhūr*). Each of these realms was inhabited by certain deities to whom sacrifice was offered, particularly Indra, the warrior god of the atmosphere, Agni the fire god, and Soma the god who is both deity and hallucinogenic plant (possibly a vine or mushroom). Of all the deities in the text, Agni and Soma are particularly important, being the links between heaven and earth, the fire conveying the sacrifice to the gods and soma inspiring the seers (*ṛṣi*) with vision from the gods and inspiration for the composition of their hymns (or, in Hindu terms, for the atunement necessary to receive the word).

The *Sāma-veda* is a book of songs or chants (*sāman*) based on the *Ṛg-veda*, with instructions on their recitation (*gāna*). The *sāman*s are songs or melodies to which different verses (*ṛc*) can be sung. The *Yajur-veda* is a further collection of hymns of short prose formulae (*yajus*) for use in ritual. There are two recensions of the *Yajur-veda*, known as the 'black' (*kṛṣṇa*) and the 'white' (*śukla*), the former being composed of formulae (*yajus*) and prose, the latter being composed entirely of verses or *mantra*s. The white *Yajur-veda* contains one book, the *Vājasaneyi-saṃhitā*, while the black *Yajur-veda* contains three books, the *Taittirīya*, the *Maitrāyaṇī* and the *Kāṭhaka saṃhitā*s, all of which are associated with the elaborate ritual of the sacrifice. Lastly, we have the *Atharva-veda*, a collection of hymns and magical formulae, compiled a few centuries after the other Veda, around 900 BCE, though some of the material it contains may well be older than even the *Ṛg* (Brockington 1981: 23). This collection tends not to have quite as high a status as the other three Vedas, and is concerned not so much with elaborate, priestly rituals, but rather with topics such as magical healing and the invoking of otherworldly beings, concerns which reflect a more popular layer of vedic religion.

These texts reflect changing religious attitudes over a long period of time, showing that the ritual of sacrifice becomes much more elaborate and complex in the later tradition. But what is most significant about the Vedas is that from the time of their composition, they have been associated with, and the first three chanted during, ritual. This was, and still is, their primary function. Indeed the vedic *Saṃhitā*s are associated with the three classes of ritual specialists who recite them during the liturgies, namely the *hotṛ*, who recites from the *Ṛg-veda*, the *udgātṛ*, who chants the *Sāma-veda* and the *adhvaryu*, the ritual director, who recites from the *Yajur-veda*.

The *Brāhmaṇa*s, manuals for the Brahmans, are attached to the books of the Veda (in the narrower sense) within the branches or schools. Thus we have the *Kauṣitaki* and *Aitareya Brāhmaṇa*s attached to the *Ṛg-veda*, the *Taittirīya Brāhmaṇa* to the *Taittirīya*

Saṃhitā, and the *Jaiminīya Brāhmaṇa* to the *Sāma-veda* and so on. These prose texts contain rules and elaborate symbolic explanations of vedic ritual, postulating various magical links (*bandha*) between the sacrifice and the cosmos. They are thus interpretations of earlier texts and begin a hermeneutic tradition which runs throughout the history of Indian religions. The *Āraṇyaka*s or 'forest books' are a development of the *Brāhmaṇa*s, speculating upon the symbolism of the sacrifice and representing the emergence of a more contemplative strand in the tradition. Dasgupta illustrates this from the *Bṛhadāraṇyaka*, where 'we find that instead of the actual performance of the horse sacrifice (*aśvamedha*), there are directions for meditating upon the dawn (*Uṣas*) as the head of the horse, the sun as the eye of the horse, the air as its life and so on' (Dasgupta 1975: 14).

With the *Upaniṣad*s the process of speculation on the meaning of the earlier ritual continues, and the seeds of later philosophical speculation are laid. Indeed, with the *Upaniṣad*s we find a turning away from ritual sacrifice, which characterised the vedic *Saṃhitā*s, and an emphasis is placed on inner, mystical experience, spoken of as the 'internalisation of the sacrifice'. The more esoteric nature of these texts is implied in the very term *upaniṣad*, which can be translated as 'sitting near,' which is suggestive of a disciple sitting at the feet of his master.

Key ideas are articulated in the *Upaniṣad*s that were to become central to Hindu traditions and that, partly due to the nineteenth-century 'Hindu Renaissance', are commonly identified with 'Hinduism': namely the doctrines of the transmigration of the soul due to action (*karma*) and its result, the liberation of the soul from this process through controlling and stilling the mind (*yoga*), and the idea of liberation as experiential knowledge of the identity of the particular soul (*ātman*) with absolute being (*brahman*).

Knowledge (*jñāna*), rather than the ritual action (*karman*) of the earlier Veda, takes precedence, a knowledge which is the means of salvation from the cycle of birth and death (*saṃsāra*). For example, rather than the performance of rituals to feed the deceased in the next, ghostly, world (*preta loka*), to ensure that it passes into the world of the ancestors (*pitṛ loka*) in a body created and nourished by food offerings, the *Upaniṣad*s begin to emphasise the prevention of re-birth through knowing the true state of reality as unitary.[3] The earliest expression of this idea is in the *Bṛhadāraṇyaka Upaniṣad* where the Brahman Uddālaka receives the esoteric teaching from the prince Pravāhaṇa Jaivali (a *Kṣatriya*), never before revealed to a Brahman, that the soul is either reborn through traversing the path of the ancestors (*pitṛ-yāna*) or is liberated through the path of the gods (*deva-yāna*) (6.2.1–16; cf. the *Chāndogya Upaniṣad* 5.3–10). What is important here is not ritual action, but knowledge as a necessary condition for liberation, by which beings 'pass into the light' (6.2.15: *te'rcir abhisambhavanti*) and thence to the gods from where there is no rebirth. This liberation is knowledge of the truth (*satyam*), which is knowledge of the identity of the particular soul (*ātman*) with the absolute being (*brahman*) (*Chāndogya* 3.14), an idea central to later Hindu soteriologies.

The *Upaniṣads*, however, are not a homogenous body of texts. The earliest, such as the *Bṛhadāraṇyaka*, the *Chāndogya*, and the *Taittirīya*, dating from about the eighth century BCE, are closely linked with the earlier *Brāhmaṇas* and contain speculation about the underlying nature of the universe as a single, abstract principle. In a later group of texts, however, including the *Īśa*, the *Śvetāśvatara*, the *Mahānārāyāṇa* and the *Maṇḍukya*, an emphasis on a more personal theistic reality begins to appear. For example, in the *Śvetāśvatara* we find the lord (*Īśa*) as the creator and sustainer of the cosmos and the soul (*ātman*), as in some sense distinct from him, becoming free through knowledge: 'the soul, not being the Lord, is bound due to the condition of being an enjoyer [of the world], (but) having known God, it is freed from all bonds' (1.8: *anīśas cātmā badhyate bhoktṛbhāvāt jñātva devam mucyate sarvapāśaiḥ*). These developments reflect theistic trends within the Hindu tradition which become particularly associated with the deities Śiva and Viṣṇu, who are elevated by their devotees to the status of the absolute. Indeed the term *bhakti* ('devotion'), which was to become so significant in later Hinduism, occurs in the last verse of the *Śvetāśvatara*, and although this verse may be a later interpolation, it is nevertheless significant in that *bhakti* is a doctrine based on sacred revelation, a view which is corroborated by the *Bhagavadgītā*.

Texts with the name *Upaniṣad* continued to be produced throughout the middle ages and into the modern period. These texts tend to reflect particular traditions within Hinduism; thus there are Śaiva *Upaniṣads*, Yoga *Upaniṣads* and so on. There is even, as Coburn notes, an Allāh *Upaniṣad* composed in the seventeenth century (Coburn 1989: 106).

There are implications here for the idea of 'sacred scripture' as inviolable. A class of texts, the *Upaniṣads*, which continue to be composed into the seventeenth century and even later, demonstrates a certain fluidity in the notion of sacred scripture, which leads Coburn to conclude that '*śruti* must be seen as [an] ongoing and experientially based feature of the Hindu religious tradition' (Coburn 1989: 112). But even so, it is nevertheless the case that a certain group of the older *Upaniṣads* were taken to be authoritative and commented upon in later philosophical and exegetical traditions, particularly certain phrases, or the 'great sayings' (*mahāvākyas*, within those texts (see below, p. 85). Indeed, while the edges of certain classes of Hindu literature may be blurred, the texts themselves, such as the *Ṛg-veda*, remain intact through the generations.

The Vedas (in the wider sense, including the *Upaniṣads*) are of extreme importance in two areas of Hindu life: in ritual, and in philosophical speculation, which takes the form of the interpretation of the revealed texts. These two routes from the Veda originate in the texts themselves, which contain material (the *mantra* portions) for ritual use as well as exegesis of the ritual (the *brāhmaṇa* portions). Ritual and speculation have thus become the contexts within which the Veda has functioned throughout the history of Hinduism, and within these routes the Veda has functioned, not as a written text, but as an oral and recited text.

Remembering the Veda

One of the most remarkable things about the Veda is that it has been handed down as an oral tradition through the generations with little or no change to its contents. Such accuracy has been due to a system of double-checking by two transmissions, in which each word could be 'checked' by the way it related to the preceding and subsequent words (i.e., by its *sandhi*). The continuous recitation of the Veda, called the *saṃhitāpāṭha*, in which the Sanskrit rules of euphonic combination (*sandhi*) operated, were checked by another system of recitation, the *pādapāṭha*, in which the euphonic combination was broken down and the recitation was made 'word for word'. These two systems were related by various rules (see Staal 1989: 37–46). To cite an example given by Staal, the sentence from the vedic *Saṃhitās*, 'the immortal goddess has pervaded the wide space, the depths and the heights', is remembered in two recensions, the continuous flow of the *saṃhitāpāṭha* ('*orv aprā amartyā nivato devy udvataḥ//*') and the word-for-word recitation of the *pādapāṭha*, stripped of euphonic combinations ('*a/ uru/ aprāḥ/ amartyā/ nivataḥ/ devī/ udvataḥ//*') (Staal 1989: 37).

Apart from these two systems of recitation, the supplementary disciplines (*prātiśākhyas*) of grammar, phonetics and definitions were developed, each vedic tradition having its own *prātiśākhya*, the earliest of which may date from around 1000 BCE. Through these disciplines, which, for example, formulated the rules of euphonic combination, the correct transmission of the Veda could be checked and assured. This practice of using the *prātiśākhya*s to ensure correct transmission is still practised. Indeed, Coward observes that after independence, the Indian government established a commission to check the transmission of the Veda through the *prātiśākhya*s (Coward 1988: 117).

Not only has the Veda been preserved in a tradition of recitation, but also in ritual, where sentences from it may be recited during private morning and evening rites, as well as at public festivals (*utsava*). Indeed, the use of the Veda during ritual is its primary function within Hinduism. These chants used during rituals are called *mantra*s. *Mantra*s are 'sacred formulae' taken from the Veda, or, to use Staal's phrase, 'bits and pieces of the Veda put to ritual use' (Staal 1989: 48). There are also *mantra*s derived from a later body of texts, the *Tantra*s, though these *mantra*s are regarded as polluting by the orthodox. The recitation of *mantra*s may make up a ritual sequence, and may not necessarily bear any relationship to the acts which they accompany other than that they accompany those acts; that is, there is no necessary semantic link between the recitation of the Veda and the ritual act (see Staal 1989: 191–7). These *mantra*s may be semantically complete or may include sequences of meaningless syllables called *stobha*s (such as *hā bu hā bu hā bu bhā bhaṃ* . . ., cited by Staal 1989: 50, 200) which are recited at different times during a ritual by different priests.

Staal (1989) argues that, as can be seen in their ritual use, *mantra*s do not share with 'language' semantic properties, though they do share syntactic and phonological properties. That is, in ritual it is not the meaning of *mantra*s which is important, indeed their meaning is often impossible to establish, but rather their correct recitation in the right place by the right person. The function of the text in ritual is thus not its meanings but primarily its uses. What the particular phrases or sentences in a ritual mean, is secondary to their place in the ritual sequence and their correct recitation. Indeed this view was rigorously propounded by the Mīmāṃsā school of philosophy, which regarded the Veda as a series of injunctions – instructions on the ritual act.

The meaning of the texts, particularly the *Ṛg-veda*, might not be understood even by the reciter, for they are in an archaic form of Sanskrit, more terse than the language of the later literature. Meanings are variable and open to different interpretations by different generations, but the recitational sequence of the text, its structure and place in ritual are invariant to a striking degree: the *Ṛg-veda* has functioned in an almost identical way in a ritual context for nearly three thousand years.

Each of the layers of the Veda is connected through the 'branches'. These branches are further related to another group of texts, the ritual *sūtra*s, concerned with ritual practice. There are three groups of these texts, the *Śrauta-sūtra*s, *Gṛhya-sūtra*s, and *Dharma-sūtra*s. The *Śrauta-sūtras*[4] were concerned with major non-obligatory rituals detailed in the *śruti* literature, each *sūtra* growing out of a particular branch of the tradition. Thus, for example, the *Baudhāyana Śrauta-sūtra*, *Vādhūla SS* and *Āpastambha SS*, all belong to the *Taittirīya Saṃhitā*. The *Gṛhya-* and *Dharma-sūtra*s, on the other hand, are concerned with domestic rites, rites of passage such as marriage, birth and funerary rites, and law and social relationships pertaining to the high caste or twice-born householder (see the chapter on Hinduism in *Rites of Passage* in this series). Developing from these texts are the *dharma-śāstra*s, the most famous of which is the *Manusmṛti* or *Laws of Manu*.[5]

Interpreting the Veda

There is no formal, centralised authority in Hinduism, akin, say, to the Catholic Church, but, in the main, different communities of Brahmans, the highest *varṇa*, have perpetuated the traditions and been the interpreters of it. While the sacred texts have been read and interpreted from different perspectives by different social classes in India, it is the Brahmans who have conveyed the traditions of Sanskrit learning and culture. A number of orthodox interpretations of the Veda developed (as opposed to the heterodox views of the materialists, Buddhists and Jains). A route from the *Brāhmaṇa* literature can therefore be traced which emphasised the interpretation of the texts rather than the performance of rituals, and which developed into the great Sanskrit tradition of philosophical commentary and sub-commentary by different schools (*darśanas*). This hermeneutical tradition shows, on the one hand, that the meanings of the Veda are plural, and on the other, that the text itself is regarded by the traditions as eternal and unchanging; what has been discovered through interpretation is not a new meaning, but the original or 'true' meaning.

What is significant about these schools is that they are not only metaphysical systems, but also methods of interpretation. The vehicle of philosophical inquiry is almost always dialogue through a commentary on an authoritative text – the *śruti* literature or some *smṛti* literature, most notably the *Bhagavadgītā* and the *Brahmasūtras*. There has been an emphasis in western scholarship on understanding the abstract philosophical systems of the schools, but it is now becoming recognised that Indian philosophy is inextricably linked to exegesis and strategies of interpretation. For example the monistic metaphysics of the philosopher Śaṃkara, in contrast to the theism of Rāmānuja, can be shown to arise partly out of the interpretative strategies they employ; or at least their interpretative strategies are bound up with their metaphysics. Mumme even suggests that 'from an Indian perspective, an orthodox metaphysical system may be only a by-product of a proper hermeneutical approach to scripture'. She goes on, 'It is certainly true that creative philosophical systems in Indian thought cannot gain the stamp of orthodoxy without equally creative interpretative approaches to scripture' (Mumme 1992: 70).

THE MĪMĀṂSĀ

The distinction between the meanings and interpretations of a sacred text on the one hand and its function on the other, are reflected in the division of the Veda itself by later philosophical schools, specifically the Pūrva and Uttara Mīmāṃsā, into the sections on ritual action (*karmakaṇḍa*) and sections on knowledge (*jñānakaṇḍa*), or into *mantra* and *brāhmaṇa* portions of the texts: those sections concerned with ritual injunctions and those concerned with the interpretations of meanings. These philosophical schools were acutely aware of problems concerning the nature of a sacred text's authority, with what the sentences and phrases of these texts referred to, and what their primary function was.

The Pūrva Mīmāṃsā[6] provided a basis for the interpretation of vedic texts. It argued that the earlier portions of the Veda – the *Saṃhitās*, *Brāhmaṇas*, and *Āraṇyakas* – are primary, being concerned with injunctions (*vidhi*) about correct and incorrect ritual and social behaviour; while the *Upaniṣads* are secondary, being concerned with the interpretation of injunctive statements. The function of the Veda is to command appropriate activity or to restrain people from prohibited actions (*niṣeda*). The Veda is about imperatives and no word has meaning unless it has reference to some action, either an action which must be performed without a particular reward, such as ritual and social duty, or action which will result in happiness in the next world or riches in this. So the interpretations or sentences of the *Upaniṣads*, if taken out of context, are by themselves meaningless, their only function is to shed light on the meaning of the vedic injunctions.

The Pūrva Mīmāṃsā has a distinctive understanding of *śruti*. For this school, *śruti* is the revealed word (*śabda*) which is discovered, as it were, or 'seen', by the sages (*ṛṣis*). This revelation is eternal, and the relationships between its words and their meanings are constant. The words of revelation do not acquire their meaning through convention (only personal names do this), but, rather, meaning is an inherent power which the words of the Veda possess. Thus the Veda is inherently meaningful; it is self-revealed and self-illumined, though its meanings may be obscured by human consciousness. The inherent meaning of the sacred texts transcends the human condition in so far as it predates and will post-date human reality. In itself the Veda is the primary source of all knowledge (*pramāṇa*), which shines independently of finite, human error which obscures its pristine validity. The task of philosophical inquiry is the retrieval of this original meaning (though there was, of course, wide disagreement as to what this was).

There is no need in this system, therefore, for a God who sustains the cosmos and who is the author of this revelation. Although the Mīmāṃsā accepted the plurality of vedic deities, it comes to regard them only as names which serve in the process of the sacrifice; their ontology is simply unimportant. The more impersonal the Veda is, the clearer its message and the more forceful its injunctions when stripped of any personal, limited will. Indeed the Veda is the prime source of knowledge because a human, personal source, which is subject to error and deceit, cannot be the source of a cognition of that which is eternal and transpersonal. As Śabara says, humans cannot make valid statements about transpersonal things for they are 'like statements on colour by persons born blind' (Pereira 1991: 87). We need the Veda to tell us of the transcendent truth of *dharma*, which, by definition, is beyond human perception and known only through revelation.

The only recourse for knowledge of the transpersonal, or knowledge of *dharma*, is through the eternal Veda. While ordinary, worldly experience is sufficient for most aspects of life, a knowledge of transcendence can only come through a trans-human revelation. But more important than knowledge of the Veda, is action (*kriyā*) enjoined by the Veda, whether its purpose (*artha*) is clearly understood or not. In the everyday world, an action is considered to be complete once the result is seen. On the contrary, with regard to vedic actions, the result may not be seen, but the action should nevertheless be regarded as complete, simply because it has been done exactly according to the text (*Mīmāṃsā-sūtra* 11.1.28). Revelation, therefore, constantly points to the transcendence which is itself. What is important, is for the Veda's injunctions to be performed for their own sake, or rather because they are so enjoined by the text. Although there is a payoff in heaven for the performer of the injunctions, this is not of primary importance. Rather, remembering the Veda and fulfilling its injunctions is its own transcendent purpose. Jaimini writes:

> The hymns (*sāmans*) are sung for the purpose of learning [the singing]; in fact they take different forms with different verses; for the purpose served by them is beyond the ordinary (*alaukiko*) because it is enjoined.[7]

The purpose of learning to sing the hymns is the singing of the hymns, which, because it is an injunction, is transcendent and therefore needs no other justification.

Reciting the text of the Veda, and performing its rituals, are therefore sacred, self-fulfilling actions in accordance with the eternal *dharma*. The Mīmāṃsā is the brahmanical philosophy *par excellence*, and although most Brahmans would not now claim to be Mīmāṃsākas, many of the ideas it expressed are maintained by contemporary Brahmans. The Veda is learned because it is sacred tradition; vedic rituals are performed because the Veda says they should be performed; a Brahman learns the tradition because it is his *dharma* to do so.

THE VEDĀNTA

In contrast to the Pūrva Mīmāṃsā, the second important brahmanical, orthodox and orthoprax philosophy, the Uttara Mīmāṃsā or Vedānta,[8] regarded *śruti* as important not so much because it enjoined action, but rather because it revealed knowledge (*jñāna*). This tradition was therefore more concerned with interpreting the 'knowledge sections' (*jñānakaṇḍa*) of the Veda, namely the *Upaniṣads*, rather than the 'sections on ritual action' (*karmakaṇḍa*). As the Pūrva Mīmāṃsā develops from the *Mīmāṃsā-sūtra* of Jaimini, so the Vedānta schools develop from the *Brahma-* or *Vedānta-sūtra* of Bādarāyaṇa (around the second century CE), a text upon which commentaries were written by all the major schools of Hindu thought. Indeed the Vedānta reveres a 'triple canon' (*prasthara-traya*) of texts, the *Upaniṣads*, the *Bhagavadgītā* and the *Brahma-sūtra*, taking them as its authority, even though these last two are not strictly speaking, *śruti*. Indeed, to begin a philosophical school or to seriously disagree with an opponent, a theologian needed to write a commentary on the *Brahma-sūtra*.

The most famous exponent of the Non-dualistic (*advaita*) branch of Vedānta was Śaṃkara (788–820 CE), who, while assuming a study of Pūrva Mīmāṃsā as a starting point, diverged widely from that school's understanding of sacred scripture.

For Śaṃkara, the sacred texts have two concerns, *dharma* and *brahman*: Hindu duty or law, and knowledge of absolute being. While maintaining that all of *śruti* is grounded in, and emerges from, the absolute (*brahman*), the earliest portions of the Veda (namely the *karmakaṇḍa*) are primarily concerned with *dharma* and ritual injunction (*vidhi*), while the later portions (namely the *Upaniṣads* or *jñānakaṇḍa*) are primarily concerned with knowledge of the absolute and the freedom (*mokṣa*) from the cycle of reincarnation, gained as a result of that knowledge. He therefore rejects the *Mīmāṃsāka* claim for the primacy of action. Performing *dharma* is, of course, important, but what is more important is the eradication of ignorance through renunciation (*saṃnyāsa*) and knowledge of the absolute.

What reveals this knowledge is, primarily, sacred scripture. As with the *Mīmāṃsā*, for Śaṃkara verbal testimony (*śabda*), which primarily refers to the Hindu revelation, is the source of knowledge about *brahman*, revelation's origin. Śaṃkara's high opinion of scripture is illustrated in his commentary on the *Brahma-sūtra*. For example, he writes:

> Brahman is the *yoni* (i.e., the material and efficient cause) of great scriptures like the Ṛg-veda etc. which are supplemented by other scriptures that are themselves sources (of various kinds) of knowledge, which reveal all things like a lamp, and which are almost omniscient. For scriptures like the Ṛg-veda, possessed of all good qualities as they are, cannot possibly emerge from any source other than an all-knowing One. . . . It goes without saying that that Great Being has absolute omniscience and omnipotence, since from him emerge the Ṛg-veda etc. – divided into many branches and constituting the source of classification into gods, animals, men, castes, stages of life etc. and the source for all kinds of knowledge. . . .
>
> (*Brahmasūtrabhāṣya* (BBS) 1.1.3, trans. Swami Gambhirananda, 1977, Advaita Ashrama, Delhi)

We see here that for Śaṃkara the Veda is not authorless and eternal, as for the *Mīmāṃsā*, but rather that it emanates, along with all other branches of knowledge incorporated in the supplementary vedic texts (the *Vedāṅgas*), from the absolute source of all.

Thus, rather than being an end in itself, the Veda is a means of knowing *brahman*. Each object of knowledge (*prameya*) has an appropriate means whereby it can be known (*pramāṇa*) and sacred scripture is the appropriate means whereby we know *brahman* as the 'object' of its knowledge. Such knowledge, for Śaṃkara, brings liberation, though such an inquiry into the absolute (*brahmajijñāsa*) cannot strictly speaking be commenced, for *brahman* is not a 'thing' in the common sense of an object of cognition distinct from a subject (see BBS 1.1.1).

The importance of scripture for Śaṃkara cannot be underestimated. Knowledge of *brahman*, which in the strictest sense is unknowable, can come only through 'the word': *brahman*, which is without qualities (*nirguṇa*), cannot be known through the senses, which can only grasp objects appropriate to their own sphere, or through mere reasoning (BSS 1.1.2). Indeed, even meditation and ritual cannot yield up knowledge of *brahman*, for *brahman* is uncaused and so cannot be attained through causes and conditions. But although in one sense *brahman* is unknowable, it is nevertheless 'revealed' through the word which emanates from it, and can be existentially apprehended 'as the content of the subject "I"' (BBS p. 3). That *brahman* is the content of the subject 'I' – the irreducibility of the subjective – is revealed particularly in the 'great sayings' (*mahāvākyas*) of the *Upaniṣads* and *Bhagavadgītā*: 'I am the absolute' (*aham brahmāsmi*), 'this self is the absolute' (*ayam ātmā brahma*), 'all this is indeed the absolute' (*sarvam khalu idam brahma*) and 'you are that' (*tat tvam asi*).

These statements were interpreted in a purely monistic sense by Śaṃkara's unremitting non-dualism, but there were other schools of Advaita Vedānta which understood these sentences in a less uncompromising way, a way which is perhaps more central to the general tendency of Hindu thought. Most significant of these is the Viśiṣṭādvaita or qualified non-dualism, made famous by Rāmānuja (*c.* 1017–1137). Rāmānuja interpreted the sacred scriptures not to mean, as Śaṃkara did, that the everyday world was unreal or illusory (*māyā*), but rather that it is a mode of expression of the absolute. He thus rejects Śaṃkara's interpretative strategy of dividing scripture into a lower and higher level of truth and relegating all statements implying dualism to the former. All parts of the Veda are of equal value for Rāmānuja, for there are no grounds internal to the Veda for maintaining the supremacy of some statements over others or for taking such statements out of their total context.

For Rāmānuja the Veda was the word of the Lord who was united with his creation, yet still maintained his transcendence. (This philosophy is therefore a 'qualified non-dualism', *viśiṣṭādvaita.*) Yet it was not the *śruti* texts themselves which provided the main authority for Rāmānuja, but rather the *Bhagavadgītā* and Bādarāyaṇa's *Brahma-sūtra*. Not only did he regard these texts as authoritative, inheriting as he did an expanded Hindu notion of sacred scripture, but he and the Śrī Vaiṣṇava tradition, of whom he was the hierarch, also revered texts of the 'tantric' Vaiṣṇava tradition of the Pāñcarātra and Tamil songs of the Āḻvārs, the seventh-century devotees (*bhaktas*) of Viṣṇu.

Indeed, the *Tiruvaimoḻī* of Nammāḻvār, a collection of his 'sweet Tamil songs', was known as the Tamil Veda and treated with as much authority as the Sanskrit scriptures. This text was, and is, believed to contain great spiritual knowledge, and is recited by the Śrī Vaiṣṇavas during daily rituals and in its entirety at weddings, funerals and other occasions (Carman and Narayanan 1989). Rāmānuja never actually composed a commentary on this text, though his disciple and cousin, Piḷḷān, did, in Maṇipravāla, a hybrid of Tamil and Sanskrit. Other commentaries followed after this into the thirteenth century.

What is significant here is that the sacred text is no longer confined to Sanskrit, but a respectable orthodox tradition has widened the boundaries of the sacred to include a text in a Dravidian language. Indeed, the *Tiruvaimoḻī* was thought to have sacred power akin to the Veda and could be taught only to a suitable disciple in the process of transmission from teacher to pupil (*ōrāṇ-vaḻi*). In contrast, however, to the Sanskrit Veda, which was restricted to twice-born males, this text could be heard by all castes, including *śūdras*, and by both genders.

We see here, then, the expansion of the idea of a sacred, revealed scripture, which is accessible to a wider community of people, in a language more easily understood. Of course the Tamil texts would not be accepted as authoritative by highly orthodox Brahmans from outside the Śrī Vaiṣṇava community, but we see here a strong sense which prevails in much of Hinduism, that 'revelation' is not something in the distant past, but is a continuing tradition, and indeed the line between revelation and compositions of human authorship is sometimes quite thin.

That which is remembered

So far we have examined the idea of revelation and seen how there are two paths which lead from it, the primary path of ritual in which the Veda functions liturgically, and the path of interpretation where it functions as an authoritative basis or source of knowledge upon which, or around which, metaphysical systems, such as the Pūrva Mīmāṃsā and Vedānta, can be built. We have also seen how there can be the expansion of the idea of the sacred text in some communities to include works which are not written in Sanskrit and which are not ancient. We shall return to this theme of revelation presently in discussing a different class of text often contrasted with the Veda, namely the *Tantra*, which again raises questions of authority and authenticity. But first it is necessary to survey briefly a vast body of literature of human authorship, 'that which is remembered' (*smṛti*), for it is this literature which is most significant at a popular level within Hinduism, and which has captured and filled the Hindu imagination.

Within this category are classed the *śāstra*s, associated with various branches of the Veda (see above pp. 73–5), the epic literature (*itihāsa*), i.e., the *Rāmāyaṇa* and *Mahābhārata*, the compendiums of mythology, ritual, yoga and doctrine called the *Purāṇa*s, and the *āgama*s and *tantra*s which are, however, regarded by their followers as being equal in status to the Veda.

THE EPICS

The *Rāmāyaṇa*,[9] traditionally composed by Vālmīki, is more concise than the *Mahābhārata*, which it predates. The story, briefly, concerns the banishment into the forest of Prince Rāma, who is an incarnation of Viṣṇu, along with his wife Sītā and brother Bālarāma, as a consequence of his stepmother's wishes. Here they live the life of hermits until the demon Rāvaṇa, from Śrī Laṅka, abducts Sītā. With the help of a monkey army of the king Sugrīva, headed by the monkey-general Hanuman, Sītā is rescued and Rāvaṇa defeated.

The importance of this epic lies particularly in the messages it presents concerning correct behaviour and duty (*dharma*). Rāma and Sītā are models of moral rectitude. Rāma demonstrates filial piety by exiling himself because his father has so asked him, even though both know such an exile is unjust, and Sītā is the ideal wife, accepting her fate when she is banished into the forest towards the end of the story because people are suspicious of her purity, even though Rāma knows she is innocent. (See the chapter on Hinduism in *Women in Religion* in this series.) Sītā and Rāma are the ideal married couple, each embodying the expected virtues of the husband and wife and demonstrating the constant Hindu idea that social duty and obligation are far more important than personal desires.

The *Mahābhārata* and the *Purāṇa*s are thought by many Hindus to have been composed by Vyāsa, a Brahman seer who appears in the *Mahābhārata* and is thought to be an incarnation of the deity Viṣṇu-Nārāyaṇa. Vyāsa taught the epic poem to his pupil who then recited it during the snake sacrifice of King Janamejaya, from whence the poem was passed down orally through the generations. The *Mahābhārata*[10] is an encyclopedic work which was begun probably in the fifth or fourth century BCE, and which was complete by about the fourth century CE. It contains a wealth of mythological, ritual and philosophical material, woven around the story of an internecine war between the five Pāṇḍavas and their cousins, the Kauravas. Yudhiṣṭhira, the heir apparent, loses his kingdom to his cousin Duryodhana at a game of dice and has to retire to the forest for thirteen years. At the end of this period, Duryodhana and his cousins do not give back the kingdom and so a war ensues in which the Pāṇḍavas are eventually successful.

The *Mahābhārata* was added to over the years, particularly by a Brahman clan (*gotra*), the Bhārgavas, and it contains many stories embedded within the larger framework. These may have originally existed independently. Perhaps the most famous of these embedded episodes, after the *Bhagavadgītā*, is the story of Nala and Damayantī. Nala, 'a tiger among men', is King of Niṣadha, while Damayantī, 'a mind agitating' beauty, is the daughter of King Bhīma. They fall in love by hearing of each other's qualities, and eventually Damayantī chooses Nala for a husband at her *svayamvara*, the free choice of a husband allowed to Kṣatriya girls. Nala, however, comes to grief by gambling away all he has (reflecting Yudhiṣṭhira's behaviour) and wanders in the forest. Eventually he wins everything back and lives happily with Damayantī.

Although the Nala episode reflects the narrative structure of the larger story, it is probable that we have here an example of the Sanskritisation of a folk tale. Indeed, the story of Nala is still found as an oral tradition in northern India, and rather than these being derived from the Sanskrit version, it is more probable that the north Indian folk tales and the epic version are both derived from an older, oral tradition.[11] This happens throughout the epic, and many episodes contained within it may have been folk tales viewed through a Vaiṣṇava lens.

Both epics are important in telling us about the kind of religious and social changes occurring in India during the periods of their composition. These texts paint a picture of life in north and northeast India during the last half of the last millennium BCE, depicting a number of small kingdoms, a hierarchical social structure and groups of ascetics living in the forests seeking release (*mokṣa*) through yoga and asceticism (*tapas*). The gods Brahmā (not the impersonal force, *brahman* of the *Upaniṣads*) and Indra are important in the text, and the text also reflects the rise to prominence of Śiva and, particularly, Viṣṇu.

The epics have been at the centre of the Hindu religious imagination, functioning to reinforce ideals of behaviour, interaction and social duty (*dharma*) of both householders and renouncers, and also reflecting the Hindu love of poetry and a good story. These texts would have been known not through the written word, but through being told by bards around the villages, and by being acted out and danced. In contemporary India the stories are still a living tradition and have captured the minds of millions of Hindus by being serialised though the medium of television, the television set becoming a shrine during their transmission. Indeed, the televised epics may well have been instrumental in the recent increase of support for political Hindu movements such as the Bhāratīya Jana Saṅgh.

THE BHAGAVADGĪTĀ

The *Bhagavadgītā* is located within book six of the *Mahābhārata*. A text originating with the Vaiṣṇava Bhagavata cult, it became a pan-Hindu authority, being commented upon by the main Vedānta thinkers, Śaṃkara, Rāmānuja and Madhva, and also by some important Śaiva thinkers such as Rāmakaṇṭha and Abhinavagupta, though undoubtedly the Vaiṣṇavas have been much more interested in this text than the Śaivas. One is even tempted to think that Abhinavagupta wrote his *Bhagavadgītā-saṃgraha*, not out of a deep respect for the text, but rather to align his monistic Śaiva tradition with more orthodox ways of thinking. Although technically *smṛti*, the *Gītā* has been treated as though it were *śruti*. Indeed, the commentators do not seem to be very concerned with this problem. The text even calls itself the *Bhagavadgītā-upaniṣad*, which Coburn says, with justification, substantiates his claim that the classification of Hindu scriptures needs to be re-examined (Coburn 1989: 126 n. 63).

The *Gītā* is a text expressing two central concerns of Hinduism, the need to perform one's duty (*dharma*) and the need to attain liberation (*mokṣa*) from the cycle of birth and death (*saṃsāra*) through detachment and love (*bhakti*) for God (Viṣṇu/Kṛṣṇa). It begins with Arjuna, one of the Pāndu brothers, being driven in a chariot by Kṛṣṇa, an incarnation of Viṣṇu, between the two armies on the eve of the great battle. Arjuna expresses a deep moral concern to Kṛṣṇa about the war, how he does not want to fight, for it means destroying the lives of so many of his relations (1.28–46).

Kṛṣṇa attempts to allay Arjuna's apprehensions by giving three reasons why he should fight in the battle. First, he tells Arjuna that to fight is the manly thing to do (2.2–3), but Arjuna is not convinced by this argument. Kṛṣṇa then presents a deeper reason as to why Arjuna should not flinch from the battle, namely that soul (*ātman*) is eternal and passes at death from one body to another (2.13); the eternal soul, being 'unborn, eternal, everlasting and ancient' (*ajo nityaḥ śāśvato 'yaṃ purāṇo*) cannot die neither can it kill (2.19–20). The existential understanding of this eternal soul and its dependence upon the absolute is, of course, liberation. But of more immediate concern is the third and most important reason for Arjuna to fight, namely that it is his duty, his *svadharma*, as a member of the warrior class (2.31). Indeed, not to fight would be to transgress his warrior's duty and would therefore be a 'sin' (*pāpa*) (2.33).

Attempting to bring together the two realms of *dharma* and *mokṣa*, the text unfolds a teaching of detachment and devotion. One can be in the world, performing one's worldly duties, but should be detached from it, dedicating the fruits of one's action (*karmaphalam*) to Kṛṣṇa in order to attain peace (2.11; 5.10–12). Undoubtedly the text's highest ideal is liberation through devotion (*bhakti*) to the theistic reality of Kṛṣṇa (18.55–7), who, as is revealed in chapter 11, is the supreme absolute creating all universes, and in whom all universes are consumed (11.15–31).

Many influences have fed into the *Gītā*, and it is a great reservoir of ideas which can seem contradictory. Indeed, the openness of the text is seen in the commentarial tradition which developed from it. Śaṃkara saw the text as propounding non-dualism (*advaita*) of the soul and absolute, while other theistic traditions read the text in purely theistic terms, maintaining a clear distinction between the soul and the absolute. One such interpretational divergence is illustrated by Patricia Mumme with regard to verse 18.66, the so called *caramaśloka*. The verse reads: 'Having relinquished all dharmas, resort to me alone as refuge. I will save you from all sins; do not fear' (*sarvadharmān parityaja / mām ekaṃ śaraṇaṃ vraja ahaṃ tvāṃ sarvapāpebhyo / mokṣayiṣyāmi mā śucaḥ*) (Mumme 1992: 69).

A hundred or so years after Rāmānuja's death, the Śrī Vaiṣṇava community had split into the Teṉkalai, the 'southern culture', and Vaṭakalai, the 'northern culture', schools. The former placed emphasis on the Tamil scriptures and the idea of surrender to God's grace as the only means of liberation, the latter emphasised the Sanskrit sources of their tradition, i.e., the Vedas, and effort as playing a part in the process of salvation (Carman and Narayanan 1989: 187–90). Accordingly, the Teṉkalai teachers understood the *caramaśloka* to be saying that there are two distinct paths, that of *bhakti-yoga* and that of surrender (*prapatti*); surrender being the superior, esoteric 'path' in which the devotee is wholly dependent on God's (Viṣṇu's) grace. Vedānta Deśika (1269–1370), by contrast, the main theologian of the Vaṭakalai school, maintained that the verse referred to two groups of people. On the one hand there are twice-born males who are liberated through the performance of ritual devotion (i.e., *bhakti-yoga*), while on the other hand there are all the others, for whom surrender (*prapatti*) is appropriate. Thus the verse 'having relinquished all dharmas' does not mean that there is a superior path to *dharma*, which means here the performance of devotional ritual, but refers to those who cannot perform ritual because they are not twice-born (Mumme 1992: 78).

This verse serves to illustrate the 'openness' of the *Gītā*, and is an example of the way in which it has functioned almost as revealed scripture in the hermeneutic traditions of Hinduism. However, it has enjoyed a wide, popular appeal among the Hindu urban classes only since the Hindu Renaissance, which began in the nineteenth century. The text also functioned to stir nationalist aspirations before Indian independence, drawing as it does on the more martial elements of the Hindu tradition. The struggle against colonialism was seen as the struggle of righteousness (*dharma*) against unrighteousness (*adharma*). Part of the *Gītā*'s popular appeal may also be due to what Bharati has called the 'pizza-effect'; namely that the *Gītā* has been exported to the West, particularly through 'new religions' such as Transcendental Meditation and the Hare Krishna movement, and then imported, as it were, back into India. Indeed, the founding *gurus* of these two movements, Maharishi Mahesh Yogi and Bhaktivedanta Swami Prabhupada, have both written commentaries on the text, one from an advaitin perspective, the other from a devotional, theistic perspective.

While the *Gītā* has undoubtedly been very influential at the level of philosophy and in modern, urban Hinduism, it does not play such an important role for rural Hindus, for whom, rather than the Kṛṣṇa of the *Gītā*, it is the stories of the erotic, youthful Kṛṣṇa of the *Bhagavata Purāṇa* which have been the source of amusement and wonder.

THE PURĀṆAS

The *Purāṇas*[12] are a vast corpus, covering a wide range of material, often derived from the *Upaniṣads*, the *Brāhmaṇas* and epics. They include mythologies of the Hindu deities and incarnations (*avatāras*) of Viṣṇu, the origins of the cosmos and of humanity, law codes, ritual, pilgrimage and so on. Traditionally there are eighteen major and eighteen minor (*upa*)*purāṇas* which overlap in content and present different versions of the same myths. This largely depends upon sectarian affiliation, as many *purāṇas* promote a particular deity, such as Viṣṇu or Śiva, over others. Indeed, local stories and traditions were incorporated into the puranic tradition in the process known as Sanskritisation: the absorption by the 'great tradition' of local, low-caste, 'little traditions'. This process of control was done by orthodox Brahmans, the Smārtas (those who followed *smṛti*).

The dating of these texts is very problematic, partly because they were composed over a long period of time and freely borrow material from each other. Indeed, these are very uncircumscribed texts, and they have always been transmitted without clearly defined boundaries, so much so that the notion of establishing critical editions is at least problematic. So while, as some scholars have argued, the search for an 'original' text in the case of the *Purāṇas* may be a waste of time,[13] we can nevertheless establish a rough chronology, with, for example, the *Brahmāṇḍa*, composed from about 350–950 CE, the *Viṣṇu* about 450 CE and the *Bhagavata* in about 950 CE (O'Flaherty 1988: 5).

Popular Hinduism has been conveyed mostly through the medium of these texts, which were performed by reciters going around the villages, for, of course, the written text would be accessible only to the literate. Indeed, there were public readings of the *Purāṇas*, for, unlike the Veda, there were no restrictions on who could hear them; they were open to all, even to the lowest class (*śūdra*) and to women. Perhaps the most popular and authoritative *Purāṇa* among the Vaiṣṇavas has been the *Bhagavata-Purāṇa*. This text depicted Kṛṣṇa's play (*līlā*) with the cowgirls (*gopīs*), and promoted the idea of the longing devotion of separation (*viraha-bhakti*) from the Lord as the means to salvation. These stories have captivated the minds of generations of Hindus, inspiring theological speculation, dance and iconographic representations of Kṛṣṇa and the *gopīs*. Indeed, rather than the monism of the *Upaniṣads*, it is the devotionalism (*bhakti*) of texts such as the *Bhagavata* which pervades popular, rural Hinduism.

THE ĀGAMAS AND TANTRAS

While the *śruti* literature and *smṛti* texts (the *Dharma-śāstras*, the epics including the *Bhagavadgītā* and the *Purāṇas*) have functioned as the authoritative source for orthodox Hindu society (particularly for Vaiṣṇavas), all mainstream schools of Śaivism revere a different group of texts. These are the *tantras* and *āgamas*, dating mostly from about the seventh to eleventh centuries.

The *tantras* and *āgamas* are a vast body of literature which generally take the form of a dialogue between Śiva and his consort (Śakti), dealing with ritual, the divine nature of the body, the female energy (*śakti*) of god, cosmology (particularly speculation on the cosmos as an emanation of energy as divine sound), and the construction of ritual formulae or *mantras*. Theoretically the *tantras* contain four sections (*pādas*), on knowledge (*jñāna*), yoga, ritual (*kriyā*) and behaviour (*caryā*), though most are not clearly divided in this way and there is much overlap in contents.

A Hindu who follows the ritual prescriptions and behaviour enjoined by the *tantras* is a *tāntrika*, in contrast to a person who follows only the vedic prescriptions, a *vaidika*. A *tāntrika* has undergone initiation (*dīkṣā*) by a *guru* into a particular school and would regard the *tantras* as a more powerful revelation than the Veda, providing an effective soteriology in the present age of darkness (*kali-yuga*). Indeed, the tantric householder would not reject the vedic rites, but would perform his tantric rites in addition, maintaining that this was a more rapid path for one desirous of liberation (*mumukṣu*). A popular dictum has even maintained that one should be a *vaidika* in one's social practice, externally a Śaiva, but internally a *tāntrika*. There was also an initiation into an alternative path for those who desired magical powers and pleasure in heavenly abodes (*bubukṣu*).

The classification of these texts is a complex matter, for as Sanderson has shown, later developments absorbed the revelations of their predecessors in an initiation hierarchy.[14] That is, the later developments regarded their revelation and ritual initiation as containing, yet superseding, the earlier revelations. One way of looking at the *tantra*s would be to divide them into 'monistic', or 'northern' *tantra*s, the authoritative source of 'Kashmir' Śaivism, and 'dualistic', or 'southern' *tantra*s, the source of Śaiva Siddhānta. Very generally speaking, the 'northern' texts tend to be called *tantra*s while the Siddhānta texts tend to be called *āgama*s. There was also a tantric Vaiṣṇava tradition, the Pāñcarātra, whose texts, called *saṃhitā*s, closely resemble the Śaiva *tantra*s in many respects. These texts were revered by the Śrī Vaiṣṇavas, and Rāmānuja defended their orthodoxy (see above pp. 85–6 and Carman and Narayanan 1989: 181).

Quite different from the more respectable, vedically aligned Pāñcarātra, we have, at the opposite end of the tantric spectrum, the Śākta *tantra*s. These were produced by groups of cremation-ground ascetics, worshipping ferocious female deities such as Kālī or one of her manifestations. These terrible (*ghora*) female deities needed to be placated by substances which were anathema to the orthodox, namely non-vegetarian offerings, alcohol and sexual fluids. In later *tantra*s these offerings became known as the 'five Ms', wine (*matsya*), flesh (*maṃsa*), fish (*matsya*), parched grain (*mudrā*) and (caste-free) sexual intercourse (*maithuna*). These substances could, for some deities, be substituted by harmless, symbolic substances such as milk and ghee etc., as was done by the more orthodox Goddess-worshipping tradition, the Śrī Vidyā, which became associated with the Śaṃkara Brahman tradition of south India.

Mention should also be made of the vast body of Buddhist *tantra*s (see chapter on Buddhism in this volume). These are mostly preserved in Tibetan, and their form is akin to the Śaiva texts which influenced them. There is also Jain tantric literature. Examining the 'intertextuality' of these Hindu, Buddhist and Jain sources (as well as the tantric material in Tamil) is a major task which needs to be done.

While the metaphysics of the *tantra*s themselves is sometimes ambiguous, the *tantra*s of the north, the authority of Kashmir Śaivism, have been interpreted by that school through the lens of a monistic metaphysics, in which there is only the reality of pure consciousness (*saṃvit*), identified with Śiva, of which the cosmos is an appearance. Śaiva Siddhānta, the older system, by contrast, maintained that there is an eternal distinction between the Lord (*pati*), souls (*paśu*s) and matter (*pāśa*). Some of the *tantra*s, such as the *Svacchanda*, have been interpreted in both ways by these schools.

Both Kashmir Śaivism and Śaiva Siddhānta had thriving commentarial traditions. Kashmir Śaivism, whose main exponent was Abhinavagupta (*c.* 975–1025), not only revered the revelations of the *tantra*s but also the independent revelation of Vāsugupta (*c.* 875–925), who in a dream was told by Śiva that on the Mahā Deva mountain he would find a secret (*rahasya*) text inscribed upon a stone for the benefit of the world. This text is the *Śiva-sūtra*, which generated a tradition of commentarial literature and intertextual dialogue. But over and above philosophy, the importance of the *tantra*s and *āgama*s lies in their use as ritual manuals and as objects of recitation. For example, the *āgama*s of the south Indian Śaiva Siddhānta are still used today in personal, daily ritual and in temple rites. In the sense that the *tantra*s are liturgical manuals, there is a strong continuity with the vedic tradition, though the deities and the *mantra*s used in ritual would be different and, indeed, regarded as polluting to the orthodox, especially if the focus of the rites is one of the terrible deities of the harder, 'left-hand' traditions.

Although not technically *śruti*, the *tantra*s and their associated literature, such as the *Śiva-sūtra*, have been revered by initiated *tāntrika*s and by the wider Śaiva communities of Kashmir, Nepal and South India. With the *tantra*s, we have another Hindu instance which demonstrates the ongoing nature of revelation within the Hindu traditions, outside of orthodox, vedic boundaries. While the orthodox Brahmans would never accept the *tantra*s or their related literature as 'canonical', these texts have been accepted by a significant body of the Hindu tradition, which would claim equal right to the term 'Hindu'.

THE VERNACULAR TRADITIONS

Not only the *tantra*s and *āgama*s, but also poetry in vernacular languages is authoritative for some of the Śaiva traditions. In a way akin to the Tamil poetry of the Āḻvārs for the Śrī Vaiṣṇavas, the southern school of Śaiva Siddhānta honoured, along with the *āgama*s, the Tamil poetry of the Śaiva poet-saints, the Nāyaṉārs. Another Śaiva school, the Liṅgayats or Vīraśaivas, established in Mysore, similarly revere the Kannada poetry of their founders, including the powerful poetry of a female initiate, Mahadevyakka (Ramanujan 1973: 111).

In addition to the Tamil poetry of the Āḻvārs, the Nāyaṉārs, and the Kannada poetry of the Liṅgayats in the south, there is also Bengali and Hindi devotional poetry (O'Flaherty 1988: 138–87). The Hindi poetry of the north is of great significance in the development of Indian religious traditions. A distinction can be made here between poetry which eulogised the Lord who possessed qualities (*saguṇa*), usually Kṛṣṇa and Rāma embodied in a temple image, and praise of a formless, transcendent Lord without qualities (*nirguṇa*). Generally, these poets were low-caste, and criticised orthodox forms of worship in favour of devotion to the transcendent Lord, through repeating his divine names and apprehending the name (*nām*) or sound (*śabad*) of God in meditation through the grace of the *guru*.

Tulsi Das' (*d.* 1623) *Rāmcaritmānas*, a Hindi version of the *Rāmāyaṇa*, was a very influential work which eulogises the saving power of God's infinite name. Among the most famous poets in the tradition of 'good people' or *sant*s, is Kabir (fifteenth century). Nominally a Muslim of the weaver caste, his poetry is terse and disparaging of traditional soteriologies, emphasising, rather, devotion to the formless absolute through repeating his name:

> I have searched all the Vedas,
> the Puranas, the Smriti –
> Salvation lies in none.
> Kabir says, 'So I repeat Ram's name –
> he erases birth and death.[15]

With the Sant poetry we have a reinterpretation of the traditional Hindu idea of the revealed word. Rather than a group of received scriptures (*śruti*), the word becomes a transcendent reality, whose power goes beyond the traditional understandings of the heard scripture, becoming a means of transformation and salvation.

The devotional poetry of the Sant tradition is very popular in north India and much of it is collected in the holy book of the Sikhs, the *Ādi Granth*. This poetry is sung with great feeling at various festivals and during the community meetings (*satsang*s) of contemporary *gurū*s (such as those of the Rādhā Soami tradition), functioning to express popular devotional sentiments and a soteriology without the necessity of caste qualification, elaborate ritual or stringent *yoga*.

In a curtailed survey such as this it is impossible to cover all genres, aspects and functions of sacred texts in Hinduism. We have seen that the heard, rather than the written, word plays a central part in Hindu traditions, as the conveyor of those traditions through time and as the pointer to how people should live their lives in accordance with the higher power of *dharma*. Revelation is not static, but while there is a central corpus of unchanging texts, the Veda, passed down orally through the generations, there is also a fluidity and acceptance of new texts. Revelation is not something in the far distant past, but is a constant and present possibility. The Hindu traditions have always reassessed themselves, introducing new ideas, though rooting them in the past, and occasionally even rejecting the old models. The received word has functioned to constrain behaviour into certain forms, and whether complied with, modified or rejected, it has been at the heart of the development of the amalgam of regional traditions, doctrines and behaviour which the term 'Hinduism' has come to designate.

NOTES

1. Bharati, A. (1982) *Hindu Views and Ways and the Hindu–Muslim Interface*, Santa Barbara, Ross Erikson, pp. 2–3.
2. The complete corpus of vedic literature has not yet been translated into European languages, and translations which are available are often inaccessible. Some of the translations are as follows. The standard translation of the *Ṛg-veda* is by Karl F. Geldner, *Der Rig-veda, aus dem Sanskrit ins Deutsche übersetz und mit einen laufenden*

Kommentar versehen (4 vols), Harvard Oriental Series 33–35, Cambridge, Harvard University Press, 1951. In English there is H.H. Wilson's *Rig-Veda-Sanhita: A Collection of Ancient Hindu Hymns* (6 vols), London, 1850–88. W.D. O'Flaherty has published a very readable translation of selected hymns in *The Rig Veda*, Penguin, Harmondsworth, 1981. W.D. Whitney produced a translation of the *Atharva-veda* (revised by C. Lanman) (2 vols), Harvard Oriental Series 7, 8, Cambridge, 1905 (repr. Delhi, 1962). Also M. Bloomfield translated some of the text in *Hymns of the Atharva Veda*, Sacred Books of the East 42, Oxford, 1897 (repr. Delhi, 1964). R.T.H. Griffith produced *The Hymns of the Yajur-Veda*, Benares, 1899. For the *Brāhmaṇas* we have J. Eggeling, *The Śatapaṭha Brāhmaṇa According to the Text of the Mādhyandina School* (5 vols), Sacred Books of the East 12, 26, 41, 43, 44, Oxford, 1882–1900 (repr. Delhi, 1963) and W. Caland's *The Pañcaviṃśa-Brāhmaṇa*, Biblioteca Indica, 1955 (repr. Delhi, 1982). For the *Āraṇyakas* see A.B. Keith *The Śāṅkhāyana Āraṇyaka*, London, Royal Asiatic Society, 1908, and *The Aitareya Āraṇyaka*, Oxford, Clarendon Press, 1909. English translations of the *Upaniṣads* are a little more accessible. Here we have Hume's *Thirteen Principal Upanishads*, 1971, Oxford University Press, New York and S. Radhakrishnan's *The Principal Upanishads*, London. Allen & Unwin, 1953.

3. Bowker, J. (1991) *The Meanings of Death*, Cambridge, Cambridge University Press, pp. 148–67.
4. For an English translation see van Gelder, J.M. (1961–63) *The Mānava Śrauta-sūtra Belonging to the Maitrāyaṇī Saṃhitā* (2 vols), New Delhi (repr. Delhi, 1985).
5. English translation by O'Flaherty, W.D. (1992) *The Laws of Manu*, Harmondsworth, Penguin.
6. The Pūrva Mīmāṃsā or 'Primary Investigation' is a 'realistic' school of philosophy dating from about the second century BCE with the *Mīmāṃsā-sūtra* of Jaimini. It was concerned with vedic ritual, the purposes of the eternal Veda as injunctions to correct action and the avoidance of wrong action, and the invisible force (*apūrva*) which gives rise to the future result of a ritual act. Śabara wrote a commentary on this text (which in turn was commented upon by Prabhākara and Kumārila. These provide the basis of two sub-schools which have some disagreements concerning the nature of verbal testimony and error (see Dasgupta 367–405, Francis Clooney (1990) *Thinking Ritually*, Vienna, De Nobili).
7. *Mīmāṃsā-sūtra* 7.2.15 translated by Clooney, F. (1990) *Thinking Ritually*, Vienna, De Nobili, p. 134.
8. The Pūrva Mīmāṃsā was so called because it concentrated on the earlier (*pūrva*) parts of the Veda which it regarded as injunctions,

whereas the Uttara Mīmāṃsā emphasised the later (*uttara*) parts of the Veda, namely the *Upaniṣads*.

9. English translations by Goldman, R. and Sutherland, S.J. (1984) *The Rāmāyaṇa of Vālmīki*, vol. 1, and Pollock, S.I. (1986) *The Rāmāyaṇa of Vālmīki*, vol. 2, Princeton, Princeton University Press. A complete translation exists by Hari Prashad Shastri (1952–59) *The Rāmāyaṇa of Vālmīki* (3 vols), London, Shanti Sadan.
10. A good, though unfortunately incomplete, English translation is by van Buitenen, J.A.B. (1973–78) *The Mahābhārata*, vols 1–3, Chicago, University of Chicago Press.
11. See van Buitenen, J.A.B. *The Mahābhārata*, vol. 2, pp. 184–5.
12. For translations of the *Purāṇas* see Dimmitt, C. and van Buitenen, J.A.B. (1978) *Classical Hindu Mythology: A Reader in the Sanskrit Purāṇas*, Philadelphia, Temple University Press. O'Flaherty, W.D. (1975) *Hindu Myths*, Baltimore, Penguin.
13. Madeleine Biardeau observes: 'The approach of historical philology will never be suitable for an oral tradition, which has no essential reference to its historical origin' ('Some More Considerations about Textual Criticism', *Purāṇa* 10, 2, 1968: 115–23).
14. Sanderson, A. (1988) 'Śaivism and the Tantric Traditions', in Sutherland, S., Houlden, L., Clarke, P. and Hardy, F. *The World's Religions*, London, Routledge, pp. 660–704.
15. Dass, Nirmal (1991) *Songs of Kabir From the Adi Granth*, Albany, SUNY, p. 128.

FURTHER READING

Brockington, J.L. (1981) *The Sacred Thread*, Edinburgh, Edinburgh University Press.

Carman, J. and Narayanan, V. (1989) *The Tamil Veda*, Chicago, University of Chicago Press.

Coburn, T.B. (1989) '"Scripture" in India: Towards a Typology of the Word in Hindu Life', in M. Levering (ed.) *Rethinking Scripture*, Albany, SUNY.

Dasgupta, S.N. (1975) *A History of Indian Philosophy*, vol. 1, Delhi, MLBD.

Coward, H. (1988) *Sacred Word and Sacred Text*, New York, Orbis Books.

Gonda, J. (1975) *Vedic Literature*, Wiesbaden, Otto Harrassowitz.

—— (1977) *Medieval Religious Literature in Sanskrit*, Wiesbaden, Otto Harrassowitz.

Levering, M. (ed.) (1989) *Rethinking Scripture*, Albany, SUNY.

Mumme, P. (1992) 'Haunted by Śaṅkara's Ghost: The Śrī Vaiṣṇava Interpretation of *Bhagavad Gītā* 18.66', in J.R. Timm (ed.) (1992).
O'Flaherty, W.D. (ed.) (1988) *Textual Sources for the Study of Hinduism*, Manchester, Manchester University Press.
Pereira, J. (1991) *Hindu Theology, A Reader*, Delhi, Motilal Banarsidass.
Ramanujan, A.K. (1973) *Speaking of Śiva*, Harmondsworth, Penguin.
Staal, F. (1989) *Rules Without Meaning*, New York, Peter Lang.
Timm, J.R. (ed.) (1992) *Texts in Context: Traditional Hermeneutics in South Asia*, Albany, SUNY.

4. Islam

Martin Forward

The most important sacred writing for Muslims is the Qur'ān, their holy scripture, revealed by God to the Prophet Muhammad (*c.* 570–632)[1] and written in Arabic. There is also a secondary level of sacred writings, the *Ḥadīth*, which means, 'speech', or 'report', but has acquired the specific meaning of Tradition, a record of the sayings and actions of Muhammad and his closest followers. The *Ḥadīth* is regarded as an important source of dogma, ritual and law, second only to the Qur'ān.

The Qur'ān contains 114 chapters (*sūrahs*). It is a little shorter in size than the Christian New Testament. The first *sūrah*, called 'The Opening', is only seven verses long. Thereafter, the *sūrahs* are arranged roughly in order of length. The longest *sūrah* (the second) has 286 verses and the shortest have only three. Each *sūrah* has a name at its head. Most Muslims use it rather than the chapter number when they point out a particular passage. The name may refer to just a few verses. For example, the second *sūrah* is called 'The Heifer', but the story of that animal takes up only five of 286 verses. Sometimes, the passage to which the name draws attention is particularly striking. For example, the denunciation of 'The Poets' at the very end of *sūrah* 26, verses 224–7, is the only reference to them in the Qur'ān. They were a much appreciated group among Arabs then, though not by God and his Prophet! But often, other parts of a *sūrah* are just as interesting and important as the verses to which the name alludes.

After the name of each chapter comes a statement about its date. This indicates whether it was revealed at Makkah (a town, now in Saudi Arabia) between 610 and 622, or thereafter in Madinah (some 200 miles from Makkah) until the Prophet Muhammad's death in

632.[2] However, Muslim scholars have always recognised that many *sūrah*s are amalgams of Makkan and Madinan revelations.

At the beginning of every chapter except one, comes the expression, *Bismillāhir raḥmānir raḥīm* (in the name of God, the beneficent, the merciful), an affirmation that belies the western caricatures of Islam as a wholly warlike religion, with God as an oriental despot. Muslims believe that this phrase belongs to God's revelation, and is not an editorial addition at some later date. *Sūrah* 9 is the one that omits it. Many reasons have been offered for this exception. One suggestion is that this *sūrah* was originally attached to the previous one, from which it somehow came apart. Another is that *sūrah* 9 begins with a formal proclamation in the name of God, which renders the *Bismillāh* superfluous. Neither these nor other explanations are especially compelling, so it is best to accept this omission as puzzling and mysterious.

Even more mysterious are the Arabic letter or letters that follow the *Bismillāh* at the beginning of twenty-nine *sūrah*s. In English 'translations' of the Qur'ān,[3] these letters are sometimes rendered in Arabic, sometimes in an English equivalent. Some of them appear in groups: for example, *sūrah*s 10 to 15 begin with *alif*, *lam*, *ra*, and 13 has *mim* as well (in English, a, l, r, and m). One possibility, therefore, is that these letters signify the name of a scribe who was responsible for collecting groups of *sūrah*s, or perhaps they were used to identify such a group. Again, it seems best to accept a degree of mystery. We cannot know why these letters exist where they do.

Verse numbers vary slightly between different 'translations' of the Qur'ān. Nowadays, most Muslims follow the official Egyptian text, though a few non-Muslim scholars still follow a text of 1834 by a western scholar, Gustav Flügel.

The opening *sūrah* and some of the later and shorter ones are devotional, fervent in belief, sometimes confrontational, and they often make compelling reading, even to non-Muslims. There are many striking images of God's grandeur and human frailty; for example, 'all things pass away, save for the face of God' (28:88). The longer *sūrah*s, too, have moments of poetic beauty. The throne verse (2:255) and the verse of light (24:35) are of surpassing beauty, even in translation, and so are many other passages.

The Qur'ān in the life of devotion

When an Arabic-speaking Muslim opens his copy of the Qur'ān, how does he do so and what does he find there? He treats it with the greatest of respect. The Qur'ān is often kept apart from other books, and nothing is ever placed on top of it. The reader may wash his hands before opening it. Unlike an English book, it is opened from right to left, and the reader scans it from right to left. The Sacred Text is often beautifully bound, and ornately and attractively written. Indeed, qur'anic calligraphy is world-famous.

Although the word *qur'ān* is found in the text at several places and with various meanings, it is never employed there to describe the whole work of scripture. Some translations read it into 42:52 (for example, Ali Ahmed's), but this is a controversial rendition. However, from the early days of Islam, Muslims have called their scripture *qur'ān*. But the Muslim reader never simply refers to it as the Qur'ān. He always uses some honorific adjective. For example, he may call it *qur'ān ṣharīf*, 'Illustrious Qur'ān', *qur'ān majīd*, 'Noble Qur'ān', or *qur'ān karīm*, 'Glorious Qur'ān'. When he speaks in English he sometimes calls it 'The Holy Qur'ān', but usually prefers to keep to Arabic, as in the sentence, 'The *qur'ān ṣharīf* is my holy scripture'.

What then does it mean for an Arabic-speaking Muslim reader to call the scripture, *qur'ān*? Most probably *qur'ān* means, 'recitation'. Muhammad is often instructed to 'recite' (Arabic, *'iqra*) the revelation he receives (e.g., 96:1). Moreover, most Muslims, after opening the Qur'ān, move their lips as they read the sacred text, sometimes barely audibly, often out loud, rarely in complete silence. They recite it rather than read it, just as it was originally recited to the Prophet Muhammad. Believers recite scripture regularly during formal prayer (*ṣalāt*), and study it at other times, either alone or in a group. During the month of *Ramaḍān*, when Muslims fast from dawn to dusk, they read one section daily so that by the end of the month, they have recited the whole of scripture. These sections are usually marked in the margins of copies. There are other divisions, into four, or into seven, and so on. These divisions are to facilitate recitation for particular periods of time.

An Arabic-speaking Muslim reader often calls his scripture other names which stress aspects of its incomparable worth. So he calls it *al-kitāb*, '*the* Book' (superior to all other books), and, similarly, *an-*

nūr, 'the Light', *al-hudā'*, 'the Guidance', and *al-furqān*, 'the Distinction (between good and evil)'. Other words in the text, which only an Arabic speaker would notice, exalt the Qur'ān. In particular, the words that are weakly translated into English as chapter (*sūrah*) and verse (*āyah*, pl. *āyāt*), have meanings for Muslims that strengthen their understanding of its unique authority. In 10:38, God challenges those who claim Muhammad is inventing scripture: 'Bring then a *sūrah* like it, if you speak the truth'. Here, the word *sūrah* has something of the force of 'revelation'. The word *āyāt* is often and richly used to describe 'signs' of God's presence in the created order, which serve as reminders to human beings of 'the Beneficent, the Merciful' (e.g., 16:10–21).

The incomparability of the Qur'ān extends to its language and style, which Muslims regard as inimitable, a standing miracle (*i'jaz*). It is often said that the whole Qur'ān is written in *saj'*, a kind of rhyming prose with assonances at the end of verses, but Muslim scholars have sometimes held that this is not so in a strict sense. Perhaps they want to distinguish its style from that of soothsayers and poets who also used rhyme (52:29 denies that Muhammad is a soothsayer, and 69:41 that he is a poet). Most Muslims heighten the miraculous quality of the Qur'ān by deeming Muhammad illiterate: 7:157 describes Muhammad as the *ummī* Prophet, which can mean 'illiterate Prophet', though it could mean 'Prophet for those without a scripture'.

At any rate, the Muslim reader, scanning the Qur'ān in Arabic, encounters a wonder of language and style, which translations can only pallidly convey. Yusuf Ali wrote about the throne-verse, 'Who can translate its glorious meaning or reproduce the rhythm of its well-chosen and comprehensive words?'[4] Even in English, some of its magnificence survives:

> God! He is the only God, Alive and eternal. Neither slumber nor sleep seize him. Everything in the heavens and on earth is his. Who can intercede with him except by his leave? He knows what is before and after them, who know nothing of his knowledge save as he wills. His throne composes the heavens and the earth, and no fatigue touches him who sustains them. He is the most-high, the incomparable.
>
> (2:255)

So the Qur'ān, for the Muslim reader, plays the role that both the

King James Bible and the works of Shakespeare did for many generations of British schoolchildren. It is the religious and literary classic of the Arabic language. However, many Muslims are not fluent in Arabic. Few have it as their mother-tongue. Nowadays, the most populous part of the Muslim world are east of the Arabic-speaking countries. Many more Muslims live in South Asia (Bangladesh, India, Pakistan and Sri Lanka), Malaysia and Indonesia (the country with the world's largest Muslim population), than in Islam's original heartland of West Asia. So Bengali, Urdu, Malay, and Bahasi Indonesian are the first languages of many Muslims. In the United Kingdom, many are more conversant with the first two of these, and with other South Asian languages such as Gujarati and Panjābi, than with Arabic. Therefore, in Britain and many other countries, Muslims often send their children to classes in the mosque (*masjid*, 'a place of bowing down', for worship and other social and religious activities) after school to learn qur'anic Arabic. (Although the Arabic text remains the same throughout the Arab world, spoken dialects vary enormously from place to place.)

Formal prayers (*ṣalāt*) in Islam consist of the recitation of qur'anic passages, so all Muslims have to acquire some knowledge of Arabic. Some Muslims are able to recite the sacred text without properly understanding it, though many acquire a considerable competence in it. For those who do not know Arabic well, an obvious solution is to seek out a translation.

The Qur'ān translated is not, however, the Qur'ān. There is an Italian pun: *tradutore, traditore* ('Translation is a betrayal'). Nuances in one language cannot easily be translated into another. Puns and idioms go for nothing. Meanings can be subtly or even wholly changed. Many Muslims are offended by the idea of translating the Qur'ān. The divine language of revelation is Arabic. To translate it is to connive at distorting the Word of God. Indeed, scripture describes itself as 'an Arabic Qur'ān, in which is no deviousness' (39:27). In this view, it is better to learn Arabic haltingly than to seek the help of a translation to understand its meaning. Nevertheless, to help other Muslims understand their scripture better, scholars have translated the Qur'ān into Urdu, English and other languages. Translators have often been careful to refrain from calling their work, 'The Qur'ān'. For example, Mohammed Marmaduke Pickthall designated his work, *The Meaning of the Glorious Koran* and wrote: 'the result is not the

Glorious Koran, that inimitable symphony, the very sounds of which move men to tears and ecstasy'.[5]

The Qur'ān in English

There is no completely satisfactory English version of the Qur'ān. (For this reason, I have supplied my own translations in this chapter.) Translators usually fall at one or more of three hurdles: exercising their prejudices against Islam; mangling the English language; or, seeking to 'improve' the format of the Sacred Text.

The earliest translations of the Qur'ān into English were by Christians. They often interpreted the text satisfactorily, even if their style now seems somewhat dated. But they wrote to denigrate Islam. They seem to have believed that reading the Qur'ān would prove to English-speakers its inferiority to the Bible, so they translated it for that reason. George Sale, in his pioneering translation of 1734, defended his work by writing that 'they must have a mean opinion of the Christian religion, or be but ill-grounded therein, who can apprehend any danger from so manifest a forgery' (*The Koran*, London, Routledge and Sons Ltd, p. v). The Reverend J.M. Rodwell rearranged the chapters according to the order in which he believed they were revealed. It is a futile endeavour, since Muslim scholars agree that many chapters have portions dating from different revelatory moments in the Prophet's career. His book was first published in 1861 and has had a long life in the 'Everyman Library'. He saw Islam as an improvement on pre-Islamic paganism, but described Muhammad as 'probably, more or less, throughout his whole career, the victim of a certain amount of self-deception' (*The Koran* (1909 edn), London, J.M. Dent and Sons Ltd, p. 14). It is hardly surprising that Muslims avoid the translations of those whose views are so antagonistic to their basic beliefs. Unless outsiders are prepared to think themselves into the devotional attitude of a Muslim who approaches the Qur'ān with reverence and awe, it is unlikely that they will be able to understand, still less convey how the text impresses itself upon believers.

Some non-Muslims have been able to 'produce something which might be accepted as echoing, however faintly, the sublime rhetoric of the Arabic Koran',[6] notably the author of that intention, Arthur Arberry, whose translation was published in 1955. Muslims have been grateful for his work, which Fazlur Rahman ranks 'easily as the best in English' (Rahman 1989:12). But it has been consistently overpraised. In chasing after poetry, it achieves obscurity. It is poorly annotated, with only every fifth verse numbered, and no explanatory notes. E.H. Palmer's translation, dating from 1880, which has had a long shelf life in the 'World's Classics' series, also strives after expressiveness at the expense of clear meaning. He seems to have modelled his work on the King James 'Authorised' translation of the Bible, believing perhaps that archaic language confers respectability or holiness.

The two most common and praised translations by Muslims into English also employ arcane language. Mohammed Marmaduke Pickthall was an English convert to Islam, a cultured man who was tutor to an Indian princely ruler's children, so it is perhaps not surprising to find in his translation, first published in 1930, an attempt to emulate the language of Shakespeare and the seventeenth-century English Bible. This work was authorised for use among English-speaking Muslims by al-Azhar ('the radiant', Islam's most famous university and mosque, located in Cairo). Official approval does not prevent it from being a dull and rather obscure read. Moreover, he calls God Allāh. True, it is the Arabic, qur'anic, word for God. But his is a translation, the English word is 'God', and the use of Allāh tends to make non-Muslims think that *Allāh* is the Muslim God, as opposed to the Christian (or some other) God or gods. Abdullah Yusuf Ali's translation of 1934 calls God, God. It is less impenetrable than Pickthall's work, but still uses old-fashioned English. This is not as surprising as it seems. The author lived in Lahore, then an important city of British India. There, English officials introduced the educated classes to the delights of cricket and Shakespeare, and even today, high-flown English is alive and flourishing in South Asia. Yusuf Ali's translation is worth acquiring. Whereas Pickthall employs few footnotes, Yusuf Ali uses 6,311, most of which illuminate the text. His work also has a much better index.

Translations that attempt to improve the original (apart from Rodwell's) include Richard Bell's, first printed in 1937, and N.J. Dawood's 'Penguin Classics' version, dating from 1956. The latter reorders the *sūrah*s into their supposed order of revelation, rather as Rodwell had, except that his reordering is different. Bell keeps to the traditional chapter order but dates sections in each, with minor rearrangements of the text. His is a remarkable achievement, but a controversial one. Moreover, the actual translation is not strikingly elegant or interesting. Kenneth Cragg goes a step farther in *Readings in the Qur'ān* (London, Collins, 1988). He omits all repetitive material, and divides the rest (about two-thirds of the original) at random into eight sections. However, the material on offer is finely translated and very readable.

A good translation is by the Pakistani poet, Ahmed Ali (*Islam: The Qur'ān* (rev. edn), Princeton, Princeton University Press, 1988). Like Pickthall's, it is wedded to the use of Allāh rather than God, and employs the occasional archaism, such as 'verily' and 'haply'. But it is, on the whole, clear and readable, and conveys something of the Arabic Qur'ān's poetic drawing power, more so than Arberry's translation.

The best translation is M.M. Khatib's *The Bounteous Koran* (London, Macmillan, 1986) which provides useful notes and was authorised by al-Azhar in 1984. It reads well, and is based on The Royal Cairo Edition of the Arabic text. It is, however, very expensive.

The origin of the Qur'ān

The Qur'ān was revealed to Muhammad, piecemeal, from about the year 610 until his death in 632. He was the husband of a wealthy merchant called Khadijah, and would often retire to a cave in Mount Hira, three miles outside Makkah, to spend time in meditation. He received a call, which might be described in 96:1–5, generally considered to be the first revelation:

> Recite, in the name of the Lord who created. He created human beings from clots of blood. Recite, because your Lord is merciful. He has taught the use of the pen. He has taught human beings what they did not know.

Muhammad went home deeply troubled, telling Khadijah that he was either a poet or a madman! But she comforted him, and her cousin Waraqa, a Christian, declared that this was the *nāmūs*, i.e., the message that had come from God to Mūsā (Moses) and *'Īsā* (Jesus). After the first revelation, he experienced a period of doubt, which may have lasted three years, when no revelation came.

Finally, Muhammad felt a strange sensation come over him. He hid himself in his cloak, and a voice said:

> You, wrapped in your cloak, get up and warn (others). Praise your Lord. Purify your clothing. Shun idolatry.
>
> (74:1–5)

Thereafter, Muhammad's doubts disappeared. He had a mission to fulfil. He made converts, despite the persecution of idolaters and other opponents. In 622, he emigrated to Madinah to build a community there, but returned victoriously to Makkah in 630 as its political head as well as its spiritual leader. He died two years later, leaving behind him a community called Islam.

What does that community believe about its revelation? All Muslims believe that the Qur'ān is divine in origin. The qur'anic revelations form part of 'the Mother of the Book' (13:39), which is also called 'the well-preserved Tablet' (85:22). The Qur'ān descended to the lowest of the seven heavens to the 'House of Protection', during the 'Night of Power', the 27th night of the month of fasting (*Ramaḍān*). From there is was revealed bit by bit to Muhammad, as God chose and circumstances demanded (97:1–5; 17:106f.). The medium of communication was the angel Gabriel (in Arabic *Jibrā'īl*, 2:97). The most important qur'anic word for revelation is *waḥy*, which conveys the idea of both revelation and inspiration. Muhammad, in the state of revelation, heard a message from God delivered by *Jibrā'īl*. But in what form did it come? The great Muslim historian, Ibn Khaldun (1332–1406), wrote that:

> The Qur'ān is alone among the divine books, in that our Prophet received it directly in the words and phrases in which it appears. In this respect, it differs from the Torah, the Gospel and other heavenly books. The prophets received them in the form of ideas during the state of revelation.[7]

Other Muslims have tried to find some more positive role for Muhammad in his reception of revelation, teasing out what it means for a prophet to be inspired with a message from God. The Indian Muslim modernist, Syed Ameer Ali (1849–1928) in *The Spirit of Islam* (London, Chatto and Windus, 1890, with many reprints) believed the Qur'ān to be quintessentially Muhammad's moral teaching. However, he was a poor scholar both of Islam and Arabic, and few, if any, other Muslims have agreed with his assumptions about its value. More interestingly, Fazlur Rahman (1919–88) wrote that

> orthodoxy . . . lacked the intellectual capacity to say both that the Qur'ān is entirely the Word of God and, in an ordinary sense, also entirely the word of Muhammad. The Qur'ān obviously holds both, for if it insists that it has come to the 'heart' [2:97] of the Prophet, how can it be external to him?

Fazlur Rahman's explanation concentrates on the meaning of prophethood:

> Now a Prophet is a person whose average, overall character, the sum total of his actual conduct, is far superior to those of humanity in general. He is a man who is *ab initio* impatient with men and even with most of their ideals, and wishes to re-create history. Muslim orthodoxy, therefore, drew the logically correct conclusion that Prophets must be regarded as immune from serious error (the doctrine of *'iṣmah*). Muhammad was such a person, in fact the only such person really known to history. That is why his overall behaviour is regarded by the Muslims as Sunna or the 'perfect model'. But with all this, there were moments when he, as it were, 'transcends himself' and his moral cognitive perception becomes so acute and so keen that his consciousness becomes identical with the moral law itself. 'Thus did we inspire you with a Spirit of Our Command: You did not know what the Book was. But We have made it a light' (XLII, 52). But the moral law and religious values are God's Command, and although they are not identical with God entirely, they are part of him. . . . The Qur'ān is thus pure Divine Word, but, of course, it is equally intimately related to the inmost personality of the Prophet Muhammad, whose relationship to it cannot be mechanically conceived like that of a record. The Divine Word flowed through the Prophet's heart.[8]

Fazlur Rahman's intriguing explanation has not convinced most non-Muslim students of the Qur'ān. Western Christians have long lived and coped with a critical study of their sacred texts, and recognise a human involvement in biblical revelation: the word of God revealed through the words of people who wrote the scriptures. So, many Christian and other western scholars have raised questions about the sources of Muhammad's inspiration. The Qur'ān tells stories of biblical figures, but to different ends. For example, Moses is an important figure in both the Bible and the Qur'ān, and his vocation to free the Jews from bondage to Pharaoh and the Egyptians is told in both. But the emphases are very different. In the Bible, he constitutes the Jews as the people of God, giving them the law on Mount Sinai. In the Qur'ān, he is a prophet to the Egyptians, not the Jews, urging Pharaoh to believe in One God and the certainty of divine judgement lest disaster overtake him and his people (10:75–92, 'We [God] sent Moses and Aaron to Pharaoh and his leaders with our signs . . .'). So Christians and Jews ask what Muhammad knew of biblical stories and how he heard about them. Fazlur Rahman's cautious explanation of revelation hardly, if at all, raises western critical concerns.

Neither has he provided a satisfactory answer for most Muslims. To be sure, some modern Muslims acknowledge a human element in scripture, but only at the level of agreeing that it contains historical references to events in the life of the Prophet. The vast majority, however, hold that an investigation into the sources of the Qur'ān is simply unbelief. God is the author of the stories about Pharaoh, as of all other scriptural revelation. What Muhammad might already have known is irrelevant.

Nevertheless, traditionalist Muslims recognise that the Qur'ān occasionally appears to contradict itself, and so they invoke a theory of abrogation (*naskh*). Since the Qur'ān is God's word, only he can revise it, as the Qur'ān itself testifies: 'God blots out or confirms what he chooses' (13:39). Muslims believe that God revises his words when they were only of temporary application. He does not replace his original words; indeed, they remain part of the Qur'ān, and are to be recited by believers. But a later revelation abrogates their force. So, for example, the command to spend much of the night in prayer at the beginning of 73 is invalidated by verse 20. The verses that are abrogated are called *mansūkh*, and the abrogating ones, *nāsikh*. It is generally agreed by the *'ulama'* (post-qur'anic scholars of the sacred text) that about twenty verses are abrogated. However, there is not complete agreement on the point. The Indian modernist scholar, Sir Sayyid Ahmad Khan (1817–98), argued that no verse is abrogated. In his view, to compare verses is unhelpful or meaningless, because the circumstances of each revelation were different.

The teaching of the Qur'ān

Why was the Qur'ān revealed? What does it say that human beings need to hear? The teaching of the Qur'ān insists upon the unity of God.

Muhammad's commitment to the One God set him apart from many of his contemporaries, who were polytheists. A relatively early *sūrah*, 'The Star', mentions three goddesses, with biting irony: 'Have you regarded al-Lāt, 'Uzzā, and yet a third [goddess] Manāt? Are yours male, and his female? That would indeed be an unfair partition' (53:19–21). Al-Lāt was revered by the tribe of Thaqif, Manāt by the Aws and Khazraj tribes, and 'Uzzā, who has been identified with the Venus star, was worshipped by, among other tribes, the Quraysh, Muhammad's own kindred.

The Qur'ān scorns idolatry. Idols are lifeless things, unable to help themselves or others (7:192ff.), fuel for hellfire (21:98), evanescent as cobwebs (19:41), dumb in this world but accusers in the next of those who worship them (19:83).

God is one. The word *Allāh* comes from the Arabic *al-ilāh*, which means literally, 'The God'. *Al-ilāh* is a word that cannot be pluralised in Arabic. God is transcendent in majesty: 'The creator of the heavens and the earth. . . . There is nothing like him; he hears all and sees all' (42:10). Yet God says: 'We are nearer to a human being than his jugular vein' (50:16).

Human beings must worship God alone. The Arabic word for polytheism is *shirk*, which means 'sharing'; humans are forbidden to share the worship of the creator with anything created. In the Qur'ān, *shirk* is the one unforgivable sin: 'God doesn't forgive bracketing other gods with him. To those whom he wills, all other sins are forgiven. Anyone who brackets other gods with God has wandered far away' (4:116).

God has sent a series of messengers and prophets, from Adam to Muhammad, to different communities, to dissuade them from the calamitous act of idolatry. The word messenger (*rasūl*) is used of those men of God who were sent to many and varied communities to tell them that he is One and that a day of judgement will befall them. It is even used, in 81:19, of an angelic visit to Muhammad. Every *rasūl* is necessarily a prophet (*nabī*); however the reverse is not true. The Qur'ān mentions twenty-eight prophets. All of them, apart from Muhammad, are men written of in the Jewish and Christian scriptures. In 33:40, Muhammad is described as 'the seal of the prophets', a phrase which probably means that he continued and reformed the Judaeo-Christian tradition, and was its final Prophet.

Muhammad certainly believed that that tradition was in need of reformation. Its progenitor, Abraham (in Arabic, *Ibrāhīm*), is the most important qur'anic prophet before Muhammad. He was an ardent proponent of monotheism. He trusted so completely in God, he was willing to sacrifice his son, Ishmael (in Arabic, *'Ismā'īl*; the Qur'ān does not mention the boy's name, but Muslims believe the text [37:99–111] implies that it was he and not Isaac, as the Hebrew Bible recounts). According to the Qur'ān, 'Abraham was neither a Jew nor a Christian. He was a monotheist (*ḥanīf*), one who surrenders to God (*muslim*), and not a polytheist' (3:67).

Muhammad was not accepted as a prophet by most Jews and Christians. Not surprisingly, then, the Qur'ān sees them as untrustworthy: 'Believers! Don't take Jews and Christians as friends. They are each others' friends' (5:54). Elsewhere, Christians are described more positively, as nearest in love to the believers, though Jews are still regarded as strong enemies (5:85).

The Qur'ān has another criticism of Jews and Christians, which arises from its message that the content of each scripture is really the same. Each book confirms the ones before it (3:84). So, all scriptures ought to agree. Tradition says that a hundred and four scriptures were given: ten to Adam; fifty to Seth; thirty to Enoch; and ten to Abraham. Furthermore, the Torah (*tawrāt*) was given to Moses (28:43); the Psalms (*zabūr*) to David (17:55); and the Gospel (*injīl*) to Jesus (5:110). Finally, the Qur'ān was revealed through Muhammad. However, there are significant distinctions between the Qur'ān and the Jewish and Christian scriptures. How is this to be explained? The Qur'ān reveals that both Jews and Christians meddled with the revelation they had received (2:140). Some Jews deliberately distorted their scripture (4:44–6), and called Ezra the son of God (9:30). Christians read out of their scripture that Jesus is God's son (9:30), indeed, one of three Gods (5:75f.).

But Muhammad brought a luminously true scripture: 'Those of the People of the Book and of the idolaters would not desist until the Clear Sign came to them, a messenger from God, reciting pure pages' (98:1f.). The Qur'ān, then, is 'the Clear Sign', the final scripture given to the last Prophet. Muslims have usually interpreted this to mean that the Qur'ān annuls all previous scriptures. A variety of reasons are given for how it does so. A very common view is that since the last revelation is the best, a 'clear' scripture, there is little point in reading inferior versions. Some Muslims believe in 'removal': except for Muhammad, all prophets took their scriptures back to heaven with them, and so any scriptures that exist other than the Qur'ān are not the original ones. Others speak of *tansīkh*, 'abrogating', but this is a controversial view, since this doctrine was at first applied only to verses of the Qur'ān. It is, however, widely held by Muslims that the Qur'ān abrogates previous scriptures. Many scholars say that *taḥrīf*, 'corrupting', took place. Some believe the corruption involved Jews and Christians changing the meaning of words in their scriptures. A more widely held conviction is that changes in the written words took place, in which case the scripture is, at least in some measure, a falsification of the original. Some Muslims hold that *taḥrīf* extends to eliminating prophecies of the coming of Muhammad from Jewish and Christian scriptures. They believe that Deuteronomy 18:15 points to Muhammad's ministry, which Jews have failed to see, and they argue that the texts of John 14:16, 15:26, and 16:7 have been changed by Christians to delete a reference to him. On this view, the Johnannine verses now read *parakletos*, 'comforter' in Greek, but originally read *periklutos*, 'the praised one', which in Arabic is *aḥmad*, or Muhammad. John 15:26 should therefore read: 'When Muhammad comes, whom I (Jesus) will send to you from the Father, the Spirit of Truth who goes out from the Father, he will testify about me'. By and large, Muslims regard the Jewish and Christian scriptures as darkened by changes in the meaning of words or even of actual written words. Thus, their clear scripture, the Qur'ān, has replaced them and all other sacred texts.

Nevertheless, Jews and Christians are honoured as 'People of the Book' (3:71). They may have interfered with their scriptures, but to some extent they are informed of God's will. The Qur'ān repeatedly recognises the existence of good people in other communities: 'Believers, Jews, Christians, Sabeans [who may be the Mandeans of Southern Iraq]: whoever believe in God and the Last Day and do good works shall be rewarded by their Lord. They shall have nothing to fear and will not come to grief' (2:62, 5:69), though some Muslim commentators have tried to toughen this generous revelation, by arguing, for example, that these are Jews, Christians and Sabeans who have become Muslims.

The Qur'ān states that humankind originally formed one

community, but that the messengers God sent showed up the divisions among them (2:213). It accepts that several religious communities will continue after Muhammad: 'If God had so willed, he would have made you [humankind] a single community, but [he has not done] to test you in what he has given you. So compete [with each other] in goodness. You shall all return to God, and he will tell you [the truth] about what divides you' (5:51).

What is the nature of such communities? The Arabic word, *ummah*, is difficult to translate exactly. It has elements of 'religion', 'community', 'nation', and 'identity'. Abraham and the other prophets were *muslim* in the sense that they 'surrendered' to God, and were 'at peace' with him. Because Jewish, Christian and other communities deviated from God's will as it was revealed to them by messengers or prophets, God called into being a new community to carry forward the message of obedience to the One God. This is Islam, and its members are Muslims. Muslims believe that, just before Muhammad's death, this revelation came: 'Today I have perfected your religion for you, and fulfilled my favour towards you, and chosen for you Islam as your religion' (5:3).

How can Muslims be sure that they will not move away from complete obedience to God, as other communities had? Much of the Qur'ān, particularly after Muhammad moved to Madinah, where he consolidated and expanded his community of believers, is given over to regulating the life of the *ummah*. So, for example, the Qur'ān institutes formal public prayer (*ṣalāt*, 30:17f. and 2:238), and fasting from dawn to dusk during the month of *Ramaḍān* (2:183–5). It prescribes laws of marriage and divorce (2:226–32), and of inheritance (2:180; 4:11–14). These and other community laws were developed and codified by later scholars.

Developed Muslim law came into being by the tenth century. It is important to note the breadth of law in Islam. Religious commands cover what believers wear and eat, whom they can marry and mingle with, detailed aspects of living and dying. Muslim Law is called the *Sharī'āt*, and there is one reference to that Arabic word in the Qur'ān. God draws the Prophet's attention to the Jews' disobedience to his clear signs, and says: 'Then we put you (Muhammad) on the way (sharī'āt) of the Command. So follow it, and not the devices of the ignorant' (45:18). Muslims' obedience is measured by their adherence to Islamic law. Faithfulness to it ensures that they will not go astray as other communities have done.

The *Ḥadīth*

The Qur'ān, the word of God, is the major source of Muslim Law, but it is not the only one. Although the Qur'ān legislates for the fledgling Muslim community, when Islam expanded into North Africa, West Asia and Western Europe, Muslims faced new cultures and situations that the revelation had not addressed. When Muslims asked themselves how they should act in new circumstances, the Qur'ān itself offered clues. It states: 'God and his angels send blessings on the Prophet. Believers, bless him and salute him with deepest respect' (33:56). It also says that 'you certainly have an excellent pattern in the Prophet of God' (33:21), who 'never speaks whimsically' (53:3).

Consequently, the words and deeds of Muhammad have become a source of inspiration second only to scripture. It became the practice of Muslims to pattern their lives upon his. It is very important to recognise that Muslims distinguish Muhammad's words from the Qur'ān. A saying of the Prophet may be held in great esteem, but it is his opinion, not God's command. Nevertheless, as the 'seal of the prophets' (33:40), his words are taken very seriously as guidance when there is no precise qur'anic injunction.

A story about the Prophet is called a *ḥadīth* (pl. *aḥadīth*), which means 'news', though the common English translation is 'tradition'. A *ḥadīth* is an oral tradition that describes a saying of the Prophet. *Sunnah* is a deed or practice. It is sometimes said that a *ḥadīth* is a vehicle of the *sunnah*. In practice, the two terms are often used interchangeably. Traditions also record sayings and deeds of the Prophet's companions, his earliest followers. It is believed that, because they modelled their lives so closely on his, their example and witness are to be believed and practised.

A *ḥadīth* or tradition of the Prophet has two parts. The first is a chain of authorities at its beginning (*isnād*), which lists people across the generations through whom the story is passed. The original authority is always a close follower, friend and contemporary of Muhammad. The main text, the substance of each story, is called the *matn*, which provides a word of guidance for Muslims then and now. Here is an example of a *ḥadīth*, without the often long list of authorities:

Narrated 'A'isha (a wife of the Prophet); God's Messenger prayed in his

> house while sitting during his illness and the people prayed behind him standing and he pointed to them to sit down. When he had finished the prayer, he said, 'The imām [leader in prayer] is to be followed and so when he bows you should bow; and when he lifts his hand you should do the same'.

Traditions provided material for lives of the Prophet. The most famous early life was that of Ibn Ishaq (*c.* 704–*c.* 767), whose material was edited into their most popular form by Ibn Hisham (*d. c.* 828). As the traditions about the Prophet increased in number and circulation, it became important to establish their truthfulness.

A genuine tradition has a number of characteristics. The narrator must have distinctly stated that something was said or done by the Prophet; the chain of narrators must be complete, with no break in it; every narrator must be trustworthy; and the content of the tradition must not run counter to qur'anic teaching or that of other sound traditions.

By the ninth century, there were many false traditions, betraying, for example, the views of deviant political groups or religious factions. So began the *'ilm al-ḥadīth*, 'the science of the traditions'. It centred on an examination of the chain, rather than the substance, of each *ḥadīth* by placing the reliability of each link-person under close scrutiny. Accepted traditions fell into, by and large, one of three categories. They were *ṣaḥīḥ* 'sound', when there was no weakness in the chain of witnesses and the witnesses were of unimpeachable integrity. Otherwise, they could be *ḥasan*, 'fair', when their narrators were not first class. Finally, some were *da'īf* 'weak', when some of their narrators were unreliable.

Six collections of *Ḥadīth* are generally accepted as authentic by Muslims, and those of al-Bukhari (810–870) and Muslim (817–875) are the most famous, especially the former. Muslims call them the two trustworthy collections, and believe that they contain only sound traditions.

Both Qur'ān and *Ḥadīth* have required tools by which they can be framed into law. One of the two most important tools is *ijmā'*, the 'consensus' of the whole Muslim community that, based upon Qur'ān and *Ḥadīth*, some new practice should be accepted. Very often, it was difficult to ascertain such a consensus, which relied on the notion that the community will not err on any matter of substance. Many believers quote a tradition in which the Prophet is recorded as having said: 'My community shall never agree upon an error'. The second crucial tool is *qiyās*, analogical reasoning. So, Qur'ān, *Ḥadīth*, *ijmā* and *qiyās* form the *uṣūl al-fiqh*, the 'roots of jurisprudence'. That this has become so is largely due to al-Shafi'i (767–820), who is widely regarded as 'the Father of Islamic Jurisprudence'. His key methodological significance was to found the law upon these four points.

How does this fourfold base of establishing law work in practice? Let us take the example of a Muslim who asks himself, what should he give to the poor. Qur'anic passages such as 9:60 and many others establish that *zakāt* (an alms tax for the poor) is obligatory upon believers. There is a sound tradition that reads: 'The Prophet of God said to 'Umar [the second caliph] that upon every five camels, the *zakāt* is to be one goat'. A consensus was established that one camel is worth eight goats. Hence, *zakāt* is one-fortieth of a person's disposable wealth. Nowadays, when many Muslims do not own goats or camels, but earn an income and own property, analogy dictates that one-fortieth of whatever they earn should be given.

The collection of the Qur'ān

The Qur'ān sees itself as a book (2:2), even though it was revealed gradually over a period of more than twenty years. How did these piecemeal utterances become the single volume of revelation we read today?

The usual explanation starts from the fact that the Qur'ān was originally preserved in the memories of the Prophet and his earliest followers. Most Muslims think that Muhammad was illiterate. He, therefore, could not write anything down himself. However, some followers acted as scribes. During Muhammad's lifetime, revelations were written down on pieces of pottery, palm leaves, leather, camel bone, and possibly even parchment. Once a year, the angel Gabriel would go over what the scribes had written to make sure that it conformed to the 'Mother of the Book'. In the last year of the Prophet's life, this was done twice. Small collections came into existence. It may be that the *sūrah*s with the 'mysterious letters' formed such groups. There was no complete collection by the time of the Prophet's death. However, the text was fixed by then, though not assembled and written in an orderly fashion. After Muhammad's death, Abu Bakr, his friend who succeeded him as political leader of the Muslims (*khalīfah*, or caliph), gave orders for an official version to be compiled. When this was done, he gave it to Hafsah, a widow of the Prophet and the daughter of 'Umar, who followed him as caliph. During the reign of 'Umar's successor, 'Uthman (644–656), this copy was used as the basis for the standard version.

This basic story is sometimes expanded. Sources tell us that five collections of revelations were circulating after Muhammad's death. Much information is given about one of these, that of Zayd bin Thabit. It is recorded that this was put together after a battle against the false prophet, Musaylimah, in 633. In that battle, several men perished who knew the Qur'ān thoroughly and who were official 'reciters'. 'Umar, fearing that the revelations would be lost forever when the last of the remaining reciters died, persuaded Abu Bakr to make a collection. The caliph charged Zayd with this responsibility. He gathered the sheets (*ṣuḥūf*) which were eventually lodged with Hafsah.

There are problems with this story. Few Muslims killed in that battle were likely to have known the Qur'ān by heart, since most were new converts. Moreover, it seems odd that an official version of the Qur'ān should be lodged with an individual, even if it be the caliph's daughter. It is clear, too, that other versions than Zayd's were regarded as authoritative in different places in the rapidly expanding Islamic empire.

Until recently, most western critical scholarship credited 'Uthman with beginning the process which produced the Qur'ān as we read it today. Muslims have tended to think that he continued a procedure begun in Abu Bakr's and 'Umar's reigns. Both groups have accepted the story that, during 'Uthman's caliphate, soldiers began arguing about the merits of different versions. The Syrians used a version of Ubayy ibn Ka'b, Iraq that of Miqdad bin Aswad, and those from Kufa, 'Abdallah ibn Mas'ud's. These disputes were possible because all the collections suffered from a script in which vowels were not written and several consonants had no markers to distinguish them from others. Hence, confusion could abound as recitations were written down. The caliph, alarmed by the prospect of a religious civil war, ordered Zayd to produce an official version. Zayd based it upon Hafsah's copy. When it was done, 'Uthman sent copies to Makkah, Damascus, Kufa and Basra, and ordered previous collections to be burned. This order was not completely obeyed. Twenty years later, different copies still circulated. It took until the end of the ninth century, two hundred and fifty years after the Prophet's death, for the Arabic text to be improved with signs for vowels and consonants. Even then, there was not complete textual uniformity. Ibn Mujahid (859–935) wrote a book entitled *The Seven Readings*. He based his work on a Tradition that Muhammad had been taught to recite the Qur'ān according to seven *aḥrūf*, which he took to mean 'seven sets of readings', though *aḥrūf* really means 'letters' (of the alphabet). He concluded that the set of readings of seven eighth-century scholars was equally valid, but only these. These conclusions have gained widespread acceptance. There was one reading each from Makkah, Madinah, Damascus and Basra, and three from Kufa. Nowadays two forms of qur'anic recitation remain: that of Madinah and one from Kufa. The first is used in Africa (except Egypt). The second, much more important one, is found in Egypt and the rest of the Islamic world.

The Qur'ān interpreted

At first, the Prophet could explain the meaning of the revelation. After his death, it was more difficult to find a consensus about disputed passages. Early exegesis (*tafsīr*) concentrated on showing where and why a particular revelation occurred. This discipline was known as 'the occasions of revelation' (*asbab an-nuzūl*), and the standard work is that of al-Wahidi (*d.* 1075). A later work in the same area is al-Suyuti's *The Substance of the Copies on the Causes of the Revelation*. In due course, it was felt necessary to explain the precise meaning of words and verses. These explanations are very cautious. Given that the Qur'ān is God's word, innovation (*bid'ah*) is a grave sin. Nevertheless, at least three great commentaries came into being.

The first is that of the historian al-Tabari (*c.* 839–923). He was a polymath, who wrote a history of the world and founded a school of Muslim law, as well as producing a commentary on the Qur'ān, which, when it was first printed in Cairo in 1903, ran to thirty volumes. He gives not only his own interpretation of most qur'anic verses, but those of other early authorities. Hence the title, *Comprehensive Assertion*.

The work of al-Zamakhshari (1075–1144), called *The Unveiler*, betrays, to some extent, his unorthodox Mu'tazilite convictions. Mu'tazila ('seceders') is an umbrella term (covering scholars who differed about many things), given to them by their opponents. But they were agreed on certain things most Muslims frown on as innovatory. In particular, they contended that the unity of God demanded the belief that the Qur'ān was created, whereas other Muslims held that it was uncreated, that God's word was eternal with him. The Mu'tazilites further believed, over against their opponents, in an allegorical interpretation of the physical attributes of God mentioned in the Qur'ān (such as his face), so this commentary removes anthropomorphisms from the Qur'ān. Although held in some suspicion by the orthodox, it shows its author's matchless grammatical and lexicological knowledge. It is uncertain when al-Baydawi lived. Possibly he died around 1291. His commentary is called *The Lights of Revelation*, and it owed much to al-Zamakhshari's work, though purged of its Mu'tazilite content.

These three are only the most important of many commentaries. Recent modernising movements in Egypt and the South Asian subcontinent have led to new commentaries being written. They interpret the Qur'ān rationally, rather than depending on *taqlīd*, 'imitation', uncritical dependence on past precedent, however revered. Two works of Sir Sayyid Ahmad Khan (1817–98), the Indian Muslim social and educational reformer, are particularly interesting: *The Exegesis of the Qur'ān* and *Freedom in the Sources of Exegesis*. Exegesis has attempted to determine the meaning of qur'anic words, verses and passages. But what meaning does the Qur'ān as a whole have for Muslims? Philip Hitti wrote:

> Not only is it the basis of the religion, the canon of the ethical and moral life, but also the textbook in which the Moslem begins his study of language, science, theology and jurisprudence.
>
> (*Islam: A Way of Life*, Henry Regnery, 1971, p. 27)

Above all, the Qur'ān is the bedrock of prayer, of belief, of deep mystical experience, and of Muslim law. The language of the Qur'ān saturates common speech. For example, people say to someone who sneezes, '*al-ḥamdu li-Llāh*' ('Praise be to God'), from the very first verse of the Qur'ān's first chapter. A person who can recite the Qur'ān perfectly by memory (*ḥāfiẓ*) is held in honour. Chanting of the Qur'ān is part of popular culture, and its best exponents can fill stadiums.

Nevertheless, the Qur'ān had been used to widely different ends by certain groups whose views are not shared by the majority of Muslims. For example, Shi'ah and Ṣūfī interpretations of scripture are often elaborate and flamboyant, and held in deep suspicion by Sunni Muslims (those who adhere to the *sunnah*, 'customary practice', of Muhammad). Shi'ah Muslims are the 'party' (*sh'iah*) of 'Ali, the Prophet's cousin and son-in-law. They think he and not Abu Bakr should have succeeded Muhammad as the political *and* religious leader of the Muslim community. They differ from most other Muslims not only on matters of succession, but on matters of law, authority and qur'anic interpretation. They are not a coherent group, so few generalisations can be drawn about them. However, a distinctive exegesis of many Shi'ah Muslims is called *ta'wīl* or 'allegory'. They trace this back to their early leaders (*imāms*) whom they believe had specialised, secret knowledge. They justify this knowledge from the verses 'God has taught the bee . . . a multi-hued drink comes from out of their bodies' (16:68f.). They believe this liquid to be the Qur'ān, and call 'Ali '*amīr* (commander) of the bees'. Some of their exegesis seems rather extreme, as when 'A'isha, a widow of the Prophet and enemy of 'Ali, is depicted as the cow to be sacrificed (2:67–71).

Ṣūfī Muslims are the mystics of Islam. They believe that the Prophet was a mystic. A very early revelation describes him as 'enmantled' (74:1), a state of dress associated with mystics. 17:1 describes a mystical visit by Muhammad, while he slept, to Jerusalem, to a mosque (not then built) on the site of Solomon's Temple. Some have argued that the mysterious letters at the beginning of some qur'anic *sūrah*s have mystic import. They may indicate the effort made by the Prophet as he began uttering God's words: noises like (for example) the letters a, l and r (found at the beginning of *sūrah*s 10 to 15) issued from his lips as he began to recite. This is a fascinating though unprovable suggestion. However, the very act of speaking God's word surely betokens mystical experience, even if some Ṣūfī Muslims may impose elaborate and unconvincing meanings on to part of the revelation.

Developed Muslim law and mysticism may have flourished into creations that seem very different from each other, but proponents of both can find in the Qur'ān justification for their positions, a point of origin for what they have become and are becoming. Despite differences between them, all Muslims are united in worship of the One God, love for his Prophet, reverence for his word. The Qur'ān underpins these convictions.

NOTES

1. Muslims date their calendar from the year 622 of the Common (or Christian) Era, when, after persecution in his hometown of Makkah, Muhammad emigrated to Madinah. They follow the lunar year, different from the Gregorian, western, system of dating based on the sun's rotation. In the text, I have used the Common Era dating. Muslim scholars often give both dates in their works. Muslims always refer to Muhammad with great respect, using an Arabic honorific formula after speaking or writing his name, meaning 'May God bless him and grant him salvation'. When they write in English they often put 'PBUH' in brackets after his name, standing for 'Peace be upon him'.
2. Madinah means 'The City [of the Prophet]'; its pre-Islamic name was Yathrib.
3. Muslims believe that the Qur'ān cannot be translated from Arabic, the divine language of revelation. Nevertheless, there are available a number of 'translations' or paraphrases into English. See pages 105–8 of this chapter.
4. Ali, A.Y. (1975 edn) *The Holy Qur'ān*, Leicester, The Islamic Foundation, p. 102, note 296.
5. Pickthall, M.M. (n.d.) *The Meaning of the Glorious Koran*, London, Mentor, p. xvii. Most Muslims prefer the spelling of Qur'ān for Koran, as they do Muslim for Moslem, and Muhammad for Mohammed, because these are better transliterations from the Arabic.
6. Arberry, A.J. (1964 edn) *The Koran Interpreted*, Oxford, Oxford University Press, p. x.
7. Rosenthal, F. (trans) (1967) *The Muqaddimah*, vol. 1, London, Routledge & Kegan Paul, p. 192.
8. Rahman, F. (1979) *Islam* (2nd edn), Chicago, The University of Chicago Press, pp. 31ff.

FURTHER READING

Khan, M.M. (ed.) (1984) *Ṣaḥīḥ al-Bukhārī* (vols 1–9), New Delhi, Kitab Bhavan.

Khatib. M. (1986) *The Bounteous Qur'ān*, London, Macmillan.

Lings, M. (1983) *Muhammad: His Life Based on the Earliest Sources*, London, George Allen & Unwin Islamic Texts Society.
Netton, I.R. (1992) *A Popular Dictionary of Islam*, London, Curzon Press.
Rahman, F. (1989) *Major Themes of the Qur'ān*, Minneapolis, Bibliotheca Islamica.
Von Denffer, A. (1983) *'Ulūm al-Qur'ān: An Introduction to the Sciences of the Qur'ān*, Leicester, Islamic Foundation.
Watt, W.M. (1970) *Bell's Introduction to the Qur'ān*, Edinburgh, Edinburgh University Press.

5. Judaism

Alan Unterman

The sacred literature of Judaism consists of a vast collection of texts, some dating back thousands of years and others composed in the recent past. In general, the older the text the more sacred it is considered to be, since it is closer to the textual revelation to Moses and the Israelites at Mount Sinai after their exodus from slavery in Egypt. Later writings are regarded as essentially interpretations and applications of the holy teachings of the past. The most up-to-date writings, though they lack the sanctity of early texts, carry great authority for Jews because they draw on the views of all the sages of the past in formulating their conclusions.

Jewish sacred literature is traditionally divided into two categories: the Written Teaching, *torah she-bikhtav*, and the Oral Teaching, *torah she-baal peh*. As we shall see, the Hebrew term *torah*, translated here as 'teaching', is used both narrowly and broadly, and may refer not only to the Pentateuch or to the Hebrew Bible, but also to the whole of the Jewish tradition.

The Written Teaching

The Written Teaching consists of the twenty-four books of the Hebrew Bible divided up into three sections: *torah* (henceforth Torah), *nevi'im* ('Prophets'), and *ketuvim* ('Writings'), known through the acronym TeNaKh. The Torah, or Pentateuch, contains Genesis, Exodus, Leviticus, Numbers and Deuteronomy (in Hebrew, *bereshit*, *shemot*, *vayikra*, *bemidbar*, *devarim*).

The 'Prophets' contain the books of Joshua, Judges, Samuel I and II and Kings I and II – known collectively as the 'Early Prophets', plus Isaiah, Jeremiah, Ezekiel and the Twelve Minor Prophets

(Hosea, Joel, Amos, Obadiah, Jonah, Micah, Nahum, Habakkuk, Zephaniah, Haggai, Zechariah, and Malachi) – known collectively as the 'Later Prophets'. The 'Writings' contain Psalms, Proverbs, Job, Song of Songs, Ruth, Lamentations, Ecclesiastes, Esther, Daniel, Ezra-Nehemiah, and Chronicles I and II.

THE TORAH

The Torah is the central text of the Hebrew Bible. It is believed to contain the primary revelation from God to the greatest of the prophets, Moses, known in the Jewish tradition as 'Moses our Rabbi', who received the divine teaching face to face in the most direct way. These Five Books of Moses are also known as the *humash* (i.e., 'fifth', a popular abbreviation of *hamishah humshei torah*) – 'the five fifths of the Torah').

The Torah tells the story of humanity from the beginning of the world to the death of Moses. The main religious motifs are the creation of the first human couple, Adam and Eve, who ate the forbidden fruit in the Garden of Eden and were expelled from Paradise; the story of Noah's ark and the flood; the call of Abraham, the first 'Jew'; the life of the patriarchs; the slavery of the Israelites in Egypt; their redemption by God through the agency of Moses; the crossing of the Red Sea; the theophany at Mount Sinai and the giving of the Ten Commandments; the worship of the golden calf; and the desire of the Israelites to return to Egypt after the report of the ten spies about the land of Canaan.

The forty years wandering in the wilderness which followed was a punishment for their lack of faith. During these years the remaining divine laws were revealed to the Israelites about subjects such as the Sacred Year, ritual purity, the Tabernacle and the sacrifices, correct behaviour between humans summarised in the command 'You shall love your neighbour as yourself, I am the Lord' (Lev. 19:18), social mores and dietary requirements. The Pentateuch ends with the death of Moses after he had led the people of Israel to the borders of the promised land.

PROPHETS

It is believed that the books of the *nevi'im* were written by the prophets through the gift of prophecy, and they tell the story of the

Israelites after they entered the promised land. The people were first ruled by judges until the prophet Samuel anointed Saul as the first king of Israel. He was succeeded by King David, who conquered Jerusalem and made it his capital. The first Temple was built in Jerusalem by David's son, Solomon, since David was not considered suitable to build the 'House of the Lord' because his hands were stained by the blood he had shed as a warrior king.

After the death of Solomon, who had taxed the people heavily to support both his building projects and his opulent life-style, the Holy Land was divided between the ten tribes in the Northern Kingdom of Israel and the two tribes who supported the Davidic dynasty in the Southern Kingdom of Judah. The Books of Kings tell of the corruption of kingly rule in Israel and Judah, where many of the kings 'did evil in the sight of the Lord'.

This culminated in the conquest of the Northern Kingdom by the Assyrians in 721 BCE and the exile of its inhabitants, who came to be known as 'the ten lost tribes'. The Southern Kingdom continued a precarious existence till 586 BCE when Jerusalem and the First Temple were destroyed by the Babylonians, and the Judeans were taken into exile in Babylonia. The religious heroes of this second section of the TeNaKh are characters from the period of the Judges like Ruth, Deborah and Samson, prophets like Samuel, Elijah, Elisha, Isaiah, Jeremiah and Ezekiel as well as minor prophets whose sayings and prophecies are recorded in the books named after them, and those kings of Israel and Judah who sought to eradicate idolatry and to live according to the teachings of Moses and the prophets.

WRITINGS

The *ketuvim* are books believed to be written under the influence of the Holy Spirit, a lesser degree of inspiration than prophecy. They contain works of Wisdom literature, like Proverbs and Ecclesiastes; devotional works like the Book of Psalms, which is much used in the later liturgy of Judaism; works in historical form, like Chronicles, Esther and Ezra-Nehemiah, which take the history of Israel up to the return from captivity and the rebuilding of the Second Temple.

According to the rabbinic tradition, Moses wrote the five books of the Pentateuch like a scribe copying from an ancient text. Indeed, the

Pentateuch, in its heavenly form, pre-existed the world and was used by God as a blueprint of the creation. Rabbinic tradition said that Moses also wrote the Book of Job, Joshua wrote the Book of Joshua and also, according to one view, the last eight verses of the Pentateuch which tell of the death of Moses.

The prophet Samuel wrote the Books of Samuel, the Book of Judges and the Book of Ruth. King David wrote the Book of Psalms. Jeremiah wrote the Book of Jeremiah, the Book of Kings and the Book of Lamentations. King Hezekiah and his associates wrote down the Book of Isaiah, and the Books of Proverbs, Song of Songs and Ecclesiastes (the last three originally composed by King Solomon). The Men of the Great Assembly wrote down the Book of Ezekiel, the Twelve Minor Prophets, the Books of Daniel and of Esther. Ezra wrote the Book of Ezra and the major part of the Books of Chronicles.

The Oral Teaching

The Oral Torah consists, in its widest sense, of the whole interpretative tradition which bases itself on scripture. It is important to note that the term 'Torah' is used here to refer to all of Jewish religious literature as well as the Pentateuch. Since 'Torah' means teaching, the term implies that God is the divine teacher who gives his teaching to the people of Israel, and through them to the world. When Moses ascended Mount Sinai he received not only the whole of scripture but also all future development of the Judaic tradition:

> At Mount Sinai Moses received the Ten Commandments, the Pentateuch, the Mishnah, the Prophets and Hagiographa, the Talmud, and even what the Scribes would innovate in the future.
>
> (Babylonian Talmud *Berachot* 5a and *Megillah* 19b)

Though of divine origin, Torah is always open-ended, and each statement, whether in the Bible, the Talmud, the codes, or theological texts, has to be interpreted and argued about by scholars. It is viewed from different perspectives rather than taken literally. By its very nature Torah has to be studied before it can be effectively implemented in the life of the community and in the life of the individual.

MIDRASH

The division between the Written Teaching and the Oral Teaching does not simply represent two parallel types of sacred literature, one written, one oral. The Written Torah does not exist as an independent literary genre, even though it is concretely expressed in the canonical text. The Hebrew Bible never stands on its own, it exists as scripture only within the context of the Oral Torah. The meaning of the written word is not given, even though there is a level of quasi-literal meaning (*peshat*) which recurs throughout the interpretative matrix.

This dependence of the Written Torah on the Oral Torah is illustrated by a rabbinic story told of the first-century sage, Hillel. Once, a would-be convert came to Hillel and asked to be converted to Judaism, but the heathen wanted to accept only the Written Scripture not the Oral Teachings. Hillel, surprisingly, agreed to accept him as a convert and began to teach him the Hebrew alphabet so he could study the written text. Next day Hillel continued with his lesson but this time he taught him the alphabet in the reverse order. The heathen objected, and Hillel replied that he wanted to show him that even to read the written text he needed to rely on oral teachings. How much more would this be true if he wanted to *understand* the written teaching (TB *Shabbat* 31a).

The point of this story is that the Bible can be approached only through tradition, albeit a somewhat open-ended tradition. Since texts are opaque or, what amounts to the same thing, highly ambiguous, their meaning and message have to be searched out. The process of this exegetical searching out (*derash*) is characteristic of Jewish thought, and it is this method which shaped a vast body of hermeneutical literature known as *midrash*.

The Pentateuch contains brief references to the main body of Jewish law (*halakhah*) which presupposes a much wider unwritten background. Around these seminal references a variety of different interpretations grew up in the rabbinic schools of Palestine, and these were collected in halakhic *midrashim*, which in the main date back to the first few centuries CE. A little later in origin are those *midrashim* which deal with the non-halakhic parts of Jewish teaching (*aggadah*). Most of the aggadic *midrashim* involve the expansion of biblical stories, bringing in a host of folkloristic and theological themes. *Midrash* in general is thought to be the earliest type of Oral Torah literature, although those works of *midrash* which have survived were finally redacted in the post-Talmudic period.

BIBLICAL COMMENTARY AND INTERPRETATION

Since the Hebrew Bible exists within a tradition of interpretation, the text is always in need of explication and from the early Talmudic period, side by side with the composition of the early midrashic collections, biblical commentaries serving specific interests began to be composed. These commentaries are the key to understanding the relevance and message of the Bible, and are the main repository of new ideas, new philosophies, and new approaches to Judaism. The earliest of these commentaries are the Aramaic *targumim*, which were composed in the early centuries of the common era for Jews who spoke Aramaic, the lingua franca of the whole Middle East. Since Hebrew had become a literary language, and the preserve of scholars, the *targumim* are in essence translations, the word *targum* actually meaning 'translation', but they vary greatly from each other. *Targum Onkelos*, the most famous *targum*, sticks closely to the text, alluding to midrashic interpretation and paraphrasing the anthropomorphisms of biblical Hebrew, while others introduce much midrashic material set among the translation of the text.

It was considered mandatory for every person to read the weekly portion of the Pentateuch twice to themselves, together with one reading of a translation. Throughout the early middle ages *Onkelos* was read regularly as the translation of the weekly Torah portion, and was indeed considered to be an inspired work. Aramaic ceased to be a spoken language, even among Babylonian Jews, after the spread of Islam brought Arabic in its wake. Many people, therefore, preferred to use the biblical commentary of Rashi (R. Shelomoh Yitzchaki, 1040–1105) which presents a somewhat literal interpretation of the text, and was written in a simple Hebrew style, using many Aramaic words, and translating difficult expressions into medieval French.

Rashi belonged to the Franco-German tradition, which subsequently gave rise to the Ashkenazi sub-culture. Ashkenazim were Jews who lived mainly in Christian Europe and whose lingua franca was Yiddish (a Jewish dialect of medieval German). When these

Jews settled in the Slavic countries of Central and Eastern Europe, they took Yiddish with them and also the literature, customs and foods of Germany and Austria. A distinctive Jewish life-style, known as *yiddishkeit*, characterised the Ashkenazi world which, in the nineteenth and early twentieth centuries, was centred in Poland, Russia, Lithuania and the Austro-Hungarian Empire.

The other main grouping of Jews in the late middle ages were the Sephardim, or Jews of Spanish origin. After their expulsion from the Iberian peninsula, in the 1490s, Sephardim took their highly sophisticated Spanish-Jewish culture to the Netherlands, North Africa, the Levant and into the Islamic world of the Middle East and Asia. Some of them preserved Ladino (a Jewish dialect of Spanish) as their lingua franca, and maintained their Sephardi identity where they settled by preserving their own customs, by marrying only into other Sephardi families and even by putting the two Hebrew letters 'S' and 'T', standing for *sefardi tahor* ('pure Sephardi') after their name.

The Ashkenazim, who became the dominant Jewish sub-group in the late middle ages, revered Rashi. In the course of time, some of the sanctity associated with *Onkelos* attached to Rashi, and his interpretation of a verse became *the* interpretation in the popular consciousness. His writings were also popular among Sephardim.

The standard Hebrew Bibles print the biblical text together with *Onkelos* and sometimes one or two other Aramaic *targumim*. They also include Rashi's commentary and that of his grandson, Rashbam (R. Samuel ben Meir, 1080–1174). The latter is more literal than his grandfather in his commentary and he does not include any midrashic stories. This, together with the fact that he sometimes criticises Rashi's interpretations, and that some of his comments run counter to traditional rabbinic exegesis, meant he never achieved a high level of popular acceptance. Many commentaries were actually written on Rashi's commentary, defending it from the criticisms of other commentators.

A number of Sephardi commentaries are also usually included in standard Bible editions. The best known are those of Abraham ibn Ezra (1089–1164), a Spanish grammarian and philosophical exegete who has harsh things to say about interpretations he disagrees with even when they are of talmudic origin, and of Ramban (R. Moses ben Nachman, 1194–1270), a Spanish mystic. Ramban had to flee Spain after defending Judaism too vigorously against Christianity when he was forced to participate in the Disputation of Barcelona in 1263. A number of super-commentaries exist both on ibn Ezra and on Ramban.

THE MISHNAH

At the beginning of the third century CE collections of halakhic material, extracted from their original location in *midrash*, were gathered together and eventually formed into the Mishnah, the first published work of the Oral Torah. It was composed in Hebrew, although it was not originally written down (since there was opposition to the writing down of oral material) but was memorised. It contains sixty tractates divided into six sections:

1. 'Seeds', covering agricultural laws and benedictions.
2. 'Festivals', covering the Sabbath, the festivals and the fasts of the sacred year.
3. 'Women', covering marriage, divorce, and vows.
4. 'Damages', covering duties and responsibilities in interpersonal and business relations, the function of law courts and the punishments meted out for crimes. This section also includes five chapters on ethical matters known as the 'Chapters of the Fathers' (*Pirkei Avot*).
5. 'Holy Things', covering the Temple, the sacrificial rite and the dietary laws.
6. 'Purities', covering categories of ritual purity and impurity.

The Mishnah is not simply a code, since it contains dissenting views mentioning the names and opinions of some one hundred and twenty eight individual authorities who are known as *tannaim*. A *tanna* is a sage of the mishnaic period, the term coming from a root meaning to 'repeat'. Originally it seems to have referred merely to someone who had memorised the text without necessarily understanding what he knew, but eventually it became a title of honour and authority.

The Mishnah also does not touch upon some central rituals which would have been included in a code. Thus there is nothing about the laws relating to phylacteries (*tefillin*), the *mezuzah* parchment on the doors of a house, the fringes (*tzitzit*) on the corners of the garment, the Torah scroll (*sefer torah*), or the liturgical formula of the *amidah* prayer which is at the centre of the daily services. The medieval authority, Maimonides, in his commentary on the Mishnah (*Menahot* 4:1), explained that all these matters were sufficiently well known to ordinary Jews from regular practice not to make it necessary to include them in the text.

Thus the Mishnah is more like a textbook for the study of Jewish law than a code which seeks to lay down the halakhic norms. We cannot be sure what actually motivated Rabbi Judah the Prince and his colleagues to edit the mishnaic text, but they presented the Jewish scholarly world with an authoritative collection of the main halakhic views, and excluded much material which they did not regard as reliable. Since they severed the dependence of rabbinic learning on the Bible text, as found in *midrash*, the redaction of the Mishnah signified a breakthrough in religious consciousness.

The Mishnah acted as a stimulus to the process of gathering material of the Oral Torah. Other collections of material similar in nature to that contained in the Mishnah have also survived. There is a work known as the *tosefta*, which is regarded by some authorities as an early commentary on the Mishnah, and there are citations of mishnaic-style material in rabbinic literature known as *beraitah* (pl. *beraitot*), 'extraneous' material which had not been incorporated in the Mishnah.

The Mishnah was regarded as having originated with the oral traditions taught by Moses to the Israelites in explanation of the Pentateuch, and as such was a holy text. Indeed, the ethical section of the Mishnah, *The Chapters of the Fathers*, opens with the declaration:

> Moses received Torah from Sinai and handed it on to Joshua, Joshua to the Elders, the Elders to the Prophets, and the Prophets handed it on to the Men of the Great Assembly. They said three things: Be deliberate in judgement, raise up many disciples and make a fence around the Torah.

The implication of this is that all the sayings of the sages about ethics, let alone those about *halakhah* and *aggadah* in other parts of the Mishnah, are aspects of the Torah which Moses received from God. Even the rabbinic enactments, most of which involved 'making fences round the Torah' were all part of the revelation at Sinai.

The study of the Mishnah was thought to help the souls of dead relatives to progress in their spiritual journey after death, the Hebrew letters of the word *mishnah*, when rearranged, spelling the word for soul, *neshamah*. A section of the Mishnah is thus studied in a house of mourning or on the anniversary of someone's death (*yahrzeit* in Yiddish). In the late middle ages one leading rabbi, Joseph Caro, was even possessed by the spirit of the Mishnah (known as a *maggid* or daemon), when he studied the mishnaic text with great devotion. This spirit conveyed messages to him from the heavenly world and Caro recorded them in a diary published as *Maggid Mesharim*.

THE TALMUD

The intense study of the Mishnah in the academies of Palestine and Babylonia led to the compilation of the Palestinian Talmud in the fourth century CE and the Babylonian Talmud one hundred years later. These two editions of the Talmud were known respectively as the *Yerushalmi* (i.e., 'Jerusalem', though the Palestinian Talmud was not actually redacted there), and the *Bavli* (i.e., 'Babylonian'). The *Bavli* became the most authoritative rabbinic text of Judaism, determining the *halakhah* and setting the agenda for aggadic ideas, since the Jewish community of Babylonia dominated the Jewish world for five or six hundred years after the completion of the Babylonian Talmud. Because of the particular interests of Babylonian Jewry, certain parts of the Mishnah, e.g., those dealing with the agricultural laws applicable essentially in the Land of Israel, were not dealt with at any length in the *Bavli*, although they do occupy a large section of the *Yerushalmi*.

The two Talmuds differ in many substantial ways. The *Bavli* is more developed than the earlier version of the Talmud edited in Palestine, since the Babylonian academies in which the material was shaped were larger and of a higher calibre than their Palestinian counterparts. Folklore, angelology and magic play a larger part in the *aggadah* of the *Bavli* than of the *Yerushalmi*, reflecting the different cultural milieu. Babylonian civilisation was heavily influenced by Persian religion, and Persian terms appear quite frequently in the Eastern Aramaic of the *Bavli*.

TALMUDIC STUDY

Since the *Bavli* was the principal subject of study in the Babylonian academies, it dominated Jewish thought in the post-talmudic period. So neglected was the *Yerushalmi* that the text has been preserved in a highly unsatisfactory condition, with many corrupt readings and textual variants. The Babylonian Talmud is in a much better state of preservation.

The *Bavli* is thought of as an ocean, and its study is like setting sail on a voyage of discovery. The more this talmudic ocean is explored the more it reveals new landscapes of the mind and of the spirit to the traveller. Sages, after years of study and experience, are involved in the talmudic adventure just as much as young boys who begin to study the text for the first time. The sage will already have studied thousands of pages of the Talmud, perhaps even knowing much of it by heart. Yet he may well spend his mature years trying to reconcile contradictory interpretations of abstruse talmudic discussions.

The beginner, by contrast, must learn how to pronounce strange Hebrew and Aramaic words, and how to translate and interpret the many technical terms and colloquial phrases which convey the talmudic outlook. Sentences such as:

'No one can make someone else an agent to commit a sin', i.e., everyone is responsible for his or her own actions and no one can say in extenuation 'So-and-So told me to do this'.

'An individual's opinion is nullified by the opinion of all men', i.e., the *halakhah* deals with normal ways of behaviour and does not consider grossly eccentric behaviour in formulating law.

'The law of the kingdom is law', i.e., Jews must accept that the civil law, but not the religious law, of the land they live in has validity for them also.

'He who wishes to remove something already in the possession of his fellow must prove his case', i.e., the law puts the onus upon the person who wishes to change the *status quo* to bring evidence.

'Property that a law court declares ownerless (*hefker*) is indeed ownerless', i.e., for the sake of maintaining justice, a properly constituted Jewish law court can actually remove property from its owner.

'One may act effectively to benefit someone even if they are absent', i.e., where real benefit accrues to a person one may act on their behalf even without their express permission.

'Someone who is half slave and half free man', i.e., the slave of two partners who has been freed by only one of them. He inhabits an halakhic no-man's-land. A number of issues are tested against this case to show where the boundaries are of slavery, of freedom, of marriage and of ritual action in general.

'A person should allow himself to be killed rather than transgress', i.e., whereas the saving of life takes precedence over the commandments in normal circumstances, there are some commandments that one must not transgress even to save one's life, and some circumstances when a Jew must be prepared to die even for the sake of something relatively trivial.

In a *yeshivah* academy the Talmud is studied by groups of two students, *havruta*, who read the text together and argue out its interpretation at the tops of their voices. This high-resonance learning is meant to aid the memory and to allow the expression of emotion as well as intellect in the learning process. The study of the Torah is both learning and worship.

This all comes as quite a shock to those who enter the study hall (*bet ha-midrash*) of a *yeshivah* for the first time, particularly if they are used to an academic library. In the *yeshivah* the ocean of the Talmud generates rivers of sound flowing across the hall as the *havruta* groups join together in fours and sixes to discuss a particularly knotty problem with each other, and then sub-divide to return to tandem study. There is the chanting and singing of the text which sometimes involves the constant repetition of key phrases till their particular significance is grasped in context.

Much of the chanting, however, is not actually words from the text but interjections from the student: 'Oi oi oi', 'Vai vai vai'. 'What kind of a question is being asked here by *Tosefot* (medieval commentators given to asking complicated questions)? Nu nu nu.' 'This is a difficult problem of Rabbi Akiva Eger (a pre-modern Talmudic commentator). Difficult, so difficult. Ai ai ai.'

Together with the ability to analyse issues, and the improvisation of traditional Talmud tunes, a further prerequisite for Talmud study is knowing how to use one's thumb to follow the thread of an argument. The hand is swung round the thumb as axis, while at the same time the thumb is tilted now to the right now to the left. There is no explanation of what exactly the thumb adds to the debate but it is widely used even by those who are silently following someone else's exposition. The head nods in agreement and the thumb tilts as the argument develops.

RESPONSA

The prestige of the *Bavli* was guarded by the leaders of Babylonian Jewry in the post-talmudic period. These sages were known as *geonim* (*gaon*= 'excellence', henceforth Geonim). The Geonim were recognised as supreme halakhic authorities by most of Jewry. They replied to questions from all over the Jewish world about the meaning of obscure passages in the Talmud, as well as about practical matters such as rules of prayer, ritual and conduct. These terse geonic answers to inquiries initiated a whole genre of responsa (*she'elot u-teshuvot*, literally 'questions and answers'), which soon became the most prolific source for the determination of the *halakhah*.

The vastness of this responsa literature came about because many rabbis penned letters to colleagues, discussing halakhic issues which raised novel points of law and seeking their colleagues' opinions. Although only a small fraction of this literature was intended for publication, responsa were collected together by pupils or members of the respondent's family and were eventually published. They reflect a wealth of social detail because of the need to discuss the realia lying behind particular problems. Part of this vast responsa literature is considered of only minor importance and rarely studied, while some collections of responsa are standard texts on the curriculum of most *yeshivah* academies.

All the major events of Jewish history are reflected in responsa literature. Thus wars and pogroms left hundreds of women, whose husbands had disappeared, as *agunot*, unable to remarry without solid proof of their widowhood. They turned to leading rabbis, seeking permission to remarry, and these rabbis had to investigate the precise circumstances under which death might have taken place before accepting that their husbands had died.

The major theological issues and movements which characterised Jewish life also find their reflection in responsa. Rabbis were asked questions on a great variety of topics. Can one study philosophy or is it a prohibited form of gentile culture? Can one teach the Bible to Christians and Muslims? What is the status of Jews who have converted to another faith, and particularly of those who have been forcibly converted? Who can engage in the study of the mystical texts of Kabbalah, and what is one to do when the prescriptions of the Kabbalah conflict with the *halakhah* as laid down in the Talmud or in the codes? How can one know if the Messiah has arrived? Can one change the Ashkenazi prayer book to bring it more in line with Sephardi practice favoured by the medieval Kabbalists? Are members of the nineteenth-century Hasidic Movement heretics? Can reforms be made to the synagogue liturgy, such as the introduction of shorter services, of choirs and organs, of vernacular prayers and a sermon to rectify the lack of decorum? Or are all such measures, which were favoured by early Reform Judaism, prohibited to traditional Jews?

CODES

Side by side with responsa the *halakhah* was shaped by the codes of Jewish law which began to be produced in the geonic period. The most far-reaching of these law books is the great code of Maimonides (1136–1204), known as the *Mishneh Torah* ('Second Torah') or *Yad Ha-hazakah* ('The Strong Hand'), which not only covers the practical *halakhah* applicable to the life of the community and the individual, but also deals with theological ideas, with the dogmatic beliefs definitive of Jewish Orthodoxy, with laws relating to the Temple, as well as the laws of the messianic age.

Maimonides says in his introduction that his book summarises all the laws contained in Talmudic literature:

> So that a person should not need to refer to any other work in the world concerning a law of the laws of Israel, but this book should be a collection of the whole Oral Torah. . . . For a person may firstly read the Written Torah and after that read this work and know from it the whole Oral Torah, and not need to read any other work in between them.
>
> (Introduction to the *Yad*)

His work was considered highly controversial because he seemed to claim that his was the final word on halakhic decision making. He was criticised because he did not include any references to the sources from which he drew his conclusions, nor any indication of how he arrived at a conclusion in areas where there was considerable dispute among earlier authorities. Traditionalists also objected to his philosophical chapters, believing that they were more Aristotle than Moses, and refused to study the theological sections of the *Yad*.

The code which today is the most authoritative guide to normative *halakhah* is the *Shulhan Arukh* (literally 'Prepared Table'). This was written by R. Joseph Caro (1488–1575), a Sephardi authority who based his conclusions on the majority views of three of his predecessors, two of whom were Sephardim. The language which Caro used was borrowed to a large extent from Maimonides' code. An Ashkenazi halakhist from Poland, R. Moses Isserles (1525–72), composed glosses on the *Shulhan Arukh* reflecting the Ashkenazi position of which Caro had not given sufficient coverage. Isserles's glosses were known as the *Mappah* ('tablecloth') and they were printed together with Caro's text. This combination of Sephardi and Ashkenazi viewpoints, coming soon after the introduction of Hebrew printing, made the *Shulhan Arukh* acceptable to wide sections of Jewry.

The fourfold division of material which Caro used was borrowed from the format of a previous code, the *Arbaah Turim*, on which he had written a learned commentary. His subject matter was thus divided up into the following:

1. *Orah haim* ('The Way of Life') dealing with prayers, Sabbath and festival rituals.
2. *Yoreh deah* ('Teaching Knowledge') containing laws of concern to the communal *rabbi* who has to decide matters affecting ritual slaughter, the dietary laws, mourning and menstruation.
3. *Even ha-ezer* ('The Stone of Helping') dealing with marriage and divorce.
4. *Hoshen mishpat* ('The Breastplate of Judgement') containing the laws of how a law court should function and the way people should behave in business.

Since the sixteenth century many commentaries and super-commentaries have been written on the *Shulhan Arukh*, and shortened or updated versions of the code have appeared. These provide easy reference for the layperson and include new technological and medical issues which affect halakhic behaviour in modern times. Unlike Maimonides' code, the *Shulhan Arukh* deals only with practical *halakhah* and ignores issues which are not germane to the life of the individual Jew or to the Jewish community and its institutions. The most popular simplified version of the *Shulhan Arukh* is the *Kitzur Shulhan Arukh* ('Shortened *Shulhan Arukh*'), written by Solomon Ganzfried (1804–86) in Hungary, which has been translated into English and into a number of European languages.

The beginnings of philosophy

Neither the Hebrew Bible nor the Talmud was particularly interested in doctrinal matters or in putting forward a coherent theology of Judaism. There are scattered references to the belief in one deity, to the prohibitions of worshipping others' gods or idols, to the authority of the revelation given to Moses and the prophets, to life after death and the resurrection of the body, to the divine justice which guides the world, punishing sinners and rewarding the righteous, and to the redemption to come in the messianic age. Particularly in the Babylonian Talmud and in midrashic literature, there are a myriad of folkloristic beliefs whose status as doctrine is never made clear.

The impetus for the development of Jewish philosophy came from Arabic translations of the writings of Plato and Aristotle, and it was essentially through the Muslim culture of the middle ages that Greek philosophy entered Jewish thought in a substantial way. In Muslim lands, where a more tolerant and intellectually liberal approach could be found than in Christendom, Jews were encouraged by the example of Islamic philosophy to apply Greek thought patterns to their own religion. This was partly out of necessity because young, intellectually aware Jews were being attracted away from their own beliefs into the neutral territory which an interest in Greek thought had created. It was also to enable Jews to justify Jewish belief to philosophically minded Muslims and Christians.

Many of the early works of Jewish philosophy were written in Arabic, which was the lingua franca of the Jews in Muslim countries. The supporters of a philosophically orientated Judaism reshaped their religion, in line with the presuppositions of rationalism. They regarded the many superstitious practices of medieval Judaism as anathema. They also prevailed upon pietists, who drew no clear distinction between religious and superstitious rites, to regard certain abstract ways of thinking about God and the world as obviously correct and indeed mandated by the Bible.

The first major philosopher-theologian was Saadiah Gaon, who was born in Egypt in 882 CE and died as a leading scholar of Babylonian Jewry in 942 CE. Saadiah wrote *The Book of Beliefs and Opinions* in Arabic to provide rational justification for traditional Jewish teaching and to counter heretical views then current in Babylonia. In this work he argued that while knowledge can be gained by philosophical investigation it can also be provided for those not inclined to philosophise from a reliable tradition. Revelation and reason are thus not in conflict but are two separate means whereby knowledge of the truth is provided. This led him to reinterpret the biblical and rabbinic teachings in rational terms, arguing that much of the language about God is not meant literally but allegorically or symbolically. This was not to make religion subservient to reason but to bring out the true meaning of religious teachings which denied that God had a material nature.

The greatest of Jewish philosophers, Moses Maimonides, who lived two centuries after Saadiah, disagreed with his philosophical approach. Yet he said of him that his writings kept the Torah alive and without him its true teachings would have disappeared from Israel. Saadiah was also a Hebrew poet of note and his religious poetry made its way into various parts of the liturgy.

Not all Jewish thinkers were enamoured of the philosophical re-interpretation of Judaism. Foremost among those who believed that rationalism, even rational religion, was no substitute for a living faith was Judah Halevi (1075–1141). Halevi was willing to speak in a philosophical idiom, but rejected the dominance of philosophy within Jewish theology. His main work, translated into Hebrew with the title *The Kuzari*, was entitled in the original Arabic ,'The Book of Argument and Proof in Defence of the Despised Faith'. In it he set out his semi-mystical understanding of the nature of Judaism, arguing against the claims of Christianity, Islam and Aristotelianism using rational methods.

The background to the book was the story of the conversion of the royal house of the Khazars to Judaism in the ninth century. The

Khazars were a Turkic people caught between the conflicting claims of Christian and Muslim neighbours. In Halevi's *Kuzari* the Khazar king invites an Aristotelian philosopher and representatives of the three great monotheistic faiths – Christianity, Islam and Judaism – to present their teachings to him. The king is convinced that the Jewish religion, which underlies the other two and is clearly superior to mere philosophy, is in fact the true religion. In accepting it, the king also accepts that the philosophers' truth is only a limited perspective on revelatory truth.

Halevi argued that the Jewish people possess the unique gift of prophecy, which accounts for their status as a people chosen by God to be the bearers of divine revelation. Religious experience is superior to rational knowledge, though the latter is useful as an adjunct to religion. Aristotelianism is based on the experience of the human senses while prophecy is based on a higher experience which comes from contact with the divine world. Whereas the philosopher-theologian can attain some theoretical knowledge of God, the prophet experiences him directly.

The teachings of revelation conveyed by the prophets set out the path of behaviour which brings a person to an experience of God. Just as the prophets are necessary for the Jewish people to perfect themselves in holiness, so the Jewish people, possessed of prophetic insight, are necessary to the nations of the world to help them draw near to divine experience. Israel is the heart of the nations, and its claim to religious truth is backed up by the testimony of the whole people at Mount Sinai when God revealed himself. The Christian and Muslim claims to prophecy are at best only supported by the private testimony of their religious founders.

MOSES MAIMONIDES

The most important medieval Jewish philosopher, Moses Maimonides (1136–1204), was also the leading rabbinic scholar of the post-talmudic period. It was said of him that, 'from Moses till Moses there was none like Moses', i.e., that his intellectual stature could be compared only to that of the biblical Moses.

Maimonides wrote an Arabic commentary on the Mishnah, in which he set out the thirteen principal beliefs which he considered essential for Jewish doctrine. This was the first serious attempt from within Judaism to define the dogmatic base of the religion. The principal beliefs that Maimonides arrived at were:

1. The existence of a perfect Creator, who is the first cause and sustainer of what exists, and on whom all creatures are dependent.
2. That God, the cause of all that is, is one – not one as we might use the term in ordinary discourse, but one in a unique sense which has no comparison in everyday experience.
3. That the one God does not have a physical nature or any physical attributes such as movement, or rest, or location. He therefore cannot be compared to any creature, and all language about him is simply analogous.
4. That the one God is the absolutely first being, preceding all other beings.
5. That human beings should worship and praise God alone, and not any of the lower beings of his creation such as angels or cosmic bodies which act only according to their nature without free will. Neither is it fitting to worship such beings as intermediaries in order to draw nearer to God.
6. That there are certain outstanding human beings, whose souls are perfected so that they achieve a spiritual level which enables them to receive prophetic revelation.
7. That Moses was the greatest of the prophets who preceded him and who succeeded him. His insight into divine knowledge was superior to that of all other persons, and he reached the level of the angels, having transcended human limitations. He was thus able to communicate with God directly without aid of the angels.
8. That the Torah was given by God through Moses, and it is all divine revelation. Anyone who claims that Moses composed part of the Torah himself is a heretic. The accepted interpretation of the Pentateuch found in the Oral Torah is also from God, so that traditional practice of the commandments is exactly as it was explained to Moses.
9. That since the Written Torah and the Oral Torah were both received from God, we may not add to them or detract from them.
10. That God knows the deeds of human beings and does not ignore what they do.

11. That God rewards those who keep the commandments of the Torah and punishes those who transgress its prohibitions.
12. That we should have a firm faith that the days of the Messiah will surely come, and will not be delayed. If the Messiah seems to tarry we should wait for him but we should not try to calculate the time of his coming by using hints found in Scripture. We must believe that he will be superior to all kings who have preceded him, and we should pray for his coming.
13. That there will be a resurrection of the dead. (Although Maimonides does not go into any detail about this belief in his list of principles, he later wrote an epistle on the subject since he was accused of doubting its importance.)

This programme of thirteen principles of faith was much criticised by later Jewish thinkers. Some objected to the very idea of reducing Judaism to a group of principles because this seemed to belittle the other beliefs of Judaism. Others subjected his particular list to philosophical scrutiny and concluded that he had chosen the wrong principles. Thus the fifteenth-century Spanish philosopher, Joseph Albo, in his *Book of Principles*, argued for only three basic principles of Judaism: the existence of God; divine revelation; and divine reward and punishment. Despite the controversy surrounding Maimonides' thirteen principles, they were incorporated in the daily prayer-book in a simplified, and somewhat inaccurate, form in the *ani maamin* formulae and the *yigdal* hymn.

Modern movements within Judaism have also parted company with the Maimonidean formula for authentic Jewish belief. Conservative and Reform Judaism did not share Maimonides' traditional views on prophecy, revelation, the Messiah and the resurrection of the dead. The Reconstructionist Movement, a radical development of Conservative Judaism, in the supplement to its prayer-book includes thirteen Criteria of Jewish Loyalty, which are very different from Maimonides' original. They are preceded by the following words:

> In view of the changed conditions in Jewish life, the criterion of loyalty to Judaism can no longer be the acceptance of a creed, but the experience of the need to have one's life enriched by the Jewish heritage. That experience should be formulated not in terms of dogmas but in terms of

wants. The following wants supply the measure by which we may in our day test our loyalty to Judaism.

(*Sabbath Prayer Book*, Reconstructionist Foundation, New York, 1945, p. 562)

Claude Montefiore, a founder of Liberal Judaism in Britain, wrote the following about Maimonides' Articles of Creed in his *Outlines of Liberal Judaism*:

> The articles leave out, or are silent about, many 'articles of faith' which Liberal Judaism regards as essential. . . . In addition to its omissions concerning the relation of God to man, the creed is also silent about the mission of Israel and the relation of Judaism to the world at large. It is silent about the salvation of all men, of the ultimate redemption and enlightenment of the bad as well as the good. It omits other important matters too, such as the relation of religion to morality, the true service of God, the relation of faith to works, and of both to religion, the place of knowledge in religion, and so on.

MAIMONIDES' PHILOSOPHICAL WORKS

In philosophising about the divinity, Maimonides gives his interpretation a decidedly Aristotelian colouring, and the personal God of the Bible and Talmud somehow gets lost among caveats and abstractions. In his code he had already declared the belief in the corporeality of the deity heretical. In response to this, Maimonides' most vociferous critic, R. David of Posquieres, commented:

> Why does he call such a person a heretic? For several people, greater and better than him, accepted such thoughts because of what they saw in Scripture and more than that from what they saw in the aggadic teachings which are misleading.

(*Yad* Teshuvah 3:7)

Maimonides' major philosophical work, *The Guide For the Perplexed*, originally written in Arabic but translated into Hebrew in his lifetime, caused even more controversy than his code and his Mishnah commentary. For in the *Guide* Maimonides set out his understanding both of the nature of God and also of the commandments.

In explaining the function of ritual in his *Guide*, Maimonides related it to the pagan practices of the past and explained how Jewish practice was meant to wean Jews away from idolatry. It seemed to Maimonides' critics that, as a consequence, once the pagan background had disappeared there would be no need to keep the commandments. This was most obvious in Maimonides' explanation of the sacrifices. According to the *Guide*, sacrifices were the main method of divine service in biblical times for both Israelites and pagans. They were adopted and prescribed by the Torah so that people would not sacrifice to idols, but since the destruction of the Temple prayer has superseded sacrifice. Such a position is problematic because Maimonides himself, in his code, codified the laws of sacrifice, which would be reintroduced in the messianic age. Some traditionalists were so shocked by Maimonides' remarks on sacrifice in the *Guide* that they denied he wrote the work at all.

Intellectuals were forced to choose between Maimonides' philosophical reinterpretation of Judaism and the traditionalism of Halevi or of thinkers who eschewed philosophy altogether. Those who chose Maimonides found that they could take the philosophical adventure even further than their master and could understand the whole ritual side of Judaism as really a symbolic way of expressing purely philosophical truths. This angered the traditionalists even more.

After the death of Maimonides there was a strong reaction against the study of philosophy, which was banned by some of the leading rabbis and only allowed to those of outstanding piety and maturity. This anti-philosophic reaction forced Jewish philosophy on to the intellectual back-burner for over three centuries. A philosophical revival took place in Judaism only in the period of the eighteenth-century Enlightenment when Jews in Germany and Central Europe, under the influence of Moses Mendelssohn, began once again to explore a philosophical reinterpretation of Judaism.

MYSTICISM AND THE KABBALAH

Jewish mystical literature goes back at least as far as the early mishnaic period if not back into the Bible itself. Prophetic visions of heaven became the subject of contemplation of Merkabah Mysticism, in the tradition known as *maaseh merkabah*. The

Merkabah mystics sought to undertake mystical journeys of the soul into the heavenly realm so that they could experience the vision of the divine throne. They were known as *yordei merkabah*, 'those who descend the chariot', since the vision of heaven granted to the prophet Ezekiel involved the chariot on which the divine figure rode. These heavenly journeys are recorded in works known as *heikhalot* texts, which provide instructions on how to pass the fiery angels who guard the halls through which the adept passes.

There was also a more speculative tradition which dealt with the structures inherent in the divine creative process. This creation mysticism, known as *maaseh bereshit*, finds its earliest expression in the *Sefer Yetzirah* ('Book of Formation'). This book, which is ascribed to the biblical patriarch, Abraham, surfaced in about the third century CE. It was believed that the book could be used to control the creative powers residing within the world, since artificial humans or animals could be created with the help of magical letter combinations referred to in the book.

The doctrine of the ten *sefirot*, or semi-divine functions, which control the world, is first mentioned in the *Sefer Yetzirah*. In the Kabbalah (as the later mystical tradition is known) it developed into a substantial feature of Jewish mysticism, particularly in the *Sefer Ha-zohar* ('Book of Splendour', henceforth *Zohar*), which first appeared in thirteenth-century Spain. The publisher of the *Zohar* manuscript, Moses de Leon, claimed that he had come into possession of an ancient text recording the teachings of a famous second-century CE Palestinian master, Simeon bar Yochai. The reputed age of the teachings, and the power of their imagery, made the *Zohar* into 'the Bible' of the Kabbalists. Parts of the work were eventually even incorporated into the prayer-book, and Jews influenced by kabbalistic teaching still chant sections on ritual occasions. The *Zohar* puts forward a mystical philosophy of Judaism in which the forces of evil are ranged against the working of the divine in the world and the commandments of Judaism are instrumental in preserving the divine harmony. The world emanates from the Godhead through the agency of the *sefirot*, and thus there is a divine underlay just below the surface of the mundane world.

One of the most remarkable developments of the Kabbalah took place in Safed, North Palestine, in the sixteenth century, when Isaac Luria arrived from Egypt and taught a new system of Kabbalah to a small circle of mystical disciples. This new system implied that each individual Jew, through his religious activities, was furthering the messianic process. This process will be complete only when all the divine sparks trapped in the world are raised back to their divine status. The alienation of these sparks came about through a catastrophic upheaval which took place in the process of emanation and left the world needing rectification.

Lurianic Kabbalah generated messianic movements which raised the mystical theology of Judaism to the forefront of the popular consciousness. This popularisation of mysticism eventually led to the Hasidic Movement, founded in the mid-eighteenth century by Israel Baal Shem Tov (the Besht), a wandering folk healer and mystic. The Besht taught that God, the merciful father, could be found everywhere in all walks of life and in all activities, not merely in specifically religious contexts. Hasidism developed its own genre of sacred literature: works of a Kabbalistic nature, story books full of wonderful tales about Hasidic Masters, Bible commentaries which playfully drew lessons from words and images at a level of popular homiletics.

The prayer-book

Many of the popular elements from Jewish literature were gathered together in the different versions of the prayer-book (*siddur*) used by various communities. Originally, prayers were considered to be part of the oral tradition of Judaism and there was some resistance to writing them down. As the prayers grew from rather simple paradigms in talmudic times, it became imperative to commit them to writing and this was first done by the Geonim in Babylonia in the eighth–ninth centuries.

The elements which go to make up the fabric of these prayer-books come from the Pentateuch, the Prophets, the Book of Psalms, the mystical hymns of the Merkabah mystics, the *Zohar* and the many liturgical poets, *paytanim*. In the prayer-book there are references to the events of post-biblical Jewish history and especially the persecution of the Jews. There are martyrologies which include hymns remembering the Jewish martyrs of York, who burnt themselves alive as far back as 1190 rather than be forcibly converted to Christianity. Some modern editions of these texts even include a dirge on the massacre of Jews during the Nazi Holocaust.

Inside the *siddur* are not only the fixed orders of public prayers, but also sections for Torah study and for private meditation, blessings for all sorts of occasions and table songs to be sung at home at the Sabbath meals. The prayer-book is also the repository of Jewish doctrine for the layperson and it includes poetic formulations of doctrine based on Maimonides' Thirteen Principles of Faith.

The traditional prayer-book is mostly in Hebrew, with some few prayers in Aramaic, a related semitic language. These were introduced at a time when Hebrew had become a literary language and ordinary people understood only Aramaic. Thus the *kaddish* prayer recited by mourners is in Aramaic. Today, with the rebirth of Israel and the revival of Hebrew as a spoken language, it is precisely the Aramaic portions of the prayer-book which are least understood. Some modern Israeli editions of the prayer-book include parallel Hebrew translations of the Aramaic.

There are translations of the prayer-book into all the major languages spoken by Jews in the Diaspora. Conservative, Reconstructionist, Reform and Liberal versions of the prayer-book contain many more vernacular prayers than Orthodox ones and have eliminated those parts of the service which seemed too archaic. Orthodox Judaism has preserved even the most anachronistic prayers (e.g., those requesting the welfare of the exilarch, an institution long abandoned) on the grounds that they have become sanctified by use over the centuries.

FURTHER READING

General

Alexander, P.S. (1984) *Judaism, Textual Sources for the Study of*, Manchester, Manchester University Press.

Unterman, A. (1991) *Dictionary of Jewish Lore and Legend*, London, Thames and Hudson.

Unterman, A. (1989) *Jews, Their Religious Beliefs and Practices*, London, Routledge & Kegan Paul.

Waxman, M. (1960) *A History of Jewish Literature*, New York, Yoseloff.

Midrash

Freedman, H. and Simon, M. (1939) *Midrash Rabbah*, London, Soncino.

Ginzberg, L. (1909) *Legends of the Jews*, Philadelphia, Jewish Publication Society.

Talmud

Cohen, A. (1949) *Everyman's Talmud*, London, Dent & Sons.
Steinsaltz, A. (1976) *The Essential Talmud*, London, Weidenfeld & Nicolson.

Responsa

Freehof, S.B. (1959) *The Responsa Literature*, Philadelphia, Jewish Publication Society.
Freehof, S.B. (1963) *A Treasury of the Responsa*, Philadelphia, Jewish Publication Society.

Codes

Goldin, H.E. (trans) (1963) *Code of Jewish Law*, New York, Hebrew Publishing Co.

Philosophy

Guttmann, J. (1964) *Philosophies of Judaism*, New York, Routledge & Kegan Paul.
Jacobs, L. (1964) *Principles of the Jewish Faith: An Analytic Study*, London, Valentine Mitchell.

Mysticism

Scholem, G. (1961) *Major Trends in Jewish Mysticism*, New York, Schocken.
Sperling, H. and Simon, M. (trans) (1934) *The Zohar*, London, Soncino.

Prayer-book

(Orthodox) *Authorized Daily Prayer Book of the United Hebrew Congregations of the Commonwealth*, Centenary Edition (1990) London, Singer's Prayer Book Publication Committee.
(Progressive) *Service of the Heart. Weekday Sabbath and Festival Services and Prayers for Home and Synagogue* (1967) London, Union of Liberal and Progressive Synagogues.

6. Sikhism

Beryl Dhanjal

As far as Sikhism is concerned, one book, the Gurū Granth Sāhib is revered above all other writings. There are other writings which can be regarded as sacred – the *Dasam Granth*, the works of Bhai Gurdas, the traditions of the *janam sākhīs*, *gur bilās*, *rahit nāmās* and an assortment of modern works on religion, but none of these works is on a par with the Gurū Granth Sāhib.

Gurū

The Gurū Granth Sāhib (the Sikh holy book) is treated with the courtesy normally shown to a living *gurū*, a teacher. The book is called Gurū because of a belief first expressed by the Sikh scholar, Bhai Gurdas Bhalla. Bhai Gurdas was a kinsman of the third Sikh Gurū, and a loyal friend to the successive Gurūs in his lifetime, which lasted until the reign of the seventh Gurū. Bhai Gurdas was the scribe who actually prepared the holy book, the Gurū Granth Sāhib. He sat with Guru Arjan and wrote. He proposed the theory that there was a unity among the Gurūs; when one went, another came, and although the physical body changed, the Gurū remained the same. He described it as being like two candles touched together, carrying the same flame. Perhaps it might be called spirit. Bhai Gurdas said that before Guru Nanak died he installed Guru Angad as his successor, 'and set the Gurū's canopy over his head. Merging his light in Guru Angad's light, the Sat Gurū changed his form. None could comprehend the mystery. A wonder of wonders he revealed: changing his body he made Guru Angad's body his own' (Bhai Gurdas, *Vār* 1.45).

When there were no more living men as Gurūs, that same spirit became resident in the book, which became the Gurū. The book contains the *bānī*, the word, which was revealed through the Gurū and will ultimately, therefore, lead back to its own source – the one beyond time, the truth, the ultimate reality – God.

The gurdwara

Extraordinary reverence is the only way to describe the treatment of a volume which normally occupies a throne. The gurdwara (literally, the Doorway to the Gurū, the place of worship) is arranged like a royal court. The Gurū Granth Sāhib is enthroned each morning, draped with richly embroidered cloths, and opened with due ceremony. For devotees it is as if sacred light floods from the pages and illuminates the gurdwara where it is sited. In fact, it is the presence of the book which creates the sacred place – for a gurdwara is anywhere where a holy volume is situated. Despite this, it needs no special building; if there is a Granth, there is a gurdwara. Nowadays, weddings sometimes take place in hotels, halls or other large hired rooms. Ceremonies can take place in homes or schools. A Gurū Granth Sāhib is enthroned, making that place a gurdwara for the ceremony.

The role of the Gurū Granth Sāhib

The Gurū Granth Sāhib is essential for all ceremonies: all worship and the life-cycle rites of devotees take place in its presence. It takes centre stage when families come together to celebrate a marriage or to name a baby, to seek comfort, or express joy. People can come and seek its advice.

It has a central cohesive role in religion and community, being universally respected, impossible to argue with, and ever present. As it occupies centre stage at all times, everything happens around it.

The Gurū Granth Sāhib is visited. People take an audience – *darśan* – with the Gurū Granth Sāhib. They cover their heads respectfully, remove their shoes, approach and prostrate themselves on the ground. They make offerings and accept *kaṛāh praśād* (a special food made and offered to all in gurdwaras). (See Sikhism chapter in *Worship*, in this series.) They speak of the book as if it were a respected and loved elder (a male, of course, like a grandfather).

If a copy of the volume has to be moved, it is carefully wrapped up, and transported in a special procession. Holy water may be sprinkled by the leader, a second man comes waving a *chaur*, a whisk, the symbol of royalty, and finally the third man comes carrying the volume, carefully wrapped up, on his head. Often people give warning that a Granth is approaching so that people may cover their heads and show respect in its presence. At some festival times, the book may be installed on a lorry and driven in procession around the town. This sometimes happens in Britain. At least one gurdwara in England has a special vehicle for transporting the Gurū Granth Sāhib. The Granthmobile (to coin a term!), pennants fluttering, makes a stately progress through the London suburbs, with the book comfortably installed inside.

It is put away (to bed, as it were) at night in a ceremony called *sukh asān* (which literally means 'to sit comfortably').

Many writers have described these ceremonies as they are carried out in the important historic shrines like the *Darbār Sāhib*, the Golden Temple at Amritsar in India, but such ceremonies also take place in gurdwaras all over the world. Some people keep a copy of the book in their own homes. If they do, they will keep it in its own separate room.

The Gurū Granth Sāhib is unique. No other Sikh book deserves similar respect. Other approved works are occasionally used in gurdwaras, but these never detract from the primacy of the Gurū Granth Sāhib. When there are congregational services, these normally consist of singing the compositions in the book. There are also readings of the Gurū Granth Sāhib. Sometimes there are unbroken readings done by a relay team of readers. Each person reads for a couple of hours. An unbroken reading is called an *Akhaṇḍ Pāṭh*, and it takes two days to complete the reading continuously, day and night. Started on Friday morning, it ends on Sunday morning. (These days are not holy days – people tend to have more time available at weekends, so it is a better time to do it.) Some people hold a reading at times of joy or sorrow. Some hold one every year. Some hold one because they have made a vow, moved to a new house, or have had some good fortune, or maybe things are not going too well and they hope that things will improve afterwards. Some people read at a more leisurely pace, reading a passage every now and then, working their way through. This is called *sahaj pāṭh* or *sādhāran pāṭh*, ordinary reading. Some people do this reading as a private spiritual exercise, reading a little every day. Recently some people have begun to use lengthy and complex reading patterns. And some have begun to do ritual readings lasting for forty days.

The book can also be consulted. A person might go every day to find out what the orders for the day are. The *hukam* (orders) are the verse at the top left-hand side of the page when the book is first opened in the morning. One gurdwara in Southall in London has a telephone line where people can telephone in to hear a verse. If an individual or a community has a particular problem, they could consult the Gurū Granth Sāhib. The Gurū Granth Sāhib has also acted as a public oracle, notably, over the question of untouchables being able to offer *kaṛāh praśād*, the holy food offered in gurdwaras.

Yet despite all of the respect, it must be firmly borne in mind that Sikhs are not worshipping the book. God alone is worthy of worship, not mere paper and ink. It is true, however, that the alphabet is regarded with reverence. It is called *Gurmukhī*, meaning from the mouth of the Gurū, and traditional claims were made that it originated from the second Gurū. It was in fact used earlier, but the alphabet is associated with the Gurū Granth Sāhib and therefore has acquired a sanctity. A magazine printed recently by a gurdwara in London had a notice reminding readers to treat the pages respectfully as they are printed in *Gurmukhī*, the holy script. Some people would not step on such printed matter, and would dispose of paper bearing any writings in the script very carefully. Some might feel anxious about vulgar matters being written down in that script.

The history of the Gurū Granth Sāhib

Poetry was, and still is, an important means of expression for South Asians. If someone has something to say, he or she produces a work of art, not a dry textbook! The religious in India wrote poetry. The first Sikh Gurū, Nanak (1469–1539), was certainly a poet. His poetry is very fine indeed. Had he not been regarded as the founder of a religion, he would in any case be remembered as a first-class poet.

Guru Nanak went on many travels with a Muslim musician called Mardana, who provided the accompaniment to the Gurū's psalms. (Mardana's descendants are still found in Nankana Sāhib in Pakistan, which was the birthplace and home village of Guru Nanak and, of course, of Mardana. Mardana's descendants have remained musicians and singers, and they still accompany the Gurū's words.) It is said that the Gurū's creations were collected together and written down.

Guru Nanak was followed by a succession of nine other Gurūs. Some of these were also poets, so a very characteristic school of devotional poetry was formed. Tradition has it that the poems were collected and written down in two volumes, and although some say that these books still exist, no one seems to know where they are. They were in the possession of Bhai Mohan, a son of the third Gurū, and were borrowed by Guru Arjan (the fifth Gurū) when he was preparing the Gurū Granth Sāhib. The first compilation of the Gurū Granth Sāhib was installed in 1604 in the original temple that stood on the site now occupied by the Golden Temple at Amritsar, and a *granthī*, a person to care for the book, was appointed.

The compilation of the Gurū Granth Sāhib

It has been said that rival claimants to the Guruship began to prepare their own volumes and, in order to supply an authoritative work, Guru Arjan (1563–1606) began to select his material to create an authentic scripture. However, some Sikhs reject this story and say that the Gurū Granth Sāhib was not compiled in response to any external events, but simply because of divine inspiration. Guru Arjan had the trusted companion, Bhai Gurdas Bhalla, sit with him and do the actual writing.

There are 1,430 pages in the standard printed edition. The copies are all alike which makes for ease of reference. It consists of 5,894 psalm-like poems; the largest number – 2,216 – are by Guru Arjan himself. The Gurū included poetry by his own predecessors, and a number of works by other poets whose writings share the theme of the philosophy of the Name, which is the central message of the Gurū Granth Sāhib.

So the Gurū Granth Sāhib is an anthology of writings by men from a wide geographical area of Northern India. The poets included come from many different sections of society, the upper crust and the lower orders – a Ṣūfī holy man, a weaver, a leather-worker, a tailor and a priest. There are 937 hymns by poets other than Gurūs – fifteen of whom are called *bhagat*s (exponents of *bhakti*, devotees) and seventeen of whom are called *bhaṭṭ*s, meaning bards of the kind found at royal courts. Surjit Hans (1988: 180) has observed that the inclusion of non-apostolic writings was 'meant to popularise the cardinal ideas elaborated in the compositions of Guru Nanak and his successors, particularly the uniqueness of Guru Nanak's position and his oneness with his successors. The inclusion of these writings in the Ādi Granth gives them a divine sanction.'

Religious traditions

It is a commonplace to say that the poetry of the Gurū Granth Sāhib was written by people from different religious traditions, meaning Hindus, Muslims and Sikhs, though how relevant modern identities, sharpened up and reified by life under the British, and fifty years of independent India, might be, is uncertain. Identities are a modern concern. The Muslims who came to India did not invade as the armies of Islam. While there were occasional demolitions of Hindu temples, it was not an everyday occurrence. Successful Sultans were not particularly Islamic in their rule. They were governed by the practical need to balance interests and retain power, and they were a minority group. The religious life of medieval Panjab was considerably richer and more diverse than might be suggested by naming three major world religions, and trying to make sense of the world in terms of their interplay. To do so is to attempt to interpret medieval India in modern terms.

Ṣūfī holy men in Panjab have sometimes used the words and imagery of other traditions, and *bhagat*s, *Nāth Jogī*s and *sant*s were at one with the ṣūfīs in praise and love of the Lord. They all suffered in separation from him and all felt ecstasy at his presence. They were all people believing in one God and in the importance of directing their devotion towards him. Nothing else mattered very much. So their beliefs and practices were very similar. The scholar, Charlotte Vaudeville, has observed that Kabir, a medieval Indian mystic whose writings appear in the Gurū Granth Sāhib, seems to be of a family of *Nāth Jogī*s recently converted to, and with a superficial knowledge of, Islam. But the traditions did not matter, the experience did, for Vaudeville (1959: 221–2) says that he uses the terms in senses that are his own.

To ask whether Kabir was a Muslim or a Hindu is to misjudge the situation: he was a weaver. Religion was not a key to understanding society. People functioned in terms of locality, village, household, lineage, family, caste, clan, etc. (Many still do.) There was simply no notion of a demarcated religious community with the institutions and concerns which that implies. That notion, that model, was imported with the colonialists.

Experience

What marks the Gurū Granth Sāhib out as special, and makes its tone so compulsive, is that those who wrote it were mystics of experience writing about ultimate reality. They were not writing textbooks, political tracts or theology. Moved by the urgency of their own experience, they were describing the indescribable! When the compilation was completed, the Gurū wrote the seal – *Mundāvanī* (Gurū Granth Sāhib, p. 1,429). It would probably not be too irreverent to call it a recipe, for Sikh Gurūs were practical people. He wrote:

> Three things have been put into this dish: truth, contentment and deep reflection.
> With them has been mixed the name of the Lord, its sweet nectar sustaining all.
> He who eats and enjoys it shall be set free.
> He who tastes this food will make it his own, for evermore.
> By clinging to God's holy feet, we cross the ocean of existence and out of the world's darkness come to the light which pervades all.

Then he wrote:

> I did not appreciate what you did for me – yet you made me worthy.
> I am full of faults – But you have taken pity on me.
> You show me compassion and kindness, and so I have found the true friend, the Gurū.
> Oh Nanak, having obtained the name, my body and soul will be refreshed.

The history of the Granth subsequently is not totally clear. There were family disputes for the Guruship. The temple at Amritsar and the book were in the hands of members of the family who were in dispute with the accepted line of Gurūs. The sixth Gurū, Hargovind, is said to have kept the volume in his house from whence it was stolen by his grandson, Dhir Mal (who presumably thought that possession of the book might advance his claims). It was recovered from Dhir Mal some years later, but the then Gurū, Teg Bahadar, told his followers to return it. It was said to have been placed in the river and recovered, unharmed. The tenth and final Gurū, Govind Singh, is said to have asked for it back, and, being refused, to have re-dictated it all from memory, adding his father's poems. This was a considerable feat of memory, and as it was done at a place called Damdama, it is called the Damdama version. All of the modern, printed, copies are copies of this version. There is another version called the Banno version, said to have been made by a man called Bhai Banno, who copied the volume, either having borrowed the original or copied it on the way to the bookbinders at Lahore. The Banno version has several extra poems.

Not much is known about the subsequent history of the Gurū Granth Sāhib. The copy claimed as the original was discovered by the British after the annexation of Panjab in 1848, in the custody of the Court at Lahore, and was restored to the family, the Sodhis of Kartarpur, who were descendants of Dhir Mal. A copy was made for Queen Victoria and this is kept in the India Office Library. The book is still kept by the Sodhi family at the mansion called the *Śiś Mahal* (Palace of Mirrors) in Kartarpur, Jalandhar, where it is opened for *darśan* on occasions. Few people have been granted access to examine the pages. Hence textual studies are difficult and there are unresolved questions. Such discussions as can take place have to be based on the descriptions made by several scholars who have seen the book at close quarters.

Arrangement of the Gurū Granth Sāhib

The Gurū Granth Sāhib is arranged in a very systematic way. It opens with a special poem by Guru Nanak called *Japjī Sāhib* (*Jap* means meditation or devout repetition of a name or a special word called a *mantra*; *Jī* and *sāhib* are words used to show respect). *Japjī Sāhib* is the only one in the collection which has no musical mode ascribed to it. This may indicate that this piece is intended for a different use – perhaps quiet reflection. It is a difficult piece, with thirty-eight long stanzas. Devout people memorise it and repeat it every morning. It begins with a short statement known as the *Mūl Mantra*, the basic credal statement, Guru Nanak's description of God. It is a twenty-two word, terse statement, almost untranslatable (for each word contains so much meaning). However, it sums up the essentials about God and his qualities and also specifies human beings' proper response to God – to remember his names and attributes.

> There is one God.
> He is the supreme truth.
> He is the Creator,
> is without fear and without hate.
> He, the omnipresent,
> pervades the universe.
> He is not born,
> nor does he die to be born again.
> By his grace shalt thou worship him.
> Before time itself, there was truth.
> When time began to run its course he was the truth.
> Even now, he is the truth
> and ever more shall truth prevail.

This statement is so important that it is given pride of place. It comes before anything else, and it also comes at the beginning of each section in an abbreviated form. Some people have begun to do *pāṭh* (reading) in such a way that every time they come to the word Gurū they read the *Mūl Mantra* again; in this fashion, the continuous reading of the whole takes a week.

In the Gurū Granth Sāhib, the *Mūl Mantra* is followed by some other pieces which have liturgical uses, and these are repeated later in the appropriate place. The main body of the book is arranged according to *rāga*, a melodic organisation. The *rāga*s are often described as scales; they are a system on which Indian music is based. The poems are then arranged according to both the poetic forms used and the authors, beginning with the Gurūs in chronological order, followed by other writers. The Gurūs all used the pen-name Nanak in their compositions, so the poems are ascribed *Mahalā*, meaning master and a number – One for Guru Nanak, Five for Guru Arjan, etc. At the end there are some miscellaneous works which do not fit the scheme.

Content of the Gurū Granth Sāhib

There are many books which describe the Gurū Granth Sāhib – how it is arranged physically, how it is treated and its centrality and unifying role in Sikhism. Fewer authors attempt to describe the contents. It is simply not possible to reduce 1,430 pages of superlative poetry, written in a very condensed form, dealing with matters spiritual, into a few flat paragraphs of English prose. We are dealing with poetry of a high order. Guru Nanak was aware of himself as a poet and ends stanzas: 'Nanak the poet says . . .'. In this case, the medium is important, not just the message.

Probably the simplest meaningful description would be to say that the poems in the Gurū Granth Sāhib are fairly similar to those in the Book of Psalms found in the Bible. They are all set to music, except the first one, and are intended to be sung.

The philosophy of *Nām* (Name) is the main thrust of the Gurū Granth Sāhib. Guru Nanak's path has been called *Nām mārg* – the way of the Name. *Nām* is clearly a concept heavy with meaning, yet, like the English word 'name', Nām denotes no mere label, but a word that sums up the characteristics and qualities of that which it describes. The *Nām* is God's revelation, by which he can be known. *Nām* sums up the entire natural order, the nature of God, all we can say about him. The Name is offered. The eternal Gurū is God, and his word can be heard in the human heart. Humans must take the initiative: they must meditate, remember, love the Name. This is the start of the discipline. The discipline is called *nām simaraṇ*, praising, remembering the Name. Disciples must listen to the word in their heart, must praise and meditate on the greatness of God. They must develop a spirit of devotion, love and surrender. From this comes true and firm belief and the way to spiritual progress. But a person is not told to go off and live as a hermit while practising this discipline. The ideal is a disciplined worldliness. Devotees should be householders and live in the world, earning a living and helping others, but they should perform their meditation and seek the company of holy persons, as there is a vision of God to be gained through the company of such people.

Guru Nanak did not say that individuals can assume that they will reach a satisfactory outcome due to mere human effort. Human beings are of limited understanding. God is the one who decides. He bestows his grace on those he chooses.

Human beings must submit to God, obey him and abandon their attachment to this world. A person who lives a life in obedience and submission to God will eventually achieve union with the divine. But the path is difficult and strewn with obstacles. These are people's deeds, their engrossing, busy activities, their delusions, and their own self-centred concerns. Me! Me! a person cries, inattentive to God. Human beings are *manmukh*, self-willed, submitting to themselves and not to God. But it is the *man*, the human heart or mind that opens the way to liberation, and to conquer the heart is to conquer the world. Once human beings can conquer their own mind, it becomes a valuable instrument and may lead them to God. Once on the path, humans climb to higher levels of understanding and experience. In *Japjī Sāhib* Guru Nanak describes five *khaṇḍ*s (realms), through which the traveller passes on his journey, the goal of which is not paradise, but is union with God. The terms used by Guru Nanak are the mingling of light with light, or the mingling of two streams. The experience can never be described. It is an experience to be achieved in this life, not in an afterlife.

Apart from the religious message, the Gurū Granth Sāhib contains little other material. There are scarcely any references to contemporary events. The invasion by Babur in 1526 merits a mention – a mere mention. There are a few other references to people or events. Some people attempt to deduce the attitude of Gurūs to the contemporary scene from the writings, but the Gurū Granth Sāhib is not a work concerned with earthly matters. The shortcomings of rulers mentioned are the shortcomings of the evil age we live in, not political commentary aimed at individuals.

Language of the Gurū Granth Sāhib

The language of the Gurū Granth Sāhib is variously described by authors, some claiming that it is an easily understood, popular vernacular, while others claim that it is very difficult to read. It is possible (with some effort) to learn to read the language, which has been called the sacred language of the Sikhs by Christopher Shackle (1983: preface). It was the language used by medieval North Indian holy men, Sant Bhasa or Sadhukari.

The script used for recording the religious literature of the Sikhs is called *Gurmukhī*, which means literally 'through the mouth of the Gurū'. It is the same script which is used for writing Panjabi in India today, though there have been some changes over the years.

There have been a number of attempts to translate the Gurū Granth Sāhib. It is an enormous and difficult undertaking. The best source to consult is *Textual Sources for the Study of Sikhism*

(McLeod 1984). This is not a complete translation but a selection of the most important pieces.

Authority

The Gurū Granth Sāhib has authority because it is regarded as the eternal Gurū. Guru Govind Singh is believed to have decreed that after his death authority should pass to the community and the scripture. The traditions are called Gurū Panth and Gurū Granth. The scripture is regarded as the manifest body of the Gurū. According to Bhai Nand Lal,

> You must accept the Granth as an actual part of me, treating its letters as the hairs of my body. This truly is so. Sikhs who wish to see the Gurū will do so when they come to the Granth.

He tells Sikhs to bathe and come, to hear the words and reflect upon them.

> Acknowledge the Granth as my visible presence, rejecting the idea that it is other than me.
>
> (Bhai Nand Lal, Prasan Uttar: translation in McLeod 1984: 75)

Several times a day people are reminded that they should acknowledge the Granth as Gurū, when they repeat the *Ardās* (literally, 'petition'). It is often called the Sikh prayer. The *Ardās* is an exception to the rule that everything recited in the gurdwara is from the scriptures, as it is the one text used in daily rituals which is not in the Gurū Granth Sāhib. It seems likely that the *Ardās* dates mainly from the eighteenth century. It says:

> From the timeless one there came the bidding
> In accordance with which the panth was established.
> To all Sikhs there is the commandment
> to accept as the Gurū the Granth.
> Accept the Granth as Gurū for it is the revealed body of the Gurūs.
> Those whose hearts are pure should seek him in the word.
>
> (Also translations in McLeod 1984: 103; *Rehat Maryādā* 1978: 3)

Dasam Granth

The Gurū Granth Sāhib contains the writings of the early poet-gurūs – Gurus Nanak, Angad, Amar Das, Ram Das, and Arjan, and at a later date, Guru Govind Singh added poems by his father, Guru Teg Bahadar. It is sometimes referred to as the Ādi Granth, meaning the original or first, to distinguish it from another less well-known volume, the *Dasam Granth*. The tenth Gurū, Govind Singh, also loved poetry and the *Dasam Granth* contains some of his works. *Dasam* means 'tenth'. The *Dasam Granth* was once part of the canon, and also bears the title Gurū. It is infused with the militancy of the warriors of yesteryear. Some say that tenth refers to the Gurū; others claim that the book is now only a tenth of what it once was, the rest having been lost.

The existence of two Granths leads to some confusion. The *Dasam Granth* should not be confused with the Damdama version of the Gurū Granth Sāhib, which is the version dictated from memory by Guru Govind Singh. The Gurū Granth Sāhib is solely concerned with the message of the divine *Nām* and liberation. The *Dasam Granth* is not in the same vein at all. It is mainly a collection of tales from the *Purāṇas*, with much emphasis on Kṛṣṇa and upon the demon-slaying mother goddess, Caṅdī. There are also some tales about the wiles of women, and most of this material seems to have little to do with religious beliefs as such. These works fill the major part of the book, and are not particularly well-known. The language of the *Dasam Granth* is mostly Braj Bhaśa, with some Persian and some Sādhukarī or Sant Bhaśa. (Braj is a language now spoken in Southwestern Uttar Pradesh, a variety of Hindi, which was used for literary writings by the élite in Panjab until the turn of the century, and Sādhukarī is the lingua franca used by Northern Indian holy men of the medieval period.)

Yet there are parts of the *Dasam Granth* which are familiar, and in everyday use among Sikhs. Poems from the *Dasam Granth* are used in the *amrit* initiation ceremony and every day, when the Sikh prayer, *Ardās*, is said, its opening lines are from *Caṅdī dī Vār*, a poem in praise of the demon-slaying goddess.

The *Dasam Granth* does not have the same status as the Gurū Granth Sāhib; perhaps it did among the warrior Akālīs of yesteryear. It was compiled over a hundred years later than the Gurū Granth Sāhib, and again there are stories about how it came to be in its present form. Tradition says that it was compiled by Bhai Mani Singh who was a companion of Guru Govind Singh. He included all of the present materials. There was a discussion subsequently about whether the book should be kept in its present form or whether those compositions for which the Gurū was personally responsible should be kept separately. There was disagreement, but a solution was offered by one Sikh who was on his way to Amritsar to kill an enemy who had committed sacrilege at the holy *Darbār Sāhib*. It was agreed that if the man were killed the book would be divided, with Guru Govind Singh's work in a separate volume from the other material. If he returned in triumph, enemy slain, the book would remain as it was. He triumphed.

There are arguments as to which pieces in the collection are the Gurū's personal writings. There are two works which may be called autobiographical. One of these is called the *Bachitar Nāṭak* (the strange miracle or amazing drama), which is about the life of the Gurū, describing the Gurū's lineage, previous existence and call from God. It tells about the period prior to his birth, when he was in the mountains practising austerities. God gave him a command, telling him how he had sent others into the world, but they had been deflected from their task and, in answer to the need, Govind Singh was to be sent to 'summon men to the path which all must follow. Preach to them the way of truth, and purge them of every evil way.' The Gurū stood, palms together, head bowed in reverence and assented: 'With your gracious aid to sustain my endeavours, I go into the world to preach the ways of truth (Das Granthī, *Bachitar Nāṭak* (n.d.): also translated in McLeod 1984: 58).

The strange miracle of the title is Govind Singh himself. It certainly appears to be autobiographical, though some people think that it may have been the work of a court poet. In *Bachitar Nāṭak*, there are stanzas in praise of God which are characteristic of Guru Govind Singh. In Guru Govind Singh's writings, God is often characterised as a warrior, all-steel, all-death, but a firm protector. God is shown in his martial splendour and awesome power. He is the Master of the Sword. In the Gurū's view, the creator sometimes intervenes to aid good in the struggle against evil. Divinely appointed instruments are entitled to use force against the wicked and in defending the claims of *dharma* (right). It was legitimate for him and his Sikhs to fight. The *Bachitar Nāṭak* describes the Gurū's own battles. It shows him as an earthly ruler as well as a religious leader.

Further evidence of his worldly role may be found in a famous letter which is also included in the *Dasam Granth*. It is called the *Zafarnāmā*, addressed to the Emperor Aurangzeb. The letter opens with an invocation to God and mentions some of his attributes. It mentions incidents in the Gurū's life and makes a series of moral points backing up the Gurū's stand in his struggles. The Gurū says that the Moghul state has departed from the demands of morality and religion and oppresses the people. It is from the *Zafarnāmā* that there comes the famous quotation: 'When all other means are ineffective, it is legitimate to take up the sword'.

The *Dasam Granth* includes other influential works expressing militant piety. They are familiar and are found in the little *guṭkā*, the prayer book that a person uses every day. They are used in the initiation ceremony and other daily worship. They include the *Jap* (not to be confused with Guru Nanak's *Japjī*, though it is also a meditative piece, reminiscent of the *Japjī*, concentrating on what we can say of God). Guru Govind Singh writes:

> God has no visible sign, no caste nor lineage.
> No one can describe his form, features or attire.
> He is immovable, self-enlightened and of infinite power.
> King of Kings; God of Gods, Master of the three worlds,
> The Lord of Creation; ruler of all beings, demigods, humans and demons.
> His indescribable nature is affirmed by the forests and meadows.
> Who can tell all of your names, O Lord?
> Only by your deeds can you be known.

Akāl Ustat (In praise of the Timeless One) concentrates on the splendour of God, fervently praising the one, all-powerful but merciful Lord. It also contains some inspiring passages in which the Gurū stresses that the differences which divide people are meaningless. Although they perform all manner of rituals and belong to various sects,

> All mankind is one and all men belong to a single humanity. . . . So too with God . . . for God is but one. . . . There is no difference between a temple and a mosque, nor between the prayers of a Hindu or a Muslim. Though differences seem to distinguish between them, in reality all men are the same.

The Gurū says that there are no differences between Gods, demons, celestial beings and human beings of different traditions.

> All are the same, none is separate; a single form, a single creation.
>
> As the sparks fly upward from a fire, each separate but then reuniting with the source, as dust disturbed flies through the air and again subsides, as water splashed from waves, so do all the living forms emerge and then return again to their source.
>
> (Das Granthī (n.d.): also translated in McLeod 1984: 55)

Of the poems about deities, the most popular and best known is *Caṅdī dī Vār*, a poem describing the demon-slaying acts of bravery of the goddess. This is sometimes claimed to be a composition of the Gurū. Although modern Sikhs reject the idea, there certainly was something of a fascination with the cult of the goddess during the eighteenth century.

The familiar pieces are a very small proportion of the whole book. The great bulk of the *Dasam Granth* consists of the myths and epics of Kṛṣṇa and Caṅdī, etc. There are 237 pages containing the poems mentioned above as against 1,185 of other material. Clearly, the material is not by one person. Some have raised the question as to why Guru Govind Singh should have wanted such material, if his ideas are truly represented in the poetry of militant piety and in the statements that all human beings are one.

The book relates to another age: it was more popular at one time than it now is. In any case, Govind Singh was an educated man, educated in Persian and Sanskritic traditions. He was a cultured man, who was interested in poetry, history, religious thought and ideas. The fact that such materials were collected does not necessarily imply endorsement of any kind. Some people have said that the writings were intended to instil warrior characteristics into his followers, others that, reading such matter, they would reject it and value their own Gurūs the more. It seems reasonable to suggest that the materials found in the *Dasam Granth* are entirely the kinds of work which might be expected from court poets and bards. In the era when this material was compiled, court bards were expected to sing legends and tales of war and valour, and to use these as a backdrop to eulogies of the family they served. In this case, the bravery and powers of deities form the backdrop for the Bedi and

Sodhi families and the adventures of their sons, the Gurūs. The ballads relating stirring battles fought by the goddess against demons, and a poetic inventory of weapons, would have provided court life with a striking musical background. Unfortunately, there has been little scholarly attention paid to the *Dasam Granth*.

Other works accepted for reading in gurdwaras

There are two other writers whose works are acceptable for reading in gurdwaras: Bhai Gurdas and Bhai Nand Lal. Bhai Gurdas Bhalla was a kinsman of the third Gurū and a close observer of the rule of at least three Gurūs, dying during the time of Guru Hargovind in about 1633. It was Bhai Gurdas who undertook the physical act of writing out the Gurū Granth Sāhib, but he was also a scholar and writer in his own right.

The first written stories about Guru Nanak appear in the *Vār*s of Bhai Gurdas. A *vār* is traditionally a heroic poem, an ode, but Bhai Gurdas uses the form to write about Sikh belief and history. (Nanak himself had used it to write about the ultimate hero – the True Gurū, God.) In his first *Vār*, Bhai Gurdas spends some time placing Nanak on the pinnacle of world history and the spiritual tree, charged with a mission. He was to preach the one true name in the age of evil. Gurdas was a theologian who recorded some incidents about the Gurūs, and was the first writer to extend our knowledge of the lives of the Gurūs and explain their doctrines. His work is viewed as the key to the Gurū Granth Sāhib. He is important because he lived during a crucial period of the development of the Sikh *Panth*. His life and times covered the period when the first institutions were developing through to the period when the *Panth* became increasingly militarised, with hostile relations with rivals and with local governments. He was a supporter of the claims of Guru Arjan against those of his brother Prithi Cand. He was a believer in the unity of the Guruship. He was a critic of all the rivals who opposed Gurus Arjan and Hargovind. He wrote of the criticism of Guru Hargovind (1595–1644):

> People say the former Gurūs used to sit in the Temple.
> The present Gurū roams from place to place.
> Former Emperors used to visit former Gurūs.
> The present Gurū was sent to prison by the Emperor.

In former times the followers found peace.
Now the Gurū is forever rushing around and terrified of nothing.
The former Gurūs used to console the Sikhs and instruct them in the arts of peace.
The present Gurū keeps hunting dogs and loves the chase.
The former Gurūs used to compose hymns and listen to them and sing them.
He does not keep the devout with him but takes enemies of faith and wicked persons.
Yet the truth cannot be concealed,
The Sikhs are enamoured of his lotus feet like bees.
He supports an intolerable burden but does not complain of it.

Bhai Gurdas was unswerving, totally committed to the defence of the line which he saw descending from Guru Nanak.

Bhai Nand Lal Goya

The other writer whose work is accepted for reading in gurdwaras is Bhai Nand Lal Goya, who was an associate of Guru Govind Singh. His works are not particularly militant in tone, and are more in the spirit of the Gurū Granth Sāhib. The authentic works are in Persian, the poetic language of the educated élite of the day, which has probably limited their popularity.

Nand Lal's name is also associated with some *rahit nāmā*s, *Khālsā* codes of conduct, though the quality of writing of the poetry and that of the *rahit nāmā*s makes it difficult to suppose that both were composed by the same person.

*Rahit nāmā*s: *Khālsā* codes of conduct

Sikhism, like other religions, has a tension between the loving, spiritual side and the legal, disciplinary side. It has produced its own codes of rules. In the early days, people would be expected to live in a certain manner, though the long lists of rules developed over a long period.

*Rahit nāmā*s lay down the *Khālsā* code of conduct. That it related to the *Khālsā* is significant, because *Sikh* and *Khālsā* were not necessarily identical. The *Khālsā* were originally persons under the direct supervision of the Gurū, not under a group of intermediaries, area organisers called *masands*, who were appointed by earlier Gurūs. The *masands* were prone to go off on their own paths and not obey the Gurū's wishes. Guru Govind Singh decided to rid the *Panth* of *masands* and make everyone a member of the *Khālsā*. According to tradition, in 1699 the Gurū called his followers together, instituted an initiation ceremony and announced a code of rules. However, there is no actual *rahit nāmā*, no code, actually written by the Gurū personally, and none which actually dates from 1699.

There are no historical sources which helpfully record all that happened at that time. Clearly, Govind Singh was interested in the nature of his own religious mission and saw himself as divinely appointed to save the *dharma*, using physical force if need be. Tradition traces the initiation ceremony back to that time. The wearing of long hair, and the bearing of arms were both early requirements (and five weapons were more common than five symbols in the early days).

The first indications of rules were recorded in some works of the early eighteenth century, the most famous being *Gur Śobhā*, a work whose primary purpose was to denounce *masands* and create allegiance to the Gurū rather than to record rules.

There are more *rahit nāmās* dating from the mid-eighteenth century onwards. An interesting and unusually lengthy version is that associated with Chaupa Singh Chibbar, a Brahman tutor and adviser to Guru Govind Singh. It contains injunctions, anecdotes about Guru Govind Singh, denunciations of the leadership of the day, warnings of disaster, but promises of ultimate triumph. The special position it maps out for Brahmans would make it suspect to Sikhs nowadays. This *rahit nāmā* has been translated by W.H. McLeod (1987). There are also four shorter *rahit nāmās* in poetic form. They are associated with Nand Lal, Prahlad Singh, Daya Singh and Desa Singh. The lines used every day in the *Ardās*, urging Sikhs to accept the Gurū Granth Sāhib as Gurū, come from Prahlad Singh. Words as oft quoted and as well known as *Rāj karegā Khālsā* (the *Khālsā* shall rule) come from the *rahit nāmā* attributed to Nand Lal. Hence, these sources should be taken seriously.

There are a couple of later, prose versions. *Rahit* is best regarded as an evolving system, growing formally and informally over time.

The concerns of the eighteenth century and those of the twentieth are hardly likely to be similar. Hence, old *rahit nāmā*s are often viewed with suspicion. Much of what they include is offensive to modern *Khālsā* taste. Older *rahit nāmā*s contain many strange injunctions. They are often very anti-Muslim, seeing Muslims as attacking the *dharma*. Another interesting point is that early *rahit nāmā*s make no mention of rites of passage. Specifically Sikh ones were not commonly used until the reform movement of the late nineteenth and early twentieth centuries.

Versions of *rahit nāmā*s appeared throughout the nineteenth century, but in the later part of that century, the reforming Singh Sabha movement emerged, and one of its objectives was the production of a satisfactory code. This was not easy. A version was produced in 1915, but it was not until 1950 that the modern, fairly short Sikh *Rahit Maryādā* appeared. This seems to have met with general approval, though not all Sikhs necessarily follow it to the letter.

*Rahit nāmā*s follow a pattern. They begin by stating the fundamental doctrines, briefly mentioning belief in the Timeless One, the Gurūs, and the Gurū Granth Sāhib. Then come rules for personal behaviour, covering practices and devotions. Some also cover rites, especially initiation, which is specifically a *Khālsā* rite – a *Khālsā*-making rite, in fact. *Rahit nāmā*s also specify sins, and punishments for wrongdoers. The worst sins are cutting one's hair, eating *ḥalāl* meat (killed in the Muslim manner), using tobacco and sleeping with anyone other than one's spouse.

*Hukam nāmā*s

*Hukam nāmā*s are commands, orders, written down as in a letter. There were *hukam nāmā*s issued by various Sikh Gurūs. Later *hukam nāmā*s were issued by Guru Govind Singh's wives and by the man Guru Govind Singh sent on a mission, Banda Bahadar, who fought on after the Gurū's death. Many historic *hukam nāmā*s were destroyed in the troubles in 1984 when the Library where they were kept in Amritsar caught fire. Official policy decisions are issued as *hukam nāmā*s from the seat of temporal authority in Amritsar, the *Akāl Takhat*, or Throne of the Timeless One. For example, in November 1973 one was issued declaring that a group called the

Sant Nirankārīs were renegades, and saying that no one should, in the traditional words, 'share food or daughters' (have relationships) with them. After the *Akāl Takhat* was burnt in 1984 there was a *hukam nāmā* similarly ostracising Baba Santa Singh Nihang and others for disregarding another *hukam nāmā*, forbidding them to undertake building work aimed at restoring the *Akāl Takhat*. *Hukam nāmā*s can be addressed to individuals or to the whole community.

Later writings

Apart from the scriptures, and the codes of conduct and orders mentioned, there are many other works which ought to be taken into account in order to understand modern Sikhism. It is a historical tradition and many writings have been produced over the years which have elapsed since the Gurūs lived. These writings show how the message changed and how the community developed throughout the years. They give it its character. They include the *janam sākhīs*, traditional tales of incidents in the life of Guru Nanak, the stories of the warrior Gurūs, and the development of *Khālsā* historiography.

FURTHER READING

Grewal, J.S. (1969) *Guru Nanak in History*, Chandigarh, Panjab University Press.

Grewal, J.S. and Bal, S.S. (1967) *Guru Gobind Singh*, Chandigarh, Panjab University Press.

Hans, Surjit (1988) *A Reconstruction of Sikh History From Sikh Literature*, Jalandhar, Abs Publications.

Juergensmeyer, M. and Barrier, N.G. (1979) *Sikh Studies: Perspectives on a Changing Tradition*, Berkeley, Berkeley Religious Studies Series.

Loehlin, C.H. (1958) *The Sikhs and Their Scriptures*, Lucknow, Lucknow Publishing House.

Macauliffe, M.A. (1909) *The Sikh Religion*, Oxford, Clarendon Press. (Reprinted (1963) Delhi, S. Chand).

McLeod, W.H. (1968) *Guru Nanak and the Sikh Religion*, Oxford, Oxford University Press.

McLeod, W.H. (1984) *Textual Sources for the Study of Sikhism*, Manchester, Manchester University Press.

McLeod, W.H. (1987) *The Chaupa Singh Rahit Nama*, Dunedin, University of Otago Press.
Rehat Maryādā (1978), Amritsar, Shiromani Gurdwara Prabandhak Committee.
Shackle, C. (1983) *An Introduction to the Sacred Language of the Sikhs*, London, School of Oriental and African Studies, University of London.
Singh, Shanta Serbjeet (1970) *Nanak the Guru*, Delhi, Orient Longmans.
Vaudeville, C. (1959) *Au cabaret de l'amour*, Paris, Gallimard.
Vaudeville, C. (1974) *Kabir*, Oxford, Oxford University Press.

7. Chinese Religions

Xinzhong Yao

Sacred writings in Chinese religion are presented in various forms in different religious traditions: Confucianism, Taoism and Buddhism. Since Buddhist sacred writings have been discussed in the chapter on *Buddhism*, what concerns us in this chapter are those of the Confucian and Taoist canons.

Confucian canon

Any survey of Chinese sacred writings must first consider those of Confucianism, which dominated Chinese political and religious life for more than two thousand years. 'Confucianism' in English is a misleading term, and even more when we talk about its sacred writings. It is true that *Kung Tzu* (Confucius) is venerated as its founder and has long been regarded as its greatest teacher. However, the term 'Confucianism' does not express the same meaning as its Chinese counterparts, *Ju Jia* (school of literati) or *Ju Jiao* (religion of literati). The extension of the latter is much wider than the 'school or religion of Confucius' and Confucians are devoted not only to Confucius' teachings but also to the teachings of all the Confucian classics. Though *Kung Jiao* (a religion of Confucius) is also a name for Confucianism, especially in its later development, Confucius is thought of as a focus of devotion much less than Jesus is in Christianity.

The sacred writings of *Ju Jia* have two sources, one originating in the pre-Confucian stage and the other in the Confucian and post-Confucian stage. Confucius thought of himself as a faithful transmitter of the ancient classics, not as a creator (Waley 1938:

123). Indeed, he was a *ju*, a member of the literati class whose main responsibilities were to preserve the ancient *li* (proprieties, ceremonies or rites) and apply the ancient knowledge to his own times. However, he was a great *ju*, because what he did was not only to preserve the ancient writings but to edit them, to transmit them and to develop them. By him, the ancient classics were systematised and were given a new spirit and motivation. From Confucius on, more and more masterpieces were added to the treasury of Confucian classics.

After Confucius, three important events were decisive for what we now know as the 'sacred writings' in Confucianism. The first was the 'burning of books' by the first Emperor of China in 213 BCE, which was a heavy blow to Confucian efforts to preserve the ancient classics. Among all the literature, only books on such subjects as medicine, divination and agriculture, and a few copies on other subjects, accidentally escaped this catastrophe. The second was the rediscovery or re-editing of Confucian classics during the Western Han dynasty (202 BCE–9 CE), when Confucians, facing the problems of the lack of reliable materials and the urgent needs of the new Empire, laboured to discover, reconstruct and even rewrite some or most of the lost Confucian classics, along with efforts to create new masterpieces. The third was the revival of Confucianism in the Sung dynasty (960–1279 CE), in which the Neo-Confucian movement re-interpreted these classics in the light of the new understanding of the world, society and human beings. This understanding was partly influenced by Taoist metaphysics and Buddhist epistemology, and partly characterised by the ideal or ideas explored in the *Book of Change*.

Since the Sung Dynasty, what have been regarded as Confucian sacred writings are 'Four Books and Five Classics', or their enlarged form, 'Thirteen Classics', most of which have been not only cherished and venerated by Confucian scholars, officials and school pupils, but also absorbed by Taoists and used by Buddhists. Due to the state-cult of Confucianism as well as to the use of Confucian classics as textbooks for the civil examination, these classics exerted a great influence on all the other religious organisations and movements, and on every aspect of the Chinese way of life.

THE FIVE CLASSICS

In Confucianism, there are two kinds of sacred writings: one is called *ching*, which originally meant the warp of fabrics, and then was extended to refer to the scripture, canon or classics, which were believed to have the same function for society as the warp had for fabrics. The other is called *shu*, which means sacred books. During their history, these Confucian classics and sacred books were presented in different combinations: in the period of the Spring and Autumn (722–481 BCE), and of the Warring States (403–221 BCE), it was the 'six classics' which were claimed as the authoritative writings. From Chuang Tzu's explanation of the six classics, we can see that at that time they were not exclusively confined to Confucianism (Watson 1968: 363). In the two Han dynasties (202 BCE–220 CE), there appeared several popular combinations of these classics: the 'five classics', the 'six classics', and the 'seven classics'. In the Tang dynasty (618–906 CE), they were developed into the 'nine classics', and by the Sung dynasty (960–1279 CE), the 'thirteen classics' were finally established, which became the most common form next to the 'four books and five classics'.

In all these combinations, the 'five classics' are the basic components, and they have been treated as the sacred records of the ancient culture, and believed to have covered its every aspect: politics, philosophy, history, poetry and religion.

First of all is *I Ching*, or *Book of Change*, which is the oldest religious handbook in China. At the centre of the text are the eight trigrams, which are composed of three lines of two kinds: the unbroken line which is the symbol of the male or positive principle, and the broken line which is the symbol of the female or negative principle. The eight trigrams compose, by putting one on the other, sixty-four hexagrams. Having divined with the milfoil, the diviner would get his or her hexagram(s). Then by consulting the *Book of Change*, an oracle message would be revealed. The *Book of Change* should have been one of the least disputed writings, since it had escaped the 'burning of books' because it was a book of divination. In fact, however, the *Book of Change* turned out to be one of the most problematic writings in Chinese literature, and its origin, author(s), symbols and commentaries have been hotly debated since the western Han dynasty. A traditional and orthodox opinion, though not without challenges and criticism, is that the legendary sage-king Fu Hsi (*r.* 2852 BCE) evolved *Pa Kua* or the 'eight trigrams' from the markings on the shell of a tortoise or the markings of a horse-dragon which appeared to him from the Yellow River; then the founders of the Chou dynasty (1122–256 BCE) formed the sixty-four hexagrams from the combination of two trigrams, and wrote some texts. It was said that at the time of Spring and Autumn, Confucius wrote several commentaries on it, so the *Book of Change* acquired two parts: text and commentaries. For a long time the *Book of Change* served both as a handbook of divination and as a sourcebook of religious and philosophical thinking.

Shu Ching, or *Book of History*, is the earliest Chinese historical book. It is composed of documents covering a period between the age of the legendary sages (third millennium BCE) and the middle of the Spring and Autumn (630 BCE). It is said that the *Book of History* was used by both Confucius and Mo Tzu to teach their disciples, and was treated as one of the sacred writings in these two schools. Originally, it had one hundred chapters. However, after the burning of books in the Chin dynasty (221–207 BCE), only twenty-nine chapters were recovered at the beginning of the western Han dynasty. (Another version of twenty-five chapters has long been regarded by most scholars as a forged work of the Han Confucians.) These twenty-nine chapters were divided into three parts, the book of *Yu-Hsia* which recorded the historical events before the Shang Dynasty (1766–1123 BCE), the book of the Shang dynasty, and the book of the Chou dynasty. Except for some documents which can be traced back to the Shang time, most of them were written by historians of the early Chou dynasty. Its contents cover four subjects: canons, counsels, announcements and oaths. It is believed that this book became one of the Confucian classics because its documents were arranged chronologically, with added prefaces, by Confucius, and because many of its ideas were regarded as the original source of Chinese philosophy, religion and politics. Confucians took it as the mirror of their own times and derived moral or religious teachings from the historical events.

Shih Ching, or *Book of Poetry*, is a collection of popular and religious poems, of which five possibly came from the Shang age, and most were written between the beginning of the Chou and the period of the Spring and Autumn. It is believed that Confucius selected three hundred and five from more than 3,000 pieces and arranged them under four headings; *feng* (wind or air), *hsiao ya* (lesser odes), *ta ya* (greater odes) and *sung* (hymns or eulogies). However, some scholars doubt that this work was edited by Confucius himself. One thing that is clear is that Confucius did use the *Book of Poetry* to teach his followers and said that all the three hundred poems could be summarised by one phrase: no evil thoughts (*Lu Yu*, see Waley 1938: 88). After that, it became a Confucian tradition that poems and other writings should be used for moral education.

Li Chi, or *Book of Rites*, is a collection of the rites, rituals and ceremonies of the Chou dynasty, most of which perhaps were written during the period of the Warring States or even later. In the western Han dynasty, a version of the *Book of Rites* of one hundred and thirty-one chapters began to circulate. What has been taken as one of the Confucian classics is an abridged edition of forty-nine chapters. Besides its religious and political significance, the *Book of Rites* got its fame both in Confucianism and in other schools mainly due to three of its chapters: *Ta Hsue* (the *Great Learning*), *Chung Yung* (the *Doctrine of the Mean*), and *Li Yun* (the *Evolution of Rites*). In the Sung dynasty, the *Great Learning* and the *Doctrine of the Mean* became two of the 'four books'.

Ch'un Ch'iu, or *Spring and Autumn Annals*, is a chronological record of the chief events in, or relating to, the state of Lu, the home state of Confucius, during the period from 722 BCE to 481 BCE. Spring and Autumn were taken as its name because each of its records was preceded by one of these two terms, which referred to the season when the event took place. According to Confucian understanding, its central aim was to set up norms for good government, to put usurping princes back in their proper places and to condemn misbehaving ministers, so that the harmony between heaven and humans, and the proper orders of the social life might be maintained or restored.

THE FOUR BOOKS

The five classics had been regarded as the most sacred writings in Confucianism until the Sung dynasty when the great neo-Confucian Chu Hsi (1130–1200) gave more attention to the four books and put them ahead of the five classics. Since then, these books, along with the five classics, were not only the most important theoretical works but also, from 1313 to 1905, were the standard textbooks for the state civil examination, which every educated person had to learn by heart.

Of these books, the first is *Lun Yu*, or the *Analects of Confucius*. Confucius spent all his life persuading the dukes or princes to adopt his political ideals, educating his disciples to pursue his *tao*, and editing the ancient literature to transmit it to later generations. He, as well as some of his immediate disciples, went from one state to another, experiencing both honours and difficulties, and making many comments on various subjects. Some of these experiences, comments and teachings were recorded and edited after his death by his disciples or followers of these disciples, and became what we know as the *Analects*. The work is composed of twenty books. Each book contains various numbers of chapters and most chapters are very short, some of them consisting of just a sentence. In the *Analects*, the systematic moral teachings were concerned with the virtues of *jen* (love or humanity), *li* (propriety and rituals), *chi* (wisdom), *yung* (courage) and *yi* (righteousness), with the ideal personality of *chun tzu* (the superior man) and *sheng jen* (the sage), and with the Golden Rule: 'Do not do to others what you would not like yourself' (Waley 1938: 162) and 'Help others get what you desire and help others reach what you want' (Waley 1938: 122). In this book, Confucius also expresses his firm will to carry out the *tao* of Heaven and his deep beliefs in Heaven and its mandate.

The second and third books, as stated above, came from *Li Chi* or the *Book of Rites*'s two chapters, that is, the *Great Learning*, and the *Doctrine of the Mean*. By absorbing certain Taoist and Mohist ideas, they formed a syncretic system of Confucian morality and cosmology, politics and religion.

The *Great Learning* is believed to be a work of one of Confucius' disciples, Tseng Tzu. It purports to teach people how to learn and practise 'the great *tao*'. In this book, the author explains what one should do if one wants to govern the whole world well. It is not achieved by arms, nor by power or law, but by moral strength. The first paragraph points out that the '*tao* of great learning' is composed of three parts: to exemplify virtue, to love people and to rest in the highest good. In order to achieve these goals, one should first cultivate one's character, which is the beginning of every progress. In particular, it outlines eight steps, which are also called the 'eight items': investigating things; extending knowledge; making the will sincere; rectifying the mind; cultivating the personal life; regulating the family; governing the state; and pacifying the world. These eight items were believed to be one of the most efficient weapons which true Confucians could use to fight against the corruption of politics and save the world from the chaos.

The *Doctrine of the Mean* is believed to be a work of the grandson of Confucius, written around the fifth century BCE. If the *Great Learning* is a search for the *tao* of governing the world, the *Doctrine of the Mean* is a search for the cultivation of an individual's personality and for becoming a sage. This *tao* is not simply to pursue the middle course, but to follow the harmonious process of the universe. In order to follow the '*Tao* of the Mean', one has to keep one's mind sincere: *cheng*. Sincerity enables people to transcend and develop their nature: those who possess sincerity achieve what is right without effort, understand without thinking, and naturally and easily embody the *tao*. Sages are those who, by their sincerity, stand between Heaven and Earth and with them form a triad. This theory was accepted as orthodox Confucianism, and the goal of the 'triad' became a Confucian ideal.

The fourth book is *Mencius* or the *Book of Mencius*, possibly edited by his disciples. Mencius (371–289 BCE) was a great Confucian thinker in the period of the Warring States, and later was regarded as the second sage in Confucianism next to Confucius himself. His book has seven chapters, and each chapter has two parts. Its central topics aim to propagate Confucian ideals and to attack heterodox teachings. In this book, Mencius, by arguing with other schools, expounds his own doctrines, such as the original goodness of human nature, the unity of humans with Heaven, the possibility for everybody to become a sage, the benevolent government, and so on. His moral teachings (for example, when life and righteousness cannot be both retained, one should give up one's life and adhere to one's moral ideal), have been regarded as a noble attitude towards life and death. In this book, the author also explains how to cultivate one's own character by accumulating *chi* (spiritual power) and *yi* (moral merit), which lends some mysticism to the book: Chi 'is most great and most strong. Being nourished by uprightness and sustaining no injury, it fills up all between Heaven and Earth' (quoted in Fung, Vol. I, 1952–53: 131). All these ideas were cherished by later Confucians, and became dominant teachings in Confucianism.

OTHER CONFUCIAN CLASSICS

Besides the five classics and four books discussed above, there are other classics which also had an important position in the Confucian canon.

Yue Ching, or *Book of Music*, was once an important classic for Confucianism. Because in Confucius' time music was related closely to the poem, it was said that when he edited the *Book of Poetry*, he arranged a musical setting for each of the poems, either revising the old tunes or composing new ones. He attached the utmost importance to the moral effect of music and believed that music could not only create harmony in one's emotions, but also bring order out of social chaos. Hsun Tzu, in his book, included a chapter 'On Music', which highlights the significance of music and takes good or evil music respectively as the reason for the universal harmony or social disorder. (Dubs 1977: 247–58). However, this book was completely lost in the period of the Chin and Han dynasties, and after that time, its position in the 'Thirteen Classics' has been replaced by *Chou Li* (the *Rites of Chou*).

Hsiao Ching, or *Book of Filial Piety*, is the shortest classic in the Confucian canon. It is supposed to have been written by some followers of a disciple of Confucius. Although its contents are very shallow and its language simple and crude, it was chosen as one of the Confucian classics in the early Han dynasty because it took filial piety as the root of all virtues and the source of moral education.

Taoist canon

'Taoism' is also a misleading word because it confuses two names of Taoism: *Tao Jia* (school of Taoist philosophers) and *Tao Jiao* (Taoist religion). The former refers to those philosophers who believed in, and practised, *Tao*, such as Lao Tzu and Chuang Tzu in the age of pre-Chin (before 221 BCE), and Neo-Taoists in the period of the Wei-Ch'in dynasties (220–420 CE). The latter refers to the theories, practices and movements of the Taoist religion, which arose in the first or second century CE. Although both of them talked about *tao* and took the unification with *tao* as their ideal, their differences were still very obvious. *Tao Jia*'s main interest was in theoretically explaining the cosmic principle and exploring the way of life, while *Tao Jiao*'s concern was the practices relating to longevity or immortality.

In the history of Taoism, philosophers, magicians and practitioners contributed thousands of writings to Taoist belief and practice. The first of the individual attempts to put these writings in order, besides the list given in Pan Ku's (32–92 CE) *Han Shu* (the *Book of Han Dynasty*), was made by Ko Hung (283–343 CE), who summarised, or listed, in his work *Pao Pu Tzu*, all Taoist articles and books which he could collect. Lu Hsu Ching (406–477 CE) first made a classification of Taoist writings into 'three caverns', which became a standard structure of the Taoist canon. The first edition of such a canon, sponsored and decreed by the emperor, appeared in the Tang dynasty, and was said to include around 3,744 or 5,700, or even 7,300, rolls (volumes); however, it was soon lost in the war and the chaos of rebellion. In the successive Sung, Yuan (1260–1368 CE) and Ming (1368–1644) dynasties, several similar editions came into being, in which the volume numbers of the collected writings ranged from more than 4,000 to near 8,000 rolls. These came to be called *Tao Tsang*, i.e., Taoist canon. The Taoist canon was organised according to the structure of 'Three Caverns' and 'Four Supplements' with different central classics; however, in fact, each of them covers almost every topic of Taoist beliefs and practices, from pure philosophical arguments to the formula of immortality. The forms of these several thousand rolls can be put, according to Boltz (1987: 319–27), into several categories, such as revelation and rituals; hagiography; topography, epigraphy and historiography; literary collections and dialogic treatises; and encyclopedic anthologies. However, the most prominent parts of *Tao Tsang* concern immortality. On the basis of this concern, its contents can be classified into three subjects: (1) the philosophical foundation of immortality, such as theories of *tao*, theories of *chi*, and theories of Nature; (2) the theological framework for immortality, such as the myths of creation, the relationship between gods and human beings, and prayer, worship, disciplines and rituals; (3) the methods or techniques for attaining immortality, such as control of breathing, alchemy, abstention from grains, gymnastics, sexual techniques, medical approaches, and so on.

TAO TE CHING

Lao Tzu, according to the famous Han historian Ssu Ma Chien's *Records of History*, was believed to have been an official of Imperial Archives of the Chou dynasty, living around the sixth century BCE. When he grew old, he felt disgusted with public life, so resigned his post to live the life of a hermit. He went to the west of China. When he passed the frontier of Han Ku, the keeper (Yin Hsi) of the frontier requested him to write something before he withdrew from this world, so that people could know, study and practise his teachings. He wrote eighty-one chapters of 5,000 characters, which were later divided into two parts. One part, starting with the concept of *tao*, was called *Tao Ching*; the other, *te*, which means *tao*'s individualisation or power, was called *Te Ching*. The whole book became what we know as *Tao Te Ching* (the *Book of Tao and Its Power*).

Tao Te Ching is the primary source for the Taoist concept of *tao*, which is the basis of all Taoist beliefs and practices. In *Tao Te Ching*, Lao Tzu describes the *tao* as the ontological reality and universal principle. In his words, *tao* existed before heaven and earth and is the 'mother of the world' (chapter 25), and is the 'Valley', because it could embrace everything (chapter 6). In Lao Tzu's mind, *tao* existed before the universe, created the universe and yet was independent. Just because *tao* is the beginning of all the beginnings, is the essence of all ordinary things, Lao Tzu thinks it impossible to talk about *tao*: 'The Way (Tao) that can be spoken of is not the constant way; the name that can be named is not the constant name' (chapter 1). Even Lao Tzu himself does not know its name, so he has to call it *tao* or the greatness (chapter 25). However, this *tao*, which cannot be named, can be practised. To learn *tao* is to identify oneself with it. Those who identify themselves with *tao* will reach eternity. In order to become one with *tao*, it is necessary to get rid of knowledge and desires, to be sincere, to be humble, and to return to one's original state. To follow the way of water is the essence of what Lao Tzu taught. Although water seems very weak, there is nothing it cannot overcome. The metaphor of water highlights *Tao Te Ching*'s philosophy of life: non-action, which means that humans should not do anything contrary to the way of *tao*.

Although *Tao Te Ching* was not originally intended to initiate a religious movement, its concept of *tao* was soon seen as a revealed message by those people who sought the ways of longevity, and was venerated as a sacred concept of a mass movement which was called *Tao Jiao* – Taoist religion. Lao Tzu was deified as the initiator of Taoist religion, and was worshipped as *Tai Shang Lao Chun* (Lord Lao the Most High), one of three embodiments of *Yuan Shi T'ien Chun* (Taoist God). *Tao Te Ching* became one of the most sacred Taoist classics, and the main source of theories and practices of Taoist religion. In the Tang dynasty, due to the same surname shared by the imperial family and Lao Tzu, *Tao Te Ching* was regarded as the book of the royal ancestor, and was commented by the emperor (Hsuan Tsung); it was one of the required texts for the civil service examination, and was a necessary possession of every family, which was partly responsible for its popularity since then.

BOOK OF CHUANG TZU

Another important classic of Taoism is *Chuang Tzu* (the *Book of Chuang Tzu*), written by the philosopher Chuang, or recorded and edited by his disciples. Chuang Tzu was a contemporary of Mencius, and held a petty official's post in his native state for a short period, but he soon resigned and moved to a mountain area, living an isolated life. His book is composed of three parts: the first seven chapters are called the *Inner Book*, which is generally regarded as the true work of Chuang Tzu himself; the second part is called the *Outer Book*, which may come from his direct disciples; and the third part is called the *Added Book*, which might have been added by later Taoists.

Chuang Tzu is an idealist who takes as his ideal absolute freedom, and thinks that this freedom can be achieved only by identifying one's self with *tao*. A person who has attained *tao* is called *chen jen* (the 'true person'). Although Chuang Tzu also used many other terms to describe this ideal personality, such as *chih jen* (the 'perfect person'), *sheng jen* (the 'holy person') and *shen jen* (the 'spiritual person'), *chen jen* is a general ideal image which was accepted by later Taoists. According to the *Book of Chuang Tzu*, *chen jen* has no worries and anxiety because now life and death are seen as nothing but the passage of nature or different forms of natural transformation: 'Life and death are fated – constant as the succession of dark and dawn' (Watson 1968: 80). Life is like spring, and death like winter; they are but the passage of nature. *Chen jen* is one with *tao*, so becoming invincible and immortal. Such a person no longer lives by bread and grain, but by the cosmic air and spiritual breath. In chapter six, Chuang Tzu says that the True Person

> could climb the high places and not be frightened; could enter the water and not get wet; could enter the fire and not get burned. . . . [The True Person] slept without dreaming and woke without ease . . . breathes with his heels . . . knows nothing of loving life and nothing about hating death.
>
> (Watson 1968: 77–8)

In Taoist religion, Chuang Tzu, as one of Lao Tzu's two immediate disciples, was granted the title of *Nan Hua Chen Jen* (the true person of *Nan Hua*) and his work became *Nan Hua Chen Ching* (the *True Scripture of Nan Hua*).

PAO PU TZU

Among the thousands of Taoist religious writings, one of the earliest and most influential is Ko Hung's *Pao Pu Tzu*. Ko Hung (284–364 CE), the most important Taoist theoretician, physician and alchemist of his time, called himself *Pao Pu Tzu*, which means 'Master of grasping simplicity', and he used this name as the title of his main work. *Pao Pu Tzu* is an encyclopedic work, collecting together most of the methods and formulae practised by various groups of Taoists at that time. The work has two sections, the *Inner Book* with twenty chapters, dealing with alchemic processes, drugs of immortality, ways of nourishing the body, prolonging life, avoiding disasters and escaping from harm; and the *Outer Book*, with fifty chapters, which deals with matters of Taoist philosophy and ethics. The significance of *Pao Pu Tzu* for Taoist religion is that, on the one hand, it systematised Taoist beliefs and practices of immortality, and on the other, combined Taoist ideas with Confucian ethics. He repeatedly talks about the accumulation of merits as an effective way to reach immortality:

> Those who seek immortality must set their minds to the accumulation of merits and the accumulation of good work. Their hearts must be kind to

> all things. They must treat others as they treat themselves, and extend their Jen (love or humanity) even to insects. They must rejoice in the fortune of men and pity their suffering, relieve the destitute and save the poor'.
>
> (de Bary et al. 1960: 262)

It is obvious that these moral teachings are far away from the earlier Taoist masters who alienated themselves from morality and social propriety but are quite near that of Confucianism.

Compared with the Confucian canon, the Taoist canon is confused and disordered. Its contents are so diverse and its dimensions are so huge that virtually nobody can read all *Tao Tsang*, which functions only as a huge 'encyclopedia', available only to a few people. Each of the Taoist sects venerates different parts, which makes it almost impossible to say which were or are the most important sacred writings of Taoism. What we have done in this chapter is to give only a brief introduction to several books which are widely accepted as Taoist masterpieces, as we did in the Confucian case. The sacred and revered writings of Chinese religions, however, are a constant invitation to further exploration and reading.

FURTHER READING

Boltz, Judith Magee (1987) 'Taoism: Taoist Literature', in Mircea Eliade (ed.) *Encyclopedia of Religion*, vol. 14, New York, Macmillan.

Chan, Wing-tsit (1987) 'Chinese Religion: Religious and Philosophical Texts', in Mircea Eliade (ed.) *Encyclopedia of Religion*, vol. 3, New York, Macmillan.

de Bary, Wm. Theodore, et al. (1960) *Sources of Chinese Tradition*, New York, Columbia University Press.

Dubs, Homer H. (trans) (1977) *The Works of Hsuntse*, London, A Probsthain.

Fung, Yu-lan (1952–53) *A History of Chinese Philosophy*, Volume I and Volume II, translated by Derk Borde, London, Allen & Unwin.

Lau, D.C. (trans) (1963) *Lao Tzu: Tao Te Ching*, London, Penguin.

Chen, Li Fu (1972) *The Confucian Way: A New and Systematic Study of the 'Four Books'*, Taipei, The Commercial Press.

Thompson, Laurence G. (1973) *The Chinese Way in Religion*, Belmont, Ca., Dickenson.

Waley, Arthur (trans) (1938) *The Analects of Confucius*, London, Allen & Unwin.
Watson, Burton (trans) (1968) *The Complete Works of Chuang Tzu*, New York, Columbia University Press.
Wilhelm, Richard (1972) *Confucius and Confucianism*, London, Routledge & Kegan Paul.

8. Japanese Religions

Ian Reader

As befits its breadth and diversity, the Japanese religious world has developed a rich and complex tradition of sacred texts and writings ranging from philosophical, theoretical, mythic and ritual texts within the established religious traditions of Shinto and Buddhism, to the collections of miracle tales and legends of the folk religious world, which express in a literary style religious messages and meanings accessible to the ordinary person. Adding to this broad textual and literary tradition are the countless sacred writings that have developed out of the Japanese new religions that represent the most striking and vibrant phenomenon in contemporary Japanese religion. Just as the founders of Buddhist sects in Japan have bequeathed a textually rich heritage to the sects they have founded, so too have the founders of such new religions produced a corpus of sacred writings that are specific to, and that have taken on the mantle of sacred writ for, the particular new religion in question. Often, too, the new religions, especially those of Buddhist orientation, have centred their teachings on particular Buddhist texts within the mainstream Buddhist tradition, giving them new and distinct emphases specific to that new religion.

Shinto: sacred texts and mythical history

The indigenous Japanese religious tradition of Shinto has, in many respects, clarified, defined and given an ethnic slant to many of the unstructured notions inherent in Japanese folk religion, notably concepts concerning the polarities between, on the one hand, purity and the inherent powers of life within the world of natural phenomena and, on the other hand, the dangerous effects of pollution, death and disorder. Shinto also expresses and crystallises, within a religious framework, implicit ideas concerning the identity and special nature of the Japanese as a race and nation, particularly concerning the relationship that exists between them and the *kami* (Shinto deities), and between the *kami*, the Japanese people and the Japanese Imperial family.

Probably the best known, and most widely commented upon texts connected with the Shinto tradition (and implicitly, with the Japanese Imperial tradition, as well as with the general parameters of Japanese religion) are the *Kojiki* ('Record of Ancient Matters') and the *Nihon Shoki* (*Nihongi*, 'Chronicles of Japan').[1] These two texts were completed in the early eighth century CE, using the Chinese writing system imported from the continent. Both were constructed at the instigation of the Japanese Court and had, as one of their underlying purposes, the legitimation of the rule of the Imperial institution. While it is fair to state that neither of these texts was widely read at any time (save at the Court and by various nationalist scholars) (Earhart 1982: 31), they are nevertheless important in that they express themes central to Shinto and Japanese perceptions of the world, outlining major Japanese cosmogonic myths and expressing, in the form of a 'mythistory' (i.e., the construction of a mythical history[2]), a sense of legitimation, identity and purpose for the Japanese people and state. As such, also, they have been used as the basis for numerous nationalistic interpretations by Japanese writers over the centuries, such as those by Motoori Norinaga (1730–1801), whose studies of these early texts and of the pre-Buddhist Japanese language formed part of an endeavour to assert the culturally unique content of Shinto.

While the *Nihon Shoki* is largely a mythological account of early Japanese Emperors expressed in quasi-historical form, it is in the *Kojiki* that the more overt motifs of religious concern are found. This text recounts the mythological formation of Japan and its people, and their descent from the *kami*, and thereby establishes, within the structure of this myth, the notion implicit in Shinto of the special and distinct nature of the Japanese.

In the mythical stories told in the *Kojiki*, Japan is depicted as being created through the union of two *kami*, the female Izanami and the male Izanagi. After then giving birth to a host of deities that give life to the land, Izanami dies while bringing forth the fire-god; this death is a reminder that mortality strikes all, even gods, and shows how chaos may lurk close beneath the surface of order. Izanagi, unable to bear life apart from his consort, goes to the underworld to seek her, and there finds her body ravaged by the pollutions of decay and death. Shocked by the sight, he reflects the basic horror of the living at the incursion of death into the world, and at the pollution it brings, by fleeing. She, reflecting the implicit notion that the spirits of the dead seek to remain near those they were close to in life, and also manifesting the view that death is contagious, dangerous, and malevolent, pursues him. He escapes from the underworld, rolling a rock across the barrier to separate this from other worlds. When she threatens to wreak havoc by killing 1,000 people a day if this separation is not ended, he promises to counter this by bringing forth 1,500 people a day. Izanagi then bathes to wash away the impurities of death, and through this bathing gives birth to a number of other deities, most importantly Amaterasu, the sun goddess, from whom the Imperial family subsequently, in the myths, was to descend. Among the various other myths recounted in the text are the descent of the first Emperor, Jimmu, from Amaterasu, and of the Japanese people.

Though texts such as the *Kojiki* were not widely read in early Japan, and although their primary focus was in legitimating the position and prestige of the Imperial Court, the myths that they contain, such as those depicted in the Izanami–Izanagi cycle, do express and give form to basic elements within Shinto and within the Japanese folk-religious perception of the universe, and it is for such reasons that they are important. In them we can discern numerous themes that run throughout the Japanese religious world, such as the close relationship between the *kami*, the land of Japan and the Japanese who are their descendants, the anthropomorphic nature of the gods who grieve and are unable to stand separation (as with Izanagi) and who show dangerous malice and desire to drag their kin off to the underworld (as with Izanami), the fearful and polluting nature of death, the affirmation of the superiority of the powers of regeneration, and the importance of ritual acts of purification, as exhibited by Izanagi's bathing, which themselves are life-producing acts. The texts also affirm that the role of the *kami* is to help in the fertile and happy development of life on earth, and this again is a paramount theme running throughout Shinto, much of the ritual focus of which is concerned with the amelioration of life in the present.

There have been other texts that have, over the centuries, assumed major importance in Shinto. Prominent among these has been the *Engi Shiki*, a tenth-century collection of government ordinances that included numerous details of ritual procedures at shrines, such as the rites for the rebuilding of the most sacred Shinto shrines at Ise, a rite pregnant with themes of regeneration and renewal that is carried out every twenty years, and the regulations for Imperial enthronement, a rite that continues to this day to be carried out in a Shinto framework. The *Engi Shiki* also contains a number of examples of *norito*, Shinto ritual prayers, that are important elements in the processes of worship and supplication. Because it functions as a guide to important Shinto rituals, the *Engi Shiki* continues to be studied by the Shinto priesthood today.

As befits a religion which is largely concerned with ritual action and practice and which has little in the way of doctrinal focus, it is in the textual reproduction of rituals and of the prayers (*norito*) that any unifying foundation approaching canonical status may be found in Shinto sacred writings (Kitagawa 1987: 63). *Norito* are recited in various situations by the Shinto priesthood when making supplications to the *kami*. They also serve to commemorate events both legendary and historical, to detail liturgies for rituals, and to express individual prayers. Those in the *Engi Shiki* for instance, include prayers for good harvests, for the prevention of calamities, and for the pacification of spirits. Many have since been composed by individual priests, while numerous shrines have developed their own styles of *norito* and ritual texts. Nonetheless, it remains common for shrines to use the collections and forms of *norito* standardised and compiled in the pre-war period and currently used by the Jinja Honcho, the Shinto Shrines Association.

A concept important especially within the traditions of *norito*, but relevant to all uses of prayers, invocations and spells in Japan, is that of *kotodama*, the sacred power of words. Certain words and sounds are considered to contain an innate power to bring about good and, as a result, the recitation of sacred words is considered to produce, through the powers of *kotodama*, a spiritual effect that influences events within the world. It is primarily within this context that the efficacy of *norito* is located. The concept of words and sounds containing power is not limited to Shinto, however, but comes out most strongly also in Japanese Buddhism, in which various *mantra*s and ritual imprecations believed to contain spiritual power are widely used in a variety of circumstances, from the exorcism of evil spirits to praying for good fortune.

Japanese Buddhism: canonical texts and sectarian writings

Japan adopted the Mahāyāna form of Buddhism, embellishing it with numerous sects that developed within a Japanese framework. Prominent among these are the esoteric Tendai and Shingon sects, and the Zen, Pure Land and Nichirenist sects. All have developed their own scriptural traditions based on the works of their founders, but they have also been deeply influenced by various texts from the Buddhist canon, in particular the *Lotus Sūtra*. This *sūtra* teaches that the only valid form of salvation is the attainment of buddhahood (a state which is not limited in space and time), and that all beings possess *buddha*-nature and thus are innately bound to become enlightened and to partake of the fruits of eternal buddhahood. The *Lotus Sūtra* further states that earlier Buddhist scriptures and teachings are merely preliminary, skilful means designed to lead people forward on to the true path of enlightenment. It forms a basis of the teachings in Tendai, a sect from which many others have developed in Japan, and it has been studied and used widely in Tendai rituals as well as in Nichiren Buddhism and Zen. In the Nichirenist sects, this text, and especially its introductory invocation, *namu myoho renge kyo* ('hail to the wonderful law of the *Lotus Sūtra*'), has become the primary focus not just of doctrinal study but also of ritual practice and worship. Various lay-centred new religions such as Soka Gakkai and Risshokoseikai that have emerged out of the Nichirenist tradition in the present century have also used invocations of the *Lotus Sūtra* as the basis of their teaching. The Nichirenist new religion, Reiyukai, has even produced a short and simplified version of this text, known at the *Blue Sūtra*, which is recited and used in rituals by its lay membership.

Besides the *Lotus Sūtra*, the most widely used Buddhist text in Japan is the shorter *Heart Sūtra*, the *Hannya Shingyo*. This short text, written in Buddhist Chinese and recited using the Japanese pronunciation of the ideograms, is used across much of the Buddhist spectrum in Japan, both as a text exemplifying the essence of Buddhist teachings about emptiness (*śunyata*) and as an efficacious ritual chant or prayer. The ideas expressed in the *Hannya Shingyo* are widely known in Japan, and have been outlined also in the countless commentaries that are available in Japan that explain, in everyday language, both this and other popular Buddhist texts, written by priests, academics and educated laymen alike. Few Japanese are unaware of the text and of such phrases as *shiki zoku ze ku, ku soku ze shiki* ('form is no other than emptiness, emptiness is no other than form'), which lie at the core of its philosophical content.

However, while many Japanese may read about the explications of Buddhist thought expressed in the text, it is not primarily for its philosophical content that it has become so widely used. It is the invocation most commonly heard being recited by laypeople when praying at Buddhist temples in Japan, and is widely regarded as a powerful incantation. Its rhythmic sound and brevity (it consists of only 262 ideograms[3]) make it easily memorised, and it takes only a few moments to chant. It also ends with a Japanised pronunciation of the short Sanskrit mantric recitation that concludes the original text, and this has long been regarded as an efficacious prayer or spell in its own right, considered by some commentators as being at the core of the text's popularity. However, it is probably more accurate to say that it is the text as a whole that has assumed, in popular perspective, the nature of a ritual incantation, and it is for this reason that it is so widely used when people – priests and laity alike – make supplications and acts of worship at Buddhist temples in Japan.

The text is also widely used in the popular Japanese Buddhist practice of *shakyo* in which people use a brush pen to copy or transcribe Buddhist texts. The practice is considered to be a way of creating merit for the practitioner, and is often performed when someone wishes to make supplications to Buddhist figures of worship. The *Hannya Shingyo* is ideal for such practices due to its brevity, and it is the most commonly transcribed text in Japan.

FOUNDERS AND SECTARIAN WRITINGS

The Japanese Buddhist tradition has also produced a strong sectarian tradition of sacred writings. Usually these have been the writings of sect founders, which outline and systematise the teachings and practice of the sect in question. Thus, in Shingon Buddhism the writings of the monk Kukai (774–835), who established Shingon in Japan, are core elements in the Shingon canon, and are still studied by Shingon priests today. These include such writings as the *Sokushin jobutsugi* ('The principle of the attainment of Buddhahood in this body'), in which he expounds the Shingon view that enlightenment is directly attainable in one's present existence.

Of the two major Zen sects, Rinzai and Soto, the former has continued to display a strong connection with the textual writings of Chinese Zen masters such as Lin Ch'i (Japanese: Rinzai). Many of such writings are in the form of *koan*, short, often seemingly nonsensical sayings or questions (possibly the best-known being the question 'What is the sound of one hand clapping?') that are used as meditational tools designed to illuminate the mind and lead it to enlightenment. Although Soto Zen has paid less attention to *koan*-focused literature, it has developed an extensive sacred canon in Japan based largely on the writings of its thirteenth-century Japanese founder, Dogen, whose numerous works are concerned as much with practical rules for every aspect of monastic life, from meditation to the way that one should wash one's face and carry out everyday actions of social etiquette, as they are with more apparently philosophical matters. Dogen's writings still serve as the primary source of legitimation for Soto to this day, especially his magnum opus, the *Shobogenzo* ('The eye and treasury of the true law'), in which he argues that practice and enlightenment are indivisible. In an attempt to make Dogen's teaching more accessible (it is written in a complex mixture of Buddhist Chinese and thirteenth-century Japanese), a simplified and abridged text, the *Shushogi* ('the principle of practice and enlightenment'), was compiled from his writings by sect leaders in the late nineteenth century. Though this text omitted important aspects such as Dogen's insistence on the centrality of meditation and taking monastic vows, it has provided a framework, through an emphasis on morality and repentance, for lay Buddhist life, and has become the basis for contemporary Soto Zen teaching to the present. Nonetheless, despite this intended simplification of Dogen's writing, it remains rather inaccessible to the ordinary layperson, and the sect has found it necessary to produce numerous commentaries and contemporary explanations of the text for its members.

The writings of Honen and Shinran, founders respectively of the Pure Land (Jodo) and True Pure Land (Jodo Shinshu) sects, with their emphasis on praising the salvific mercy of the Buddha of the

Pure Land, Amida, have been core elements in the developments of those traditions. They have also been influential in establishing the recitation practices of the *nembutsu*, the invocation of praise to Amida, that are central to these sects. The writings of Nichiren are equally prominent in the sect he founded, and have contributed very much to its nationalistic orientations. Nichiren considered there to be a special and sacred relationship between the Japanese people, the state and the *Lotus Sūtra*. This nationalistic interpretation was first developed by Saicho, the founder of the Tendai sect, who argued for a state run along Buddhist principles with the *Lotus Sūtra* as its guiding precept and as its spiritual protector. Nichiren took this further, not only considering the *Lotus Sūtra* to contain the essence of all Buddhism, but also seeing it as a source of spiritual power designed to give strength to the Japanese state, and inciting people to chant it when the country was faced by danger. This idea has been expressed in various guises by some of the Nichirenist new religious movements in the contemporary era. Nichiren further expressed his views in writings such as the *Rissho Ankokuron*, in which he not only urged the state to adopt the *Lotus Sūtra* as a national creed and to accept his teachings, but also criticised other sects including Zen, Shingon and the Pure Land sects.

While the writings of such founders have framed the outlooks and nature of those sects, it is fair to say that they have not been all that widely studied outside sectarian bounds. Though there has been a continuing sectarian tradition of textual commentary and interpretation, this has largely been the preserve of the priestly and intellectual élites, and has rarely involved or affected the rank and file laity. In recent years, however, a gradual and emerging tradition of academic and philosophical study of some of these founders, notably Dogen, has developed, and some attempts have been made to discuss them outside of sectarian borders and to examine their universalistic dimensions. Nonetheless, it is still fair to say that the majority of the sacred writings that have emerged within the Japanese Buddhist tradition remain locked within sectarian bounds, and more specifically, largely within the confines of the priestly élites.

Folk tales and miracle stories

Besides these official textual traditions, there has developed in Japan a whole host of popular religious texts and stories which express basic folk-religious perceptions and ideas. A large number of these can be classed as folk Buddhist, and range from *engi*, foundation legends detailing how temples came to be founded and outlining the apparently miraculous powers of the Buddhist figures enshrined at them, to *setsuwa*, tales that recount miraculous and mythical events in order to teach some moralistic lesson and promote Buddhist devotion.

Both *setsuwa* and *engi* were used by itinerant preachers to spread the messages of Buddhism and to promote the powers of specific temples and *buddha* figures. Among the most important examples of this popular tradition is the *Nihon Ryoiki*, a collection of miracle tales written in the ninth century by the Buddhist monk, Kyokai, that especially focused on the intercessionary powers of the Buddhist figure of mercy, Kannon. The *Nihon Ryoiki* abounds with stories of Kannon's merciful interventions to save people from all sorts of woe along with tales of retribution that occur when people break moral laws.[4] The tradition of *setsuwa* and miracle stories remains alive in the present, especially in connection with the popular Japanese practice of pilgrimage, while many temples continue to produce collections of *engi* and *setsuwa* to inspire their visitors.

Such writings are inspirational and populist in nature, and have often been used as the basis for sermons and as devices to put religious messages across to wide audiences. Although perhaps not canonical in the sense in which the writings of Buddhist or new religions' founders have been, they have still played a very important part in the development of the popular, folk-based Buddhism that remains alive in Japan today.

Texts and sacred writings in Japanese new religions

Like Shinto and Buddhism, the Japanese new religions have also developed their own traditions of sacred writings. In particular, the writings of the founders of new religions have often assumed canonical status within the particular religion concerned, though rarely having much impact outside it. An example would be the *Ofudesaki* (literally, 'writing from the tip of a brush'), the copious volumes of inspirational, automatic writing by Nakayama Miki, the illiterate nineteenth-century foundress of the new religion Tenrikyo, which were 'dictated' to her by a possessing deity considered, in Tenrikyo, to be the creator of the universe. In Tenrikyo the

Ofudesaki are considered to be revelatory sacred writings that contain the essence of its religious teachings and of its explanations of the nature of the universe. They have ever since formed the basis of Tenrikyo's teaching, with numerous commentaries being written about them by Tenrikyo teachers and officials to this day. Oomoto is another new religion that regards the automatic revelatory writings of its foundress, Deguchi Nao, as sacred writings at the core of its religious teachings.

Many new religions, especially those that have developed out of the Buddhist tradition, look to the Buddhist canon for their sacred texts, often adopting a specific Buddhist text as their core religious scripture. Thus, as has been mentioned earlier, Soka Gakkai and Risshokoseikai both use the *Lotus Sūtra* as their central religious teaching. Often the text concerned has been chosen by the religion's founder as a result of some inspirational insight, as has been the case with the founder of Shinnyoen, Ito Shinjo, when he made the *Nirvāṇa Sūtra* Shinnyoen's primary scripture, or with Kiriyama Seiyu of Agonshu, who considers that the *Āgama Sūtra*s are the key texts of Buddhism and has made them the basic texts used in Agonshu rituals.

Besides these official textual traditions within the new religions, many have also developed their own populist traditions, based in particular on collections of miracle stories and testimonies of members who have been cured or who have achieved personal salvation through the religion concerned. Such collections of stories are similar in many respects, both in style and in the roles they perform, to the collections of *engi* and *setsuwa* of the folk Buddhist tradition mentioned earlier.

The power of words and texts as ritual objects

One final issue that needs to be mentioned in any discussion of the uses of sacred writings in Japan is the extent to which many of them have been used as ritual objects containing inherent spiritual powers and magical efficacy to affect situations. This point has been mentioned in the earlier discussion of *norito* and of Buddhist spells and texts; it is also found to a great degree, too, in the new religions. Thus new religions in general do not ask their members to study the meanings of such texts; adherents are expected to remain content with the interpretations provided by their leaders. It is the uses made of the texts in ritual settings that are important. Thus in Agonshu the primary emphasis on the *āgama*s is in their use in ritual settings, as objects of power which, when chanted, are believed to bring about such results as pacifying the spirits of the dead.

The concept that words and sounds possess an innate power has much to do with the ways in which sacred texts have developed as ritual objects. This has been emphasised further by the inaccessibility of the language of so many sacred writings in Japan, whether Shinto texts or *norito* that have been written in ancient Japanese, or Buddhist texts, which are generally written in Buddhist Chinese which is understood by very few apart from textual specialists. This inaccessibility has tended to emphasise their incomprehensibility and, therefore, somewhat ironically, to enhance their status as means and tools of religious power and efficacy. This is why followers of a new religion such as Soka Gakkai may well state that it is the incantation of portions of the *Lotus Sūtra* that is the key to personal amelioration, rather than close textual study of their meanings.

Such issues need to be borne in mind when discussing the uses and nature of sacred texts in Japan. As this chapter had demonstrated, there is, in the Japanese religious world in general, a highly developed and rich tradition of sacred writings, some of which are specific and have contributed to the development of one of the elements within that world, whether Shinto, Buddhism or one of the new religions. Beyond, and perhaps more important than, the philosophical and teaching content that such texts may contain, is the role that sacred writings may play as objects of power used in ritual and in acts of worship. In Japan certainly this has been, and remains, central to the nature and use of sacred writings.

NOTES

1. Both texts are accessible in an English translation: the *Nihon Shoki* by Aston (1972), and the *Kojiki* by Philippi (1968).
2. This point is discussed at length by Ebersole (1989: 3–16). This question of mythistory, and of the role and meaning of these texts within this issue, is further explored in the chapter on Japanese Religions in *Myth and History* in this series.
3. This number fluctuates very slightly depending on different textual versions.

4. An excellent translation of this collection, along with a perceptive introduction, is to be found in Nakamura (1973).

FURTHER READING

Aston, W.G. (trans) (1972) *Nihongi: Chronicles of Japan from the Earliest Times to AD 697*, Rutland, Vt., Tuttle.

Earhart, H.B. (1982) *Japanese Religion: Unity and Diversity*, Belmont, Ca., Wadsworth.

Ebersole, G.L. (1989) *Ritual Poetry and the Politics of Death in Early Japan*, Princeton, NJ, Princeton University Press.

Kitagawa, J.M. (1987) *On Understanding Japanese Religion*, Princeton, NJ, Princeton University Press.

Nakamura, K.M. (1973) *Miraculous Tales from the Japanese Buddhist Tradition: The Nihon Ryôiki of the Monk Kyôkai*, Cambridge, Mass., Harvard University Press.

Philippi, D.L. (trans) (1968) *Kojiki*, Tokyo, University of Tokyo Press.

Tsunoda, R., de Bary, W.T. and Keene, D. (trans) (1958) *Sources of Japanese Tradition*, New York, Columbia University Press.

Index

Abhidhammapiṭaka 11, 13–6, 18, 19, 27–9, 39
Ādi Granth 1, 3, 5, 7, 8, 97, 151–63, 165–70
āgamas 43, 87, 93–6, 197
aggadah 1, 129, 133, 134, 145
Akhand Path 153
Analects 178
Ananda 13, 15
Arabic vii, 5, 101–10, 112–5, 120, 123, 130, 140–2, 145
Aramaic 130, 131, 134, 135, 149
Arjan 151, 155, 159, 163, 167
Ashkenazi 130, 131, 138, 139
authenticity 7, 12–6, 33, 34, 87, 117
avadāna 31

Bachitar Nāṭak 164
Bhagavadgītā 6, 76, 80, 83, 85, 88–93
Bible 1–8, 44–6, 51–3, 57–69, 71, 105–7, 111, 113, 160
Book of Change 174–6
Book of History 176
Book of Rites 177, 178
Brahma-sūtra 6, 80, 83–5
Buddha 3, 4, 8, 10–5, 17–22, 27, 30, 31, 33, 34, 37–40, 42
Buddhaghosa 14, 27, 32

Catholic 58, 59, 62, 79
chanting 7, 39–41, 62, 74, 78, 121, 136, 147, 192, 194, 197
Chinese 5, 6, 12, 21–7, 35–8, 43, 197
Chuang Tzu 175, 180, 183, 184
commentaries 6, 10, 27–9, 41, 51, 52, 59, 60, 80, 83, 86, 90, 92, 95, 98, 120, 121, 130–3, 136, 139, 142, 145, 148, 175, 176, 183, 192–6
Confucius 7, 173, 174, 176–80
Conservative (Judaism) 144, 149

Dasam Granth 151, 163, 165–7
Dhammapada 5, 16, 29, 30

engi 195, 196
Engi Shiki 190
epistles 46–50, 53, 57, 58, 62, 68, 69, 144

fundamentalism 58, 60, 61

gospels 6, 8, 47, 53, 54, 57, 58, 62, 63, 68, 69, 109, 113
Greek 46, 68, 140
Govind Singh 3, 158, 162–6, 168–70
Gurdas, Bhai 151, 167, 168

Gurmukhī 5, 154, 161
Gurū Granth Sāhib *see* Ādi Granth

ḥadīth 1, 4, 8, 101, 116–8
halakhah 1, 129, 132–40
Heart Sūtra 7, 191, 192
Hebrew 5, 68, 125, 129, 130–5, 139–41, 145, 149
Hebrew Bible 1, 3–8, 44, 45, 46, 68, 113, 125–31, 133, 138, 140, 141, 145, 146, 148

interpretation 2, 3, 6, 8, 9, 44, 45, 58, 61, 66, 75, 77, 79–1, 83, 85, 86, 90, 95, 96, 120–2, 125, 128–31, 135, 136, 141, 174, 194, 196
isnād 116

janam sākhīs 151, 171
Japanese 5, 12, 197
Japjī 8, 158, 161, 165
jātakas 11, 16, 30, 31, 39
Jesus 2, 6, 8, 45–57, 61, 63, 66, 68, 108, 113, 114, 173

Kabbalah 138, 146–8
Kabir 96, 156
Kojiki 188, 189, 197
Kṛṣṇa 90, 92, 93, 96, 163, 166

Lao Tzu 180, 182–4
Liberal (Judaism) 145, 149
Lotus Sūtra 191, 194, 196, 197

Mahābhārata 87–9
Mahāyāna 4, 8, 10–12, 20, 22–8, 31, 33, 34, 39, 40, 191
Maimonides 133, 138–46, 149
Manusmṛti 79
Mencius 179, 183
Milindapañha 19
Mishnah 8, 128, 132–4, 142, 145
Moses 4, 46, 108, 111, 113, 125–8, 133, 139, 140, 143
Muhammad 1, 3, 4, 101, 103, 104, 106, 108–20, 122, 123
music 7, 63, 159, 160, 167, 180
myth 25, 72, 87, 88, 92, 166, 181, 187–9

Nagarjuna 28
Nanak 151, 154–61, 163, 165, 167, 168, 171
New Testament 3–7, 46, 47, 52-6, 60, 62, 68, 69, 101
Nichiren 191, 194
Nihon Ryoiki 195
Nihon Shoki 188, 197

Old Testament 3, 6, 7, 44, 46, 47, 55, 60, 62, 67–9
Oral Torah 2, 125, 128–30, 132, 133, 138, 143
Orthodox (Judaism) 4, 138, 149

Pāli 10, 11, 29, 31, 34, 37–9, 43
Panjābi 5, 105, 161
Pao Pu Tzu 181, 184
Paul 6, 46–50, 55, 56
Prajñāpāramitā 20, 21, 24, 25
Prākrit 17, 29, 31, 35, 37, 38
Prophets (*Nevi'im*) 4, 46, 125, 126, 128, 148
Protestant 51, 52, 58, 59, 62, 63, 68, 69
psalms 62–5, 69, 113, 126–8, 148, 154, 160
Purāṇas 5, 87, 92, 93, 96, 163
Pure Land 25, 191, 193, 194

Qur'an vii, 1, 3–8, 101–23

Rahit Maryādā 170
rahit nāmās 151, 168–70

Rāmānuja 80, 85, 86, 89, 91, 94
Rāmāyana 87, 96
Rashi 130, 131
recitation 4, 7, 11, 13, 39–42, 72, 74, 77–9, 82, 88, 91, 93, 95, 103, 105, 119, 120, 190, 192, 194
Reconstructionism 144, 149
Reform (Judaism) 138, 144, 149
Ṛg-veda 71, 73, 74, 77, 79, 84
revelation 2, 3, 27, 33, 34, 45, 56, 67, 71, 72, 76, 77, 81–7, 91, 93-7, 101, 102, 104–6, 108, 109, 111–16, 118, 120, 122, 123, 125, 126, 133, 140–4, 160, 181, 196
Romans 6, 49–52, 60, 61

Śaṃkara 80, 83–5, 89, 90, 94
Sanskrit 5, 11, 17, 25, 27, 29–31, 34, 35, 37–9, 43, 71, 72, 77, 79, 80, 85–8, 91, 166, 192
Sephardi 131, 138, 139
Septuagint 68
setsuwa 195, 196
Shi'ah 122
shu 2, 175
Shulhan Arukh 139, 140
Śiva 76, 89, 92, 93, 95
smṛti 2, 72, 80, 87, 89, 92, 93, 96
śruti 2, 3, 5, 8, 72, 77, 79–81, 83, 85, 89, 93, 95, 97
Ṣūfī 122, 155, 156
Suttapiṭaka 11, 14, 18, 19, 27

Talmud 1, 8, 128, 130, 131, 134–8, 140, 145
Tamil 71, 86, 91, 95, 96
tantras 10, 12, 26, 27, 33, 78, 87, 93–6
Tao Te Ching 182, 183
Tao Tsang 181, 185
Theravāda 10, 19, 27, 34, 37, 38, 41, 43
Tibetan 6, 12, 21, 25–7, 34–8, 42, 94
Tipiṭaka 10–12, 17, 22, 32, 33, 43
Torah vii, 4, 5, 7, 46, 109, 113, 125, 126, 128–30, 133, 136, 138, 141, 143, 146, 149
translation 5–7, 44, 45, 67–9, 102, 104–8, 130, 135, 161
transmission 4, 6, 11, 32–6, 39, 73, 77, 78, 86

Upaniṣads 8, 73, 75–7, 81, 83, 85, 89, 92, 93, 99
'Uthman 3, 119

Vajrayāna 10, 26
Vasubandhu 27, 28
Veda 3, 5–8, 71–5, 77–87, 91, 93, 96–9
Vedānta 83, 86, 89
Vinayapiṭaka 11–14, 17–9, 27, 31
Viṣṇu 76, 85, 88–92

worship 7, 26, 42, 45, 49, 62–4, 66, 69, 181, 190, 192, 197
Writings (*Ketuvim*) 4, 46, 125–7

Yiddish 130, 131, 134

Zen 191, 193, 194

Zohar 147, 148